LEGACY OF
THE LIONS

LEGACY OF
THE LIONS

LESSONS IN LEADERSHIP FROM
THE BRITISH & IRISH LIONS

THE BRITISH & IRISH
LIONS
— SINCE 1888 —

GAVIN HASTINGS

with PETER BURNS

POLARIS
PUBLISHING

POLARIS PUBLISHING LTD
c/o Aberdein Considine
2nd Floor, Elder House
Multrees Walk
Edinburgh
EH1 3DX

Distributed by Birlinn Limited

www.polarispublishing.com

ISBN: 9781913538378
eBook ISBN: 9781913538385

British Library Cataloguing-in-Publication Data
A catalogue record for this book is available on request from the British Library.

Designed and typeset by Polaris Publishing, Edinburgh
Printed in Great Britain by CPI Group (UK) Ltd, Croydon, CR0 4YY

CONTENTS

To Diane and my family,
who I love more with each passing day.

PROLOGUE

EDEN PARK. SATURDAY, 8 July 2017.

A light rain was falling, visible against the bright lights that illuminated the green stage before us. It was a field I had played on in the blue of Scotland and the red of the Lions. But I wasn't playing now. Those days were long behind me. I was seated in the stands, watching a new generation of Lions battling to make their mark on history, their red shirts contrasting wonderfully with the black of New Zealand, which seemed to absorb the light like a collapsing star. The packed stadium was hushed as Owen Farrell, the Lions' No.12, lined up a shot at goal. Forty-eight metres out, just off-centre of the posts, the pressure of four nations on his shoulders. He had kicked sensationally throughout the tour – and in the Test series in particular – and despite the significance of these three points, he looked calm and assured as he ran through his kicking routine, as if he were on a training ground back home rather than at the epicentre of the rugby world.

He hit the kick, the ball sailed true. It was 15–15.

Less than three minutes remained on the clock – the final moments of a thrilling, exhausting, pulsating, extraordinary three-match Test series that was locked at one game-all.

Forget the pressure of four nations, as the teams regrouped for the restart there was the pressure of over a hundred years of history between the Lions and the All Blacks pressing down on the shoulders of every player on the field, on the bench and on the coaching staff on the sidelines, while 50,000 sets of eyes gazed from the stands, millions more watched on TV. Only once in all those years had the Lions emerged victorious in a Test series against the All Blacks. Now Sam Warburton's men were, perhaps, just over two minutes away from scoring the points they needed to secure a win that would give them rugby immortality. But so too were the All Blacks just a score away from maintaining the great legacy of their predecessors.

Huddled against the cold of that dark midwinter Auckland night, I struggled to sit still. The excitement, the energy of these moments – it was everything that makes Test-match rugby the remarkable spectacle that it is.

'*Li-ons, Li-ons, Li-ons . . .*'

The chant reverberated around the ground. Eden Park, a stronghold that hadn't seen an All Blacks defeat since 1994, was awash with red. 'It was like that the whole series,' Kieran Read, the All Black skipper, told me later, with a shake of his head at the memory. 'I remember getting a real shock when we ran out for the first Test. We don't normally get many away fans down here in New Zealand, but it felt like the whole bloody place was dressed in red. I still don't understand how they got so many tickets. Three Tests at home and each time most of the crowd were Lions fans.'

The clock hit seventy-eight minutes as Beauden Barrett, the magician in the All Black No.10 shirt, spun the ball in his hand on halfway and prepared to kick off. 'Right, win this restart,' commanded my old Lions teammate, Stuart Barnes, commentating for Sky Sports. Meanwhile, in the New Zealand commentary box, former All Black scrum-half Justin Marshall noted: 'Whoever gets the ball gets the last chance.'

Barrett nudged the kick to his right. It hung for a moment and then dropped just over the ten-metre line. A perfect restart for his chasing forwards to contest – and it spooked the Lions, who scrambled desperately to get into position to reclaim possession. The Lions full back Liam Williams, who had been stationed nearby, backpedalled and leapt for the ball just as Miles Harrison, Barnes' co-commentator, said, 'It's all about the restart—'

Kieran Read had led the All Black charge and arrived almost simultaneously to Williams, his huge hand reaching up between Williams' arms towards the ball, managing to throw the Welshman off from catching it cleanly. The ball tipped off Williams' hand and tumbled forward. Ken Owens, the Lions hooker, had also been racing back to cover the kick. He caught the ball before reason and his knowledge of the laws registered that he was in an offside position. He dropped the ball as if it were suddenly made of molten rock and threw his hands in the air to signal his innocence. *Nothing to see here, sir . . .*

But referee Romain Poite blew his whistle, his arm raised in the All Blacks' favour.

My stomach lurched. *Oh my God . . . It's a penalty. He's offside.* I can still feel that moment. The Lions team I had captained to New Zealand in 1993 had suffered a similar fate in the dying moments of the first Test and Grant Fox, the All Blacks' No.10, had kicked the contentious penalty to win the game.

History was about to repeat itself.

But we didn't have video referees in those days. Back in 1993, once the referee had made his decision, that was it. In 2017, however, the Lions still had a sliver of hope.

'I was on the other side of the pitch for that restart and didn't see what had happened,' Warburton recalls when I later asked him about the incident. 'I just remember Owen Farrell and Johnny Sexton going nuts, and then I saw the referee's arm was up.

'I always made it a point of my captaincy to keep my chat with the ref to a minimum. If you're constantly in his ear, your words can become white noise. And worse than that, you can start to annoy him. So I always kept my queries to the ref to a minimum – maybe three times a half; maximum four times.

'In that Test, I'd hardly spoken to Romain during the second half, because there had been no need to. So when his arm went up, I thought, "Fuck, I've got nothing to lose, I've hardly spoken to him all game." I thought I'd just calmly walk up to him without throwing my arms up in the air. I didn't know what I was asking for, but I remembered straight away the instance in the quarter-final of the 2015 World Cup when Scotland got knocked out by Australia when they should have won and gone through to the semi-final. I remember Craig Joubert got that accidental off-side wrong and I always thought afterwards, "Whenever there's a massive moment like that in international rugby, I think a ref will learn from that instance and just take a step back and make sure he makes the right decision." So I went up to Romain and said, "You have to check." I didn't want to say what for, but I remember just saying, "You have to check the video. You've got to have a look."'

Poite considered Warburton's words for a moment and then drew a rectangle in the air to signal that he wanted to speak to the television match official, George Ayoub. The match clock paused on seventy-eight minutes, thirty-four seconds. Turning his back on the players, Poite casually strolled to the near touchline so that he, Ayoub and assistant referee, Jaco Peyper, could have a confab.

'And that was it,' remembers Warburton. 'I thought, "Right, I can't do any more than that, he's going to have another look, and this decision now will be made by the TMO."'

Ayoub began to replay the incident in slow motion on the stadium's big screen and the three officials talked through what they were seeing.

'He's in an offside position, number sixteen,' said Poite, referring to Owens. 'Red [number fifteen] touched the ball in-flight and sixteen got the ball in front.'

'Romain, those are all the angles,' confirmed Ayoub.

'Are you happy for the knock-on challenge in the air – it was fair?' asked Poite, just as Warburton appeared to his left.

Wanting to ensure the referee wasn't swayed by the presence of the Lions captain, Read made his way over to join them.

'And a penalty kick against red sixteen?' continued Poite, seemingly unaware of the two huge men now looming beside him.

'Yes, I am,' said Ayoub.

Warburton and Read were now talking.

It's over, I thought to myself. It's all over . . .

All around the stadium, Lions fans had their heads in their hands. So close. The Lions had been so close. It would be twelve more years before they would get another crack at the All Blacks.

Poite turned around to address the captains. But then he heard a voice on his in-ear radio.

'Oui, Jérôme?'

It was the other assistant referee, Jérôme Garcès, stationed on the far touchline.

From the television footage, we cannot hear what Garcès said to Poite. But as Poite made his way back to the mark where the infringement took place, his pace slowed. Read, believing that the decision had clearly been made for a penalty, returned to his teammates.

Warburton started to shout to the Lions that they should set themselves for a quick tap, just in case the All Blacks tried something unexpected.

But then Poite called the captains to him.

'We have a deal,' he said. 'We have a deal about the offside from sixteen . . .'

'Yes,' said Read, nodding decisively to confirm the penalty decision, yet there was an edge to his voice. He could tell something was up.

'Sixteen red,' continued Poite. 'He didn't play immediately the ball. It was an accidental offside.'

'No, no,' interjected Read. 'No.'

'It was an accidental offside,' repeated Poite. 'We go for a scrum for black.'

Read put his hand on Poite's shoulder. 'Romain,' he implored. 'Romain. In the rules, it's not an accidental offside—'

'He'd blown for a penalty straight away,' remembers Read when I asked him about these electric, nerve-shredding moments. 'So I was immediately like, "That's the rule, that's how it's been ruled for a long time, it's a clear penalty." And then this bizarre sequence of events unfolded, because a decision like that is generally never overruled by a TMO or a touchie. From my perspective, I didn't think twice about it because I felt that he'd made the right call and I didn't get why the TMO was even looking at it.'

The incredulity was clear on Read's face as he tried to convince Poite to stick with his original decision.

'But there was no way he was going to change back,' says Read, the incredulity once again returning to his face despite the passage of time since the event. 'Getting a ref to change his initial decision is hard enough – but to change it again? Not a chance.'

Poite waved the captains away and sets the mark for the scrum.

'That was good captaincy from Sam,' reflects Read. 'But as All Black captain in that situation you just have to park the fact that the decision has gone against you and reset yourself for the next phase. We had a scrum in their half, two minutes left on the clock and we could still win the game. That is always your mindset as an All Black: clear away what has happened, focus on what happens next; what do we have to do now to score and win this game?'

Seventy-eight minutes, thirty-four seconds into the game, Poite restarted the clock and instructed the players to set for the scrum. If you thought the noise in the stadium had been loud before, it was on another level altogether now.

'The typical All Black fan, especially at home, tends to sit there and watch the game and doesn't get too excited, doesn't sing, doesn't yell too much,' explains Read. 'But I think we learned a lot of lessons from the Lions about how to support your team. It was an absolutely awesome atmosphere over those three Tests, and you could feel the vibe every second of each game. I think that was one of the best things to come out of the tour – that New Zealanders began to appreciate the fan experience a little more. They said, "Hey, this is what it's all about. Let's have fun. It's not just about winning and losing, it's also about being part of this whole experience." The final few minutes of that third Test, the noise was just going up and up and up. It was incredible.'

All Black scrum-half TJ Perenara fed the ball into the scrum. The two packs heaved and pumped their legs. The All Blacks shifted forward, slowly at first and then at speed. The front-rows began to rotate and Read, the ball now at his feet, had to dribble it to keep control. It looked for all the world like Poite was going to signal for a penalty in the hosts' favour, but before the whistle hit his lips, the ball popped loose. Perenara reached to pick it up, just as Lions scrum-half Rhys Webb stabbed at it with his toe. The ball bobbled away from Perenara and then bounced up into Webb's arms and the Welshman was away. He was quickly closed down by Beauden Barrett, so he popped the ball to his left to the supporting No.8 Taulupe Faletau. It was a poor pass and Faletau was unable to control it. Out went Poite's arm. Another scrum.

Seventy-nine minutes, sixteen seconds on the clock.

By the time the packs got set and finally engaged, the wail of a siren had cut through the din to signal that regulation time was over. When Perenara fed the ball in, the clock read: eighty minutes, sixteen seconds.

'There is a special page in rugby's history waiting for this match,' said Miles Harrison in commentary. 'We just don't know how this story is going to end.'

Again, the ball was at Read's feet. This time he exerted complete control. Peranara spun it left and the All Blacks crashed into midfield, just inside the Lions' half. Two phases later, the ball was in Read's hands and he carried strongly over the ten-metre line. Substitute centre Malakai Fekitoa burst on to a flat pass from Barrett and punctured the Lions' defensive wall, making it as far as the twenty-two before he was hauled down. The forwards punched for two more phases to break a few yards into the twenty-two and then the ball was whipped wide to the right. Aaron Cruden stepped, shuffled and drew two defenders to him before floating a basketball pass over Lions' wing Elliott Daly's head to Jordie Barrett. Daly scrambled back to halt the younger Barrett brother but was easily fended off by the rangy full back, who ploughed on down the touchline, eating up the yards. Liam Williams was the last man in defence and dived desperately for Barrett's ankles. He just managed to catch him. As the two men slid along the damp grass, just inches from the line, other Lions defenders arrived on the scene like a thundering cavalry and dived on Barrett, the collective weight and momentum of Owen Farrell, CJ Stander and Ben Te'o sliding the All Black into touch. The ball was out. The game was over.

It was breathless, heart-pounding stuff. My hands still shake with adrenaline as I rewatch those final minutes and write these words. Sitting in the stands that night, I thought my heart was going to burst out of my chest. The whole stadium was on its feet, roaring the players on, like a scene from the Coliseum reborn.

But that couldn't be it over, surely? I thought, my head spinning. *That can't be the end of the game?* There was no doubting the sense of bewilderment that was rippling around the stadium. 'Do we not go to extra time?' I asked, voicing the question on everyone's minds around me.

'I think we would all have been happy to carry on playing until there was a winner,' Warburton later tells me.

'Golden point or something would have been good,' agrees Read.

'I think all the players on both sides felt the same,' continues Warburton. 'You're so close to making history – you want a chance to win the thing, not just finish on a draw. Maybe they'll do that in future. But, at the time, you just had to accept it for what it was.'

'We were ready to go, to keep going,' concurs Read. 'I think if you'd asked the guys out there, every last one of us would have wanted to play it out until it was decided. But that's the nature of the beast.'

It had been one of the most epic encounters I'd ever seen. The series was like three World Cup finals in a row and, at the end, neither side could be separated. A draw was an unsatisfactory result for many, but it was probably the fair outcome of an engrossing series that had been played out by two outstanding teams, fighting tooth and nail for every second of the three Test matches.

Warburton had handled the situation with Poite superbly, but so too had his opponent. Read and the All Blacks' dignity in the aftermath has always remained hugely impressive. I'm not sure how dignified the response would have been in Britain and Ireland had the situation been reversed and Poite had downgraded a potential series-winning penalty for the Lions to a scrum . . .

'It's important not to be a cry baby over a referee's decision,' reflects Read. 'As an All Black, as a leader, as a captain, I had to put on a brave face for our team and our nation, because it was the nature of a series that was so tough and tight that you just have to accept these decisions and move on.

'But there was a lot of emotion at the final whistle. You wait twelve years to get a chance to play the Lions – and many players don't get that chance at all, so you know how lucky you are. But we were there to win, and although we didn't lose, it was a bizarre feeling to deal with the series being drawn. I just had to pull the players in straight away and get their heads up. And then I began to prepare myself mentally to face the cameras to talk about what had just happened.'

'Kieran and I caught up after doing our TV interviews on the pitchside and said that we should get both teams mixed in together for the trophy presentation,' says Warburton.

'We said, "Let's get everyone up and celebrate what the series was,"' says Read, 'because we knew it had probably been a good series to watch and it had been very special to have been a part of it.'

The photo that followed is iconic: Read and Warburton smiling as they raise the series trophy, the players from both teams mixed in around them. It is a moment in time – the very essence of what makes a Lions tour so special. That Lions team had never played together before and they would never play together again. Yet their fleeting existence as a team will remain in people's minds more vividly than many sides that have been together for years and played in scores of Test matches.

As we headed out of the stadium and into the Auckland night, I kept going over those last few chaotic moments in my mind and the coolness shown by the leaders on both sides. Later, when I was able to watch the replay with the benefit of the audio, I marvelled still further at how the situation was handled. That three-minute passage of play is not just a wonderful window into different aspects of leadership – from both captains and, indeed, from the referee, who didn't want the series to be decided by a potentially controversial penalty, as well as Farrell's coolness to kick the final points – but it also encapsulates the Lions experience for me.

It's hard to describe the pressure of those moments in international rugby – which are intensified a hundred-fold when put in the context of a Lions Test series. In that cauldron of fire and fury, Warburton and Read were able to call on all their years of experience to remain calm and clear in a moment that both knew could define their entire lives. Make no mistake – winning a Lions series sets you on a sporting pedestal for all time; like winning a World Cup or an Olympic gold medal, these moments mark your name forever.

It has always fascinated me how various Lions teams function – successfully or otherwise – and that is not just because I was fortunate enough to captain the tour of 1993. There is something so magical about a Lions tour, so unique, so enthralling. Every four years the players from England, Ireland, Scotland and Wales come together with minimal preparation to take on one of the best teams on the planet in their own backyard to try and win two out of three Test matches. It is an extraordinary challenge full of potential pitfalls and uncertainties which can brutally expose human flaws and frailties. But it can also create legends in the jersey and bonds of friendship and respect that last for a lifetime. Therein lies the magic and majesty of the Lions – and so too the inspiration for writing this book. While drawing on my own experiences, I also wanted to speak to other players, captains and coaches to explore what lies at the heart of the Lions experience, to examine what makes it so unique.

The next tour is always the most important tour and as future players set out to add to the magic, the mystique, the glory and the honour of being a Lion, this book looks to offer a window into the past to explore the lessons that can be learned from those who have gone before, whether they enjoyed the glory of victory or suffered the agony of defeat. It has been an insightful, heart-warming, often hilarious and always illuminating process that has reaffirmed everything that I love about the red jersey and what it represents.

ONE

CHALLENGE-SOLUTION, CHALLENGE-SOLUTION

1989

THE HAIR THAT was once the colour and texture of iron filings is now soft and white; the hard, steely gaze I grew so accustomed to seeing when we took the field together has now mellowed. Whenever I see him these days, his face immediately cracks into a grin, his eyes glinting warmly and we spend most of our time laughing.

When it came to conducting interviews for this book, there was only one place to start – my old captain, my outstanding teammate, the man who Brian Moore once described as 'a fucking warrior'. My great friend: Finlay Calder.

Fin cuts the figure of a wise and gentle soul these days, but the warrior spirit is still there, just simmering beneath the surface. When we talk about the Lions, the passions quickly stir, his voice rolls and I can feel myself tumbling back through time to a glorious past.

We won our first caps together against France in 1986 – alongside my brother, Scott, Jeremy Campbell-Lamerton, Matt

Duncan, and David Sole. Scott and I became the forty-first set of brothers to play for Scotland. Fin also joined that list, following his twin, Jim, into the blue shirt. Ironically, it was Jim's shirt that he took. Both Jim and Fin would finish their careers as greats of the game north of the border – a Lions tour and a Grand Slam each to their names. But, amazingly, the two never played a Test match together. Jim had toured with the Lions in 1983 and won the Grand Slam with Scotland, scoring the winning try against France in the final game, in 1984. He played his final season in the 1985 Five Nations and then slipped away from the international game, usurped by his twin brother.

Fin was named Scotland captain for the 1989 Five Nations and we did pretty well that season, drawing with England at Twickenham and beating Ireland and Wales at home as France won the Championship. Not that I was involved – I missed the whole Five Nations with injury and was lucky to still be in the mix for the Lions that summer. Peter Dods had played brilliantly in my place at full back and he and I were vying with the Welsh captain, Paul Thorburn, for a place on the tour. Luckily, Ian McGeechan knew me well. He'd been my under-21 coach, had coached me for Scotland B and had been assistant coach with Scotland before taking the step into the top job in 1989. Geech had been named as head coach of the Lions for the first time for that tour and told me that, if I could get fit, he would take me. I played a couple of games for London Scottish in April and he was true to his word. Peter Dods and I were in. There were nine Scottish lads named in the squad, including my brother, which was another special moment for us. And Fin was named as captain.

'How did you find out?' I ask him, as we reminisce about the old days, more than thirty years later.

'In many ways, it was kind of by default,' he replies, his head shaking, his eyes wrinkling with a wry grin. 'Will Carling was absolutely nailed on to be the captain, but he had shin splints and had to withdraw from selection. Philip Matthews was captain of Ireland, but they didn't pick him in the squad. Paul Thorburn was captain of Wales, and they didn't pick him either.'

'So you were the last man standing?'

'Pretty much! And to be honest, I had very little experience as a captain. By 1989, the only side I'd ever captained had been the Scottish Corn Trade team when we played a game in October 1988. Somehow, despite playing dreadfully in the Scottish trial at the start of '89, I was named Scotland captain for the Five Nations. I always thought of it as a caretaker role, though. David Sole was the man for the future, we could all see it; he just wasn't quite ready for it that season, but we all knew his time would come. So I saw it as an interim role until Soley was ready.'

'Tell me about the Lions, then. Who called you?'

'Geech.'

Ian McGeechan. Geech. A man so steeped in Lions lore that it's now hard to separate him from the red jersey whenever his name is mentioned. He had been part of the 1974 Invincibles – the Lions team led by Willie John McBride who had gone unbeaten on their tour through South Africa, a draw in the final Test of the series against the Springboks the only blip on an otherwise perfect record. Geech had toured again, on an unhappier and notably less successful tour to New Zealand in 1977. Then, in 1989, he was handed the head coach position for the tour to Australia.

'He phoned and asked if I would be interested in captaining the Lions,' says Fin. 'What a question! Of course I was. The honour. God, does it get any bigger?'

I'm biased, but I don't think it does. Playing for the Lions is the ultimate. To captain them? The stuff of dreams.

1989 was a tour that was notable for several reasons. For ninety years, Australia had been little more than a stop-off for the Lions on their way to a longer tour of New Zealand; now they were hosting the tour entirely on their own for the first time since 1899.

This was also the first Lions tour for six years. They had been due to visit South Africa in 1986, but the trip had been cancelled even before a squad had been picked as a protest against South Africa's apartheid regime.

'We had to relight the Lions,' mused Fin. 'Because of that cancelled tour, the concept had kind of gone into hibernation. Usually you had any number of guys who had toured with the Lions before, knew each other, and understood what the Lions was and how it all worked. But because of those fallow years, I think only two guys had toured before in 1983 – Robert Norster and Donal Lenihan. So one of the first things we had to do was to try to break down the barriers between the teams. You have to do that on every Lions tour, but it felt particularly important in 1989 because we really didn't know each other at all.'

He swats me away with a wave of his hand when I say that his personality had been key to this – but it was true. Right from the first moment we met up as a squad, Fin pulled us all in and did as much as anyone to break down those barriers to help us bond as a team. He spent time getting to know every player and he was the life and soul of the party when we had a big piss-up early on in the preparation week. He was a character; he had supreme self-confidence and belief, and everything was fun for Fin. The training and team-building were a challenge, but he made it fun and he was clearly enjoying himself in that environment. As an example of this, I remember him challenging Chris Oti, the lightning-fast England wing, to a race after one of the training sessions. We were at one end of the pitch at London Irish and

Fin said, 'Come on, Chris, round the posts at the other end and back here. I'm gonna beat you.' And we all just thought, 'What is this guy doing, challenging Chris Oti to a race?'

'I think back on that,' I tell him, 'and there was no way you were going to beat Chris Oti. Not a chance. But you, in your usual way, just hung in there and hung in there and he beat you by a couple of paces and all the guys were cheering you on. And I think in that one, fleeting, two-minute incident, you showed that you weren't prepared to give up, no matter what. You chased him down and chased him down and chased him down. That was just you being you and saying to the rest of the squad, "Right, it doesn't matter how tough the challenge is, I'm up for it and I'm never giving in." That was great leadership.'

'I was well supported by Geech as head coach and also by Roger Uttley as forwards coach and Clive Rowlands as the manager,' replies Fin, deflecting the compliment. 'We had a good synergy between us all.'

'Was there not a bit of a clash between you and Roger?' I remind him.

'There was a small one. It was right at the start of the tour and we were trying to decide how we were going to play out in Australia. The beauty of the Lions is that you get to pull all these different strengths from the four nations into this new team, but deciding which tactics to use to fully exploit those strengths can be tricky. Roger wanted us to play to the strengths of the English pack by mauling the ball and slowing the game down; I thought our backs were so dangerous that we should make sure they had quick ball, so I said we should go with the Scottish tactic of quick rucks.'

'And what happened?'

'We agreed on a hybrid.' Then he shoots a grin. 'But you may recall getting the ball in your hands quite a lot on that tour, no?'

He was right, on those hard grounds in Australia, we had the ability to rip sides apart with our backline play. If ever Fin proved his mettle as a captain to the rest of the squad, it was by standing up to his coach early on and making sure his opinion was heard. All the predictions before the tour had stated that we would pick a heavy-duty pack to stifle the Australian teams – and, on occasion, we did. But the pack that emerged ahead of the Test matches was a mix of athletes as well as big men. A small but dynamic front row – a tactic that Geech would later use with similar success in 1997 – of David Sole, Brian Moore and Dai Young was supported by a more powerful back five of Englishmen Wade Dooley, Paul Ackford, Dean Richards and Mike Teague – plus Fin. And as he intimated, we had a very dangerous set of backs. Ieuan Evans and Rory Underwood were flying machines on the wing, my brother could provide power and dynamism in the centre, we had great options at scrum-half in Robert Jones and Gary Armstrong and guys like Mike Hall and Brendan Mullin were class acts. The best of them all, however, was a young kid who had only ever played one Test match in his life – and that had been against Romania in Bucharest. Jeremy Guscott had burst on to the international radar in that game, scoring three tries, to show that he could transfer the incredible performances he had been putting in for his club Bath to the Test stage. When Carling had been forced to withdraw from contention for the squad because of injury, his place was given to his centre partner – and if ever there was a player that looked to the manner born in a Lions jersey, it was Jerry Guscott.

When he appears on the Zoom call to reminisce about the three tours of duty he did with the Lions, he's just finished a Peloton workout and, but for the grey-white hair, he looks fit enough to still be playing.

'I really didn't expect to go on the tour,' he says as I ask him about his call-up to the squad. 'And to be honest, in 1989 I didn't really know too much about the Lions, the history of the Lions, either. I kind of knew a little bit because by being a Bath supporter as a kid I would see the likes of Gareth Edwards and Barry John and all those Welsh legends of the '70s coming over to play against Bath for the likes of Llanelli and Cardiff and Neath and Swansea and you'd hear tales about them with the Lions, but that was about it. But going on tour with the Lions in 1989? It wasn't even a thought in my mind. All I was focussed on was playing another game for England so I wouldn't be stuck on one cap.'

'I think we all knew pretty quickly that that wasn't going to be a problem!' I say.

'Ah, it's funny though,' he says, shaking his head. 'You just never know. I had all the confidence in the world in my ability, but you never know for sure whether a coach is going to like you or not. But Geech backed me and Fin quickly took me under his wing and looked after me. He was very much a lead-by-example type of captain, but he was also a brilliant communicator. I'd probably say of all my Lions captains, he was the best communicator and he was mature beyond his years. He was funny and he could be quite weird sometimes, but in a really encouraging, good way. I remember sharing a room with him at the first hotel in Australia. We got back after training and we hadn't showered or changed yet, so we were still in t-shirts and shorts, and he looked down and said, "My legs are bigger than your legs." And I looked at his skinny chicken legs and I went, "There's no way your legs are bigger than mine," and we had a sort of thigh-off and started measuring each other's legs to see who had the biggest thighs! Now, I'm not sure if you could ever class that as some kind of classic leadership method, but do you know what, it was bloody funny and we had a good laugh about it and suddenly I was feeling comfortable around this slightly eccentric guy who was my captain and I felt good and we were having a proper laugh. And that kind of sums him up. You know, he probably wasn't regarded as a really brilliant player outside of Scotland. I think a lot of neutrals would have picked Andy Robinson over him as a player, but Fin was brilliant on that tour and his leadership was key to getting us all to gel. He made people feel relaxed and he had a laugh with them, but he could also inspire them with the way he talked and he would work his bollocks off in training and give everything he had out on the field. It was the perfect combination and you could suddenly see why Geech had wanted him as captain. That's exactly the kind of leader we needed on that tour.'

'That's a great summary of Fin,' says Geech. 'And he was great to work with. He challenged you, which was good, but he also listened. And he inspired people around him. As a leadership group, we worked very well, and Clive was a great manager.'

'The role of manager has changed over the years,' I say. 'It's more ceremonial now, whereas I remember Clive having a much more active presence.'

'That's exactly right,' says Geech. 'The managers that I worked with all sat in on squad and team selection, but in the professional era they sit back more and more because the detail we have on each player is so much deeper and the game has changed a lot from when they played. But in '89, '93 and '97, the manager was really involved and Clive was fantastic. He took a lot of pressure off my shoulders. Roger and I would meet with him for a drink in his room every night before dinner and he would ask, "How did today go? How are the players? Is there anything I can do?" And I might mention something about a training ground not being very good, or the food wasn't great or something – and he would just take care of it. That was huge for me because I was still very inexperienced as a head coach. I'd been an assistant with Scotland until 1988 and then only done one Five Nations as head coach in 1989 before the tour. In many ways, I still felt more like a player than a coach in those days, so to have someone like Clive as a steady hand to help out and guide and take care of things was absolutely invaluable.'

We eased our way into the tour in Perth, beating a pretty weak Western Australia team 44–0 in the opening game. The romp in the sun came at a cost, though, with poor Paul Dean injuring his knee just twenty-seven minutes into the game. Paul had to fly home and we called up Rob Andrew to replace him.

'That was very, very tough for Paul,' says Fin. 'But it turned out to be fortuitous, let's be honest. Rob came out and was exceptional from the moment he arrived.'

In game two, we faced Australia B in a storm in Melbourne. 'We picked a heavyweight English front five to cope with the conditions, which were dreadful,' remembers Fin. 'It was a tough game that one, but we battled to a 23–8 win. Wade Dooley said to me afterwards that he'd never seen anyone in his life like Gary Armstrong, who played at scrum-half. Gary scored in that match, handing off players left, right and centre, and afterwards the English lads just said, "Who is this guy?" It was a great moment for the tour because you could see players earning each other's respect. Gary would end up playing second fiddle to Robert Jones, but he was so good on that tour that he could easily have played in the Tests.'

We flew to Brisbane to play Queensland at Ballymore. That was a tough, tough game. Brutal at times. Mike Hall, the Welsh centre, got kicked to pieces by the Queensland forwards at a ruck. I remember Mike lying on the ground getting some treatment from Smurf – our physio, Kevin Murphy – when Fin called us all in. 'That's the last time something like that happens on this tour,' he said. 'We get that sorted now.'

As Brian Moore later said: 'And with that, the whole feeling of the tour changed. There was a palpable shift in the attitude among the whole party. We wouldn't start anything; but if it started, we would finish it.' We won that game 19–15 and no side bullied us again.

Like many great leaders, Fin has a charisma that is infectious, a voice that can send shivers down your spine when he gives a team talk and a sense of humour that makes spending time with him one of life's great pleasures. Crucially, he has an innate gift for understanding people. Take Brian, for example. To many in Scotland, he was Brian Fucking Moore. The Pitbull. Brian and Fin didn't know each other from Adam before the tour and there is no doubt that Mooro probably thought he would have made a better captain than Fin. There was potential for real friction between them that could have sent poison seeping through the rest of the squad. But it never happened. A great friendship began on that tour that has only strengthened over the years. 'Finlay Calder is my soul brother,' said Mooro recently.

'I love that man,' says Fin, gently. 'He is very, very precious to me. He has had a difficult life, as he has discussed in his autobiography; but when we met – and for years afterwards – I had no idea about any of that. I remember when I first saw him at training with the Lions, though, I could see that there was a darkness in him, something that was eating him inside, and it made him the most competitive bastard I've ever met. Christ, he was on a different level.'

'And the challenge to your leadership?' I ask. 'Did you ever get a sense that guys like Mooro were challenging you for it?'

'I think that what made a difference on that tour was that I didn't try to be all things to all men,' says Fin. 'And I didn't try to take everything on myself. Before we met up, I got a lovely letter from Geoff Windsor-Lewis from the Barbarians, congratulating me on my appointment. "One tip, though," he wrote. "Don't do everything yourself. The squad will become tired of the same voice," and I took that on board very quickly. Delegation was the key. I quickly recognised that Brian knew far more about forward play and rugby in general than I ever would. So I said to him, "I want you to lead the forwards. You call the lineouts, you decide scrum moves, because you're in the thick of it. I'll toss the coin and do the team talks and the press conferences, but when it comes to what's happening on the park, nobody understands it better than you, so you call it." And by doing that, it empowered him and channelled his energies in the right way. Brian craves acceptance. That's what he wants in life: he wants to be respected and accepted, and that's what I gave him.'

'And it wasn't just him that you empowered,' I note.

'No, I suppose that's right. We had a leadership group – although we didn't call it that at the time. It was me, Robert Norster from Wales, Dean Richards from England, Donal Lenihan from Ireland. And Donal was crucial to that tour.'

'Donal's Donuts.'

'Exactly.'

Donal Lenihan became the captain of the midweek team – the dirt-trackers, as they're more commonly known. Under his guidance the dirt-trackers not only went unbeaten through the tour but had a hell of a good time doing it – on and off the field. They had t-shirts made emblazoned with 'Donal's Donuts' and it got to a stage where you wanted to play for the midweek side so that you might get a t-shirt and enjoy the night out with the boys afterwards. That enthusiasm spread through the whole squad, yet there was never a 'them-and-us' attitude between any of the players.

'By having a representative from each country in that inner group of senior players, it meant that no one in the wider squad ever felt isolated. The idea was that if a lad from Wales felt he wasn't getting a fair go and he didn't feel comfortable coming to me to talk about it, he could go to Robert; and similarly, with England or Ireland they could go to Dean or Donal. It made sure that all the players were fairly represented and it adhered to that piece of advice from Geoff Windsor-Lewis: "Don't do everything yourself," and I did my best to stick to that. Geoff also added in that letter: "Because of the role of captaincy itself, you have to become slightly distant from the rest of the players," and that, too, is true, because I was involved in selection for the games. There were four of us: Clive Rowlands (the manager), Roger, Geech and myself.'

'Was that ever difficult for you?'

'I think we were really lucky that there wasn't a single player on tour that shouldn't have been there. That's not always been the case on a Lions tour. Often someone might have a niggly injury, or be out of form, or be a coach's favourite from their national team, and they're carried through the tour – and that can often have a serious impact on the rest of the squad. If someone is down or feels slightly separate from the tour, it can leach into other players. That didn't happen in '89. Every single player could have played in the Test team and every single player got a chance to fight to be in that team.'

'Yeah, Andy Robinson played bloody well on that tour,' I say of the main rival for Fin's place in the Test team.

There's a roar of laugher. 'Well, that's right, I know, he did! And let's not kid ourselves: that's where the Lions tours have sometimes fallen down in the past, if your captain isn't an absolute nailed on first-team player. It can be hard if there are question marks around your captain. And to be fair, there were question marks around me, especially after the first Test.'

The first Test. That was one of the toughest days I've ever spent on a rugby field. After the victory over Queensland, Donal's Donuts had rolled over Queensland B, 30–6; the Saturday team came through another tough encounter to beat New South Wales 23–21; and the dirt-trackers then saw off New South Wales B 39–19 ahead of the first Test. We were unbeaten and feeling great about ourselves.

We knew the Wallabies would be dangerous, though. They'd achieved a rare Grand Slam in 1984 on their northern hemisphere tour with one of the finest rugby teams ever assembled, and when they came over again in 1988, although England had beaten them 28–19, they had easily beaten Scotland 32–13. In the summer of 1988, England had lost both Tests in Australia fairly substantially, so we knew they were still a good side – but we were confident that we would do a job on them in Sydney. Mike Hall had recovered from his shoeing against Queensland to play really well throughout the rest of the tour and Brendan Mullin was electric on the hard grounds. They went in as the centre pairing, while my brother Scott was discounted as he had a pulled hamstring. I was delighted to be named at full back alongside Ieuan Evans and Rory Underwood on the wings. Craig Chalmers was selected at stand-off next to the outstanding Robert Jones at scrum-half, while the pack consisted of Sole, Moore and Young in the front row, Ackford and Norster in the second row, and Richards and Derek White alongside Fin in the back row.

When researching this chapter, I came across the diary I had kept on the tour.

Saturday, 1 July 1989. Sydney.

I got up for breakfast about 9.00 a.m. and joined the early core whilst reading the papers, which were quite favourable to our chances. I then went to catch some fresh air with Dai Young and Fin in the early morning freshness of Camperdown – it was a bright morning full of anticipation and promise which was carried on at the mid-morning team meeting.

We had a light lunch and then relaxed for a while prior to the meeting in the team room where Geech gave an inspirational talk. He stressed that July 1st could and would be one of the most important days of our lives and we would have the chance of going down in history.

We got on the team coach and sat down and concentrated on the task ahead as we travelled the half-hour to the stadium. On arrival there were hundreds of people milling around and we dropped our kit off in the spacious double changing rooms before trekking down the long tunnel and out on to the touchline of this modern amphitheatre. Randwick were playing Easts in the curtain raiser and we could see the Australian players stripped and ready for action. We made our way back up the tunnel and into the dressing rooms to prepare for the match; we weren't to know at that stage that we would go back in two hours later with our heads lowered, reeling with the sickness of defeat and the knowledge that we'd blown it – humiliated by an Aussie side who had performed really well and had us under intense pressure for the majority of the match.

Everyone knew that we had performed poorly and there was little chat in the changing room for ten minutes or so after we got back. The management arrived with sorrowful looks on their faces and Clive tried to get us going by vowing that we would come back at them in the next two Tests and that we must accept defeat with honour but never forget what had happened that afternoon.

'That was a hard day,' says Fin, quietly. 'We got caught short. There was no question about that. From the first kick-off to the final whistle, we were second in every aspect of the game. We just didn't turn up. I was responsible for that: of course I was responsible; I was captain, for goodness' sake. And there was a lot of soul-searching.'

'I remember Clive getting us all together afterwards,' I say, 'and he didn't give us a bollocking, he didn't need to give us a bollocking. We all knew that we'd played crap and we were absolutely distraught about it. But when he came in, and all the replacements were in there, too, he said, "Come on, boys; from now on, the badge only gets bigger." He pointed to the Lions crest on his blazer. "It gets bigger and bigger from now on."'

'I remember being interviewed by Nigel Starmer-Smith immediately after the game,' says Fin. 'And he said, "Finlay, what do you say to all the people who have got up in the middle of the night to watch this in the UK and Ireland?" and I said, "Get up next Saturday morning. We'll sort it out." Where the fuck did that come from? I don't know. But I suppose I knew that we hadn't turned up and we wouldn't make that mistake again. We were in a dogfight now and we were going to sort it out.'

'I thought he was incredible in that sense,' says Jerry, 'because he did not, from my memory anyway, seem flustered. He must have been under enormous pressure after that loss and with lots of people in the press saying that Andy Robinson should be playing. But Fin never showed any anxiety about that to any of us. He just seemed focussed on the next couple of games and seemed absolutely certain that we would turn it around.'

'I remember sitting on the flight down to Canberra for the ACT game,' says Fin, 'and they were showing reruns of great sporting moments on the TV. One of them was Sebastian Coe coming back to beat Steve Ovett in the 1500m in Moscow, and David Coleman saying, when Sebastian Coe came back to win, "You don't become a bad runner overnight." And that struck a chord with me because we hadn't become a bad team overnight.

I thought, "He's absolutely right." We had a good side, we had all the components to be a *great* side, but we just hadn't turned up for that first Test.'

'ACT was a big game next, though,' I say.

'It was huge. *Huge*,' says Fin. 'If we lost that game, the wheels would really have started to come off the tour.'

And early on in the match, that was exactly what looked like happening. We went behind 18–4 and then 21–11. I remember sitting in the stand as ACT began to rack up the points in the first half and thinking, 'Oh, for fuck's sake, what's going on here?' There are moments in a tour where you're at a tipping point – and that was a tipping point. We were in danger of falling off a cliff.

'We were, we were,' agrees Fin. 'But there was a steeliness to that whole squad. And it reiterates the point that we weren't carrying anyone on that tour – every player was of Test calibre and when you have that, you can dig yourself out of a hole. Your brother was a big part of that. I remember I went to see him on the Sunday after the first Test, and he was in his bed with his hamstring injury, and I said, "Scott, you're playing on Wednesday." He said, "Ah, I'm not sure, I'm just not quite ready. Maybe next Saturday." And I said, "Scott, if you don't play on Wednesday, you'll be watching the second Test from Edinburgh; you have to play." And he did and he played very well. Rob Andrew played very well. They gave Mike Teague a cortisone injection to help with the injury that kept him out of the first Test and he came through. Soley was playing on the flank. What an athlete. How many props can play on the flank? He was sensational in that game. And Jerry showed just how good a player he was as well. Christ, everything looked so easy for him, even then.'

'As a player,' says Jerry, 'I always looked at the next task in hand, I very rarely looked back. And that's true in my life as well. My thought process has always been to look at the next challenge ahead of me and to find a solution to it. Challenge-solution, challenge-solution, challenge-solution. Any disappointment, I delete it; I don't like negativity and I don't dwell on things. We were down in that game and one-nil down in the series, but it was just a case of putting all that behind me and focussing on what I could do next that would overcome the immediate challenge in front of me. After losing the first Test, I didn't even think about it again. I just rebooted and thought about what was next. Win the next game, win the next game, win the next game. I remember being on the attack near ACT's line and I tried to get a little grubber through to get in behind their defence – but it didn't come off. They got the ball and cleared it.'

'That was a nice ambitious piece of play,' I note, raising an eyebrow. 'And the fact it didn't work on that occasion didn't mean it was the wrong thing to try.'

'And the fact it didn't work didn't bother me,' he says. 'It was just on to the next task.'

'That sums up the player that Jerry was,' says Fin. 'He had a million tricks up his sleeve to unpick defences. They didn't always work, but it kept the defenders guessing all the time. Just a class, class act. He was one of several players who put their hand up for selection in that game for the second Test.'

From 21–11 down Donal's Donuts ended up winning 41–25, with Guscott spearheading the comeback. The non-playing members of the squad rushed down from their seats to applaud the players off the field. Clive Rowlands had spoken about the badge getting bigger – it was certainly growing after that performance.

'The unity which the dirt-trackers found that day was brought into the whole squad,' says my brother.

'Winning that game against ACT was so important because the ship that had been listing dangerously was suddenly righted,' says Fin. 'We got our confidence back and there was a different attitude going into the second Test.'

'The biggest two things a Lions squad needs is a collective buy-in and collective intelligence,' says Geech. 'If you've got a group of people who are all prepared to share their knowledge and their experiences, then you have 99.9 per cent of all your answers. You can sort anything out. Share knowledge and communicate and then trust and honesty will follow. But you can only achieve that by turning up with an open mind and throwing yourself into the collective effort.

'Every Lions team's different, and the Lions rugby on every tour is different, because it reflects that group of people. It reflects what they take on to the field and what they've done off the field and reflects that whole collective environment. In 1989 there was a genuine respect amongst players for what each player could do, and what they brought to the game, and it was a hugely competitive group as well. It was that competitive drive that pulled us out of the slump of the first Test and going behind against ACT. And as a result of the way some guys played in that ACT game, they forced us into the rethink about the starting line-up from the first Test. It was a big call, but we made a lot of changes for the second Test.'

One-nil down, it was do-or-die time. No Lions squad had ever come back and won a Test series having been one-nil down. Ever. Before or since. Selection would be key to shake things up and give the Lions a chance.

'I went to see Clive that week,' says Fin, 'and I said, "Let's be absolutely clear on this: the success of the Lions is far more important than my personal success. If the management want me to step down for Andy Robinson, then I'm prepared to do it, because it's far more important that we win the second Test than it is for me to play. It's as simple as that, and if you want me to stand down, I'll stand down." And Clive looked at me and he said, "Finlay, if you stand down, I must stand down also. There is no more to be said." That's just what I needed to hear. That's leadership. It comes down to moments like that. He had my back and he put his faith in me and I was going to repay it.'

'And what about other selections?'

'We changed the centres,' says Fin. 'Scott came in and so did Jerry. What a talent that boy was and it was a great combination: Scott with his power and his huge engine, then this genius beside him. Jerry was totally untested at that level but God, his talent was out of this world.'

'Dooley came in for Bobby Norster and Mike Teague for Derek White in the pack,' I say. 'And Rob Andrew came in for Chick [Craig Chalmers].'

'Frankly, Craig was probably too young to cope at stand-off at that level,' says Fin. 'In fairness, he was only twenty at the time. In the first Test, none of us played very well, and Craig was one of the sacrificial lambs that got chopped, and Rob came in for him. Rob was magnificent in the next two Tests. He was a great filter at No.10 and he was very clever in the way he used the power of Scott and the silky skills of Jerry, the pace of the electric wingers and this big dafty at full back.'

'Thanks very much.'

My diary recalls a hot and humid night at Ballymore Stadium in Brisbane where we prepared to battle for our rugby lives against one of the great teams of the era.

'I've been in some amazing changing rooms in my life,' reflects Fin, 'but nothing comes close to the second Test for belief before we went out. It was just: "We are going to do this. We are going to do this." We all knew it, could all feel it.'

LEGACY OF THE LIONS

'We were pumped up,' I say, 'although that atmosphere didn't suit everyone.'

'No, you're right,' says Fin. 'The group of Scots on that tour used to really get riled up. It's what we had to do every time we played a Test match. We were usually physically smaller than other international teams, and *always* smaller than the likes of England, France and the southern hemisphere teams, and so the only way we could possibly compete with them physically was to really hype ourselves up, to be virtually foaming at the mouths as we ran out. But Dean Richards absolutely hated that kind of atmosphere. I remember him coming to me in the changing room just before kick-off in the second Test and saying, "Sorry, Fin, all this kicking and screaming isn't really my thing, do you mind if I go and stand outside?" I look around and I can see you and Scott going absolutely ballistic; I've been just about headbutting everyone. But I got that that wasn't for everyone. "Of course," I said. "No problem at all, Deano, off you go. We'll see you out there." And out he goes. I think he went and did a lap of the pitch with Clive Rowlands.'

'It's an interesting scenario,' I say. 'If the Lions lose that game, does that moment get pinpointed as the reason? Does it show the team spirit splitting because Deano didn't want to be in there with everyone else?'

'History spins these things one way or another, doesn't it?' says Fin, with a soft smile. 'If he plays badly and we lose, then maybe that would be the narrative. But Deano . . . what a player. He was incredible in that game. He was so strong. I always remember playing for Scotland against England and if Dean and Rob Andrew were playing, I knew we were sunk. Rob would kill us with his boot, and Deano would get the ball and never give it up. If one of them was missing, we had a chance. And luckily for us, on that Lions tour, we had them both in the form of their lives.'

Both Geech and Fin had repeated before kick-off that we couldn't afford to take a backwards step or come off second-best in the collisions as we had done the previous week. At the first scrum, Robert Jones set the tone by standing on the foot of Aussie captain, Nick Farr-Jones, and a huge brawl broke out.

'It was an important moment,' says Fin. 'You could see some of the Australians going, "Wait a minute here, I don't think I signed up for this!" It was an extraordinarily physical game. But, you know what, there had been a few physical matches: Queensland was physical – very physical – and I don't think they should have been surprised at what was coming. Did they honestly think we were going to lie down for another three weeks in Australia, having been beaten in the first Test? I don't think so.'

We matched them physically in that game, which we had failed to do in the first Test, but we were still down 12–6 going into the final quarter – not that I remember a great deal about it. Farr-Jones caught me with a huge haymaker right on half-time and Kevin Murphy came on the field to check I was okay. I said, 'Smurf, where are we?' and he said, 'You're in Australia.' I said, 'What are we doing here?' and he said, 'Oh, I think you've been concussed.' I said, 'What happens if I come off?' He said, 'You're going home.' I said, 'I'll stay on, then, shall I?' He said, 'Good idea.' Not the sort of behaviour that would happen now, of course, and thank goodness – but it was a different time back then.

'It was a different time and concussion was treated very differently back then,' says Fin. 'But by God I was glad you stayed on. Five minutes to go, you break through, hand off Dominic Maguire and score – and we're ahead.'

'Then Jerry scores an incredible try to seal it,' adds Geech.

'Reboot,' says Jerry. 'The grubber hadn't worked against ACT but I'd been watching a lot of rugby league on the TV on that tour and it was a tactic that worked very well against a flat rush defence like the one the Wallabies were using – so I tried it again. This time it worked. Challenge-solution. I don't know who was around me, I just remember dropping the ball on to my foot and running through. The ball, fortunately, bobbled up for me, I caught it, two or three more steps, and I scored. And from that moment on, it's probably the weirdest moment I've ever experienced in rugby, because it was like the way people describe their life flashing before their eyes after a near-death experience. Obviously, this was totally different, but as I ran back after scoring, my mind was literally like a slide show of mini-rugby, junior rugby, Spartans rugby, Bath United rugby, Bath first-team rugby: just little flashes, moments of players, of people scoring tries, all *vum-vum-vum-vum* in a number of seconds, a very few seconds. It was really fucking weird.'

'I remember looking up from a ruck when he grubbered it through behind the Aussie backline,' says Fin, a note of wonder in his voice. 'And he just glided through and picked it up off the bounce to score. What a class act.'

'It was funny,' says Jerry, 'but I never got nervous when I played. A lot of players might look at that situation – a first Test start for the Lions in a must-win game, only your second ever international match – and go, "Oh, God, I'm shitting myself. What if I make a mistake?" All I ever thought was: "Do you know what, if I make a mistake, I've got fourteen world-class internationals around me; how wrong can it go?" I just couldn't wait to get out and play. I knew that if I knocked the ball on, one of those guys around me would sweep it up before it hit the ground, and nobody was going to have noticed. I just thought: "Fucking hell, this is amazing! *Nothing* can go wrong. I've got too many good players around me." I was really excited, nervously excited, but not in a way that clouded my thinking; my attitude was: "Give me the ball, I want to run, I want to attack these fuckers and really have a go at them. We're 1–0 down, but we're going to win it."'

'He's a Test match animal,' says Geech, grinning. 'Perhaps the greatest Test match animal there's ever been. There was never a scintilla of doubt in that boy's mind.'

'One-all in the series,' says Fin. 'We were still alive. Like ACT, the comeback was on.'

'Do you know,' I tell Fin, 'I've got this photo from later in the tour; we're in a clubroom somewhere and you've got this look on your face. You're looking at the camera, and you've got this look on your face that tells me: "It's going to be okay, Gav. We've got this, we've cracked it, it's going to be okay next week." It's just utter confidence. Geech talks about there being a look between Lions, a special look. And that's it.'

We headed up to the Gold Coast after that game and had a fairly easy week before the deciding Test. The team was unchanged for the match in Sydney.

The night before the game, I wrote in my diary: *No matter what else is written about this tour, we are on the cusp of matching what was achieved by the Lions in New Zealand in 1971 and South Africa in 1974. However hard it must have been for them then, for me, this is equally as tough, with what we've had to deal with, with the press and some of the violence we've come up against and the quality of the Australian team.*

Lions teams have traditionally found it incredibly tough to back up one win with another. Since the turn of the twentieth century, only two Lions teams had managed to win a Test series, and only one of those managed back-to-back victories. It wasn't a surprise that most of the press had written us off before kick-off.

'I think it came down to belief,' says Fin. 'We picked the same side again. Scott was just getting fitter and stronger, and Jerry was growing in confidence all the time. Mike Teague had been outstanding in the second Test and he was even better in the third. Graham Mourie, the great All Black captain used to say: "Ripeness is all." If your team is ripe, if everyone is playing at the top of their game, you can beat anybody. And by the third Test, we were ripe. We won by a point, but I felt like we were in complete control of the match the whole way through. I honestly believe that after that match, we were the best team in the world and could have beaten anybody.'

'Yeah, we were very good. But we got some luck,' I point out.

Shortly after half-time, and with Australia leading 12–9, Rob Andrew attempted a drop-goal that went horribly wide. It bounced up in the in-goal area and the Wallaby winger, David Campese, who had tracked back to gather it, suddenly found himself in a two-on-one with his full back, Greg Martin, up against Ieuan Evans who was the only Lion who had chased the kick. Although he was a hundred yards from the other try line, Campese could see that it was on. He let Ieuan run until he was right on top of him and then flicked a scissors pass to Martin to release him into space – but the pass was a horror. Martin knocked it backwards and then leapt to regather it, just as Ieuan pounced. Ieuan was the first to get a hand to the ball as they collided in a heap. Try to the Lions. It was a freak incident, a total gift, and it proved decisive.

I added a penalty midway through the second half that pushed us into a seven-point lead and I suppose there was an element of us sitting back a little after that. Fin was right, we felt in control. The Aussies managed to eke out a couple of late penalties to take it to within one point with six minutes to go, but that was as close as they got. We kept them pinned in their half and they never got near our line or our posts again.

When the final whistle went – my God, what a feeling. Make no mistake, that was a sensational Australian team. Two years later, they won the World Cup – and their coach Bob Dwyer said that was largely down to the Lions tour and the lessons they learned from it. What we had done, to win a Test series having been one-nil down, was historic, incredible, something none of us will ever forget. Every player had done his bit, the management had been fantastic, and at our head had been Fin. He had taken some flak but he had been unbowed and he had earned the trust and respect of every one of his teammates. What a leader. What a group of men. What a tour.

TWO

COMMITMENT ISSUES

1993

IT WAS SIX o'clock on a Sunday evening when the phone rang. Diane and I both shouted for the other to answer it. Our flat in Edinburgh wasn't very big, but I was slightly closer to the phone. 'Ach, all right, I'll get it.'

I was always going to get it. The Lions squad was being announced in two days' time. I'd learned never to expect anything in life – but that's not to say there wasn't a large bubble of hope roiling around in my stomach.

'Hello?'

'Hi, Gavin, Geech here.'

'Geech, how are you?'

'I'm good, I'm good. Now listen, we're just in the selection meeting.'

'I thought you probably would be.'

'I've been asked to ask you: if you were offered the captaincy of the Lions, would you accept it?'

I paused. 'Geech, why are you phoning me? You know the answer to that question.'

'Well, I've just been asked, because obviously your name's been put forward. Will Carling's name has been put forward and so has Ieuan Evans'. But we want to know: would you be happy to be considered as captain?'

'Geech, you know the answer to that question.'

I hung up on him.

I stared at the phone, my heart racing, then went back to the sitting room and talked with Diane.

An hour later, the phone rang again. It was Geech.

'I've been asked to ask you—' he began.

'Geech, we've had this discussion,' I said, and hung up.

A few minutes passed. Maybe twenty. The phone rang for a third time.

'Hello?'

'Congratulations, Gavin, we're going to name you as skipper of the Lions on Tuesday.'

*

It was an amazing honour. Playing for the Lions in 1989 had been an incredible experience; I'd worn the red jersey made famous by my heroes and I'd performed well in it, we'd won a Test series for the first time in fifteen years and I'd forged bonds of friendships that would last for the rest of my life. Fin Calder had been a magnificent captain. And now it was my turn.

I felt ready. As I said to Geech, 'You know the answer.' I was absolutely confident in my own abilities, there wasn't a doubt in my mind that I was the best full back in Britain and Ireland and that we would be good enough to take on the All Blacks and win. That may come across as appallingly arrogant, but I knew I would be in the Test team, captain or not. And I knew what was coming for us out there. I had spent a lot of time in New Zealand; I'd played there in the 1987 World Cup and then stayed on afterwards, playing for Auckland University for a season where my teammates included Sean Fitzpatrick and Grant Fox. I'd gone back again in the summer of 1990 with Scotland, a Grand Slam under our belts, and we had very, very nearly beaten the All Blacks at Eden Park. We *should* have beaten them. I was back there again in 1992 as part of a World XV, where I experienced victory for the first time against the All Blacks. New Zealand held no fear for me.

And that was the key to my preparation: I really relished the challenge. I was absolutely convinced that the Lions could go down to New Zealand and win the series – and become only the second Lions team in history to do it. I looked around at the other three nations and saw the quality that was available and felt certain that our top side was capable of really taking the game to the All Blacks and going out there and being competitive in every game. I knew that we would need some luck when it came to injuries and the odd refereeing decision, but that was true with any tour, or with any game.

I knew it was probably going to be a toss-up between me and Will for the captaincy. All those experiences in New Zealand probably counted in my favour as Will hadn't yet played there. Ieuan had, but Wales had endured a tough Five Nations that year. In fairness, it hadn't been a vintage season for the Home Nations. England, Scotland and Ireland had all won two and lost two and France had claimed the title, while Wales had only managed one win. There's no doubt that the final game, where Ireland had beaten England 17–3 at Landsdowne Road, had probably counted against Will in the final reckoning.

'I wanted you as captain,' says Geech. 'You were the stand-out full back in the Home Nations at the time, so you were guaranteed a place in the Test team. I knew that other players would respond well to you as a person, would respect you as a player and would therefore follow you as the leader.'

These are kind words and without sounding arrogant, that's how I felt about it at the time. I was entirely confident in my own ability and I felt secure in the knowledge that if I played to my usual standards, I was a certainty for the Test side. I think that is a confidence that all Lions captains should have. I was also sure that, once the decision had been made and despite the rivalry that existed between Scotland and England – which at that point was as fierce as it had ever been in our shared history – I would have Will's backing as captain as well; and I would also have Ieuan's, my old pal from 1989. When it comes to the Lions, the first thing you have to do is set aside your national rivalries and forge a new, united identity – and I knew that we could work together to do that.

While I was conscious that Will might struggle a bit in an environment where he wasn't the main leader, I didn't want to treat him too differently from the rest of the squad. I was the captain, I was the leader and while it was important to share leadership responsibilities, I couldn't be seen to kowtow to anyone else in the squad. But that's not to say that I didn't want him involved as a senior player because he had a mountain of experience – and we needed him at his best, because at his best he was one of the most lethal players on the planet. And he was a winner.

I had no say in the make-up of the rest of the squad and there's no doubt that some of the selections that emerged when it was announced were a little bemusing to rugby critics and to the public at large.

When I ask him about it, Geech shakes his head at the memory of the squad selection and there's a pained expression in his eyes, as if he's back in that meeting room in 1993.

'Selection meetings are often pretty drawn-out affairs for Lions tours,' he begins. 'You're looking at every position, weighing up the pros and cons of one player against another and another and another, then looking at how they might fit into various combinations on the field, how they might play and get on with other guys you've selected, what they might be like in that environment, whether they have the right mindset and personality for touring. It's back and forth, back and forth among the various selectors and it takes a long, long time. But in 1993 it was something else altogether. The captaincy thing, that didn't take too long to decide. The rest of the tour party? Interminable. There was a lot of horse-trading. We'd get to a player and, say he was an English back, you'd get the selectors from Ireland, Wales and Scotland going, "Oh, I don't know – *another* Englishman? You've already got nine in the pack. We've only got two Irish guys so far, let's have this Irish player over that English guy instead. Or, if you want that back, you have to take out one of the English forwards and swap him for someone else." It had nothing to do with who was the better player or the better tourist or the better fit in a combination, it was all about balancing the books for each country.'

'That's unbelievable,' I say. 'I knew that there were some guys in there who were a bit of a surprising choice, but I didn't know it was a trade-off between countries like that.'

That was naive of me, maybe. Looking back, how could I not have seen it? I don't want to single out any players for direct criticism, but to illustrate Geech's point, it was remarkable that Jeff Probyn wasn't selected to tour. Probyn had won two Grand Slams for England (and nearly won a third) and had played in a World Cup final. He was a master scrummager, a hard bugger and had given nightmares to every prop in the international game. But he had been overlooked because he was English and there

42

were deemed to be too many Englishmen in the squad. Talk about cutting off your nose to spite your face. At times throughout the tour, the pack struggled at the set piece and the knowledge that Jeff Probyn was sitting at home twiddling his thumbs sent ripples of discontent through the English contingent in the squad.

'Probyn should have gone,' says Jerry Guscott. 'There's not a doubt in my mind about that. He was hugely respected by every front row player in the Five Nations and all the England guys knew how good he was – and how important he had been to the success that we were enjoying during those years in the late eighties and nineties. I remember thinking at the time that he hadn't been selected because they were looking for quicker, more mobile props. But the ones that were selected were hammered up front and it soon became apparent how much we could have done with having him there to shore the whole thing up. There were too many other English guys, so Probyn missed out. But as a result, ultimately so did we.'

'It was very difficult,' reflects Geech. 'To be fair, I didn't think it was going to be as big a problem as it turned out to be, but there were at least half a dozen players in that squad who I wouldn't have taken.'

'Half a dozen? That's twenty per cent of your squad!'

'I know, I know.' He grimaces. 'And I'm sorry for you and for the other guys that I had total faith in, because those decisions probably cost us. Maybe not in the Test teams themselves, but with the general success and harmony of the tour group. When the Lions asked me to be head coach again in 1997 I said that I would do it on two conditions. The first was that I wanted to pick my assistant coach. That had always been decided for me before. And the second was that me, my assistant coach and Fran Cotton, the manager in '97, would pick the squad – and there would be no one else involved in that.'

'Dick Best was your assistant in '93,' I remember.

'Yes, and in fairness to Dick, I thought he was good. Geoff Cooke was the tour manager, then we had Kevin Murphy and James Robson as our physio and doctor-cum-physio respectively. They were a great bunch, but that was our lot.'

'Now they've got a cast of thousands in the back-room staff.'

'They do – and they need it. We probably needed it then as well, though!'

We fetched up at Weybridge for the traditional squad get-together – a few days of training and getting to know one another before we flew to New Zealand. Everyone got on well and was hugely excited. Rory Underwood was put in charge of organising roommates, a judge was appointed, a fines master, the usual nonsense that greases the wheels of a tour. There was no sense then of the cracks that would appear later – but I suppose that was only natural at that stage. More than half the tour party was English, which was probably to be expected considering how they had dominated the Five Nations over the previous two seasons. For all of Geech's talk of horse-trading, it was interesting that despite Ireland's big win over England, only two Irish players were selected in the initial squad – prop Nick Popplewell and lock Mick Galwey. But there was also a wealth of experience in the squad too, with former tourist Peter Winterbottom back after an outstanding tour in 1983, as well as Mooro, Jerry, Deano, Ieuan, Wade, Rory Underwood, Mike Teague, Rob Jones, Rob Andrew and my brother Scott from 1989. Together with new tourists Martin Bayfield, Ben Clarke, Jason Leonard, Scott Gibbs, Dewi Morris, Tony Underwood and, having missed out on '89 with shin splints, Will Carling. You can understand my belief that we could do something special out in New Zealand.

We had a testing schedule ahead of us. Thirteen matches, including three Tests against the All Blacks. There were no easy games and it was also the last time that all the opposition's Test players would be released to play for their provinces against us. It was the ultimate challenge, just like the ones our predecessors had faced on earlier Lions tours.

We flew into Auckland and the tour started very well. We put thirty points on North Auckland, twenty-nine on North Harbour, came through against a strong Maori team 24–20 in Wellington having been twenty points down at half-time, and then had a major win over Canterbury, sticking twenty-eight points on them. They didn't come close. On paper, things were looking really great, but there was a schism starting to form in the party that would eventually come to define the tour, despite the magnificent play we sometimes produced on the field. I can't pinpoint exactly when it started, but there began to be grumblings among some of the midweek players that they weren't getting a fair crack of the whip and were being sidelined as the Test team began to take shape.

Touring with the Lions is hard. You arrive at a hotel, you unpack, you train, you go to some official function, you train, you play, you pack, you move to the next hotel. It sounds great – and it is great – but it's exhausting. And there are no easy games in New Zealand. It's grown-up rugby out there and every time you take on a provincial team, it's like it's their World Cup final. The majority of them will never play a bigger game in their lives than against the Lions. They want to beat you so badly for their own legend and they want to take your head off before you play the All Blacks to help the national effort. In a scenario like that, there's no room for you to be off your game. If you are, you can fall down the pecking order very, very quickly.

So we were getting big results, some players were flying, some players were loving it, but other guys were struggling. Certain individuals weren't playing brilliantly and the pecking order was shifting. That's how it goes on a Lions tour and some players react well to it and some don't. You have to remember, these guys are all used to being the number one player in their position in their respective countries. They're leaders in their teams, the big boys. Suddenly they find they're third choice in a squad; if that happens they have two choices: suck it up and work harder to get back up the pecking order, or sulk about it and go off-tour, give up and just go through the motions. I couldn't ever imagine doing the latter – not with any of the club sides I played for, not with Scotland and certainly not with the Lions, the team we'd all dreamed about playing for since we were kids. But I saw it happen with some guys on that tour. They just couldn't hack it, they just weren't mentally tough enough.

We had our first real setback of the tour when we played a shadow Test team against Otago at the House of Pain in Dunedin and lost 37–24. The only consolation from that painful lesson was that we had seven days to get things right before the first Test. Injuries to key players – including my brother Scott, Will Carling and Martin Bayfield – had hampered our performance but Otago had completely outplayed us, both in the forwards and with the way they attacked us in the backs. John Timu, John Leslie, Mark Ellis, Stephen Bachop and Josh Kronfeld were all outstanding and they scored five fabulous tries. There's not much that you can take from a game like that other than to use it as a wake-up call to refocus the minds as we turned our attention to the serious business of the Test series. Those three matches were ultimately why we were there. It wouldn't matter if we lost all the provincial games but won the series – that's all we would be remembered for.

The midweek boys got the show back on the road with a big win over Southland in Invercargill and then it was the countdown to the first Test at Lancaster Park in Christchurch.

Captains aren't involved in Test selection any more – Martin Johnson was the last player to have a say – but I think they're potentially missing a trick by not including them. As a captain, you're training and playing and socialising with the guys on tour every day and I would see how my teammates were, and maybe get an inkling if someone was struggling a wee bit or someone was going off-piste a little bit, little nuances that the coaches might miss. As Fin says of his role in 1989, as the captain you have to separate yourself slightly from the rest of the group so that loyalties to certain individuals don't cloud your selection judgement. Scott and I had not discussed Test selection before we left the UK, but we both knew that sentiment would never play a part if it was a close call between him and Will Carling or Scott Gibbs for the centre position. As it transpired, thanks to Otago, that never materialised as a problem.

I had my own room in '93 for this very reason. My door was always open and I made it clear that anyone was welcome for a chat at any time, but it was important that I didn't get swayed by a selection one way or another because I'd shared a room with someone.

Whenever I went into a selection meeting, I always had the starting XV written down for the next game. And do you know what, every time the team took the field the next day, it was the same XV as I had in my note book. There were no hiding places on that tour and it was obvious to me if someone needed a rest or someone needed to play. Again, that emphasises why I believe the Lions captain should be involved in selection. He's appointed to a position of trust; if you don't trust the guy to offer a view based on his experience and knowledge and just general wherewithal, then you could argue that he's the wrong choice as leader. I played nine of the thirteen games on that tour and I felt I knew every player inside out and what their strengths and weaknesses were.

Rory, Ieuan and I got the 1989 back-three band back together. I loved playing with those two; we ended up playing six consecutive Tests for the Lions together, which is pretty special. The back row, half-backs and midfield were all English and we felt confident with that combination at our core. Will hadn't set the world alight on the tour, but we thought of him as a big-game player and so he and Jerry were picked in the midfield, with Rob Andrew and Dewi Morris at half-back, and Deano, the outstanding Peter Winterbottom and the even more impressive Ben Clarke in the back row. Martin Bayfield was about twenty feet tall and built like a house, so he went into the second row along with Andy Reed, who was a good lineout operator. In the front row we went with Nick Popplewell and Paul Burnell at loose and tight head respectively and Kenny Milne at hooker.

It was a side that I was very comfortable with. Again, it was the side that I had in my head going into the selection meeting, even though there were some big calls there – like including Carling over Scott Gibbs, who was tearing up trees, and leaving Mooro out and going for Kenny.

And do you know what, I don't think we got it too far wrong because we very nearly bloody did it – we very nearly beat the All Blacks in that first Test. Like the Scotland game in 1990 at Eden Park, we *should* have beaten them. One particularly outrageous call went against us, and another controversial one settled the result. The first occurred in the opening two minutes when Grant Fox sent a bomb up deep into our twenty-two and Frank Bunce was awarded a try despite Ieuan clearly having control of the ball as they went over the line together. But these things happen, you just have to call everyone in, reset and move on. We had seventy-eight minutes to put it right.

We played some great stuff throughout that game and whenever we got into a good position in their half, they pretty much gave a penalty away to kill our attack. I kicked six penalties that day. It should have been enough. We were all over them. But we were letting them back into the game with our own indiscipline around the breakdown and Grant Fox was kicking as well as I was.

I kicked my sixth penalty from the left-hand touchline to put us 18–17 in front with only a few minutes remaining. No All Blacks side has ever lain down, though, and they upped the intensity to fever pitch. Michael Jones broke through a mass of bodies in our twenty-two and made it to the five-metre line and they whipped it wide where a try looked a certainty, only for Jerry to make a great read on Walter Little, forcing him to knock on. We cleared our lines from the scrum and pushed them back upfield. Time was almost up. They had a lineout on our ten-metre line and one last throw of the dice. We pushed up in defence and looked comfortable containing them. Rob Andrew chopped down Frank Bunce and Deano pounced on the ball. He wrestled with Bunce, who didn't release; it should have been our penalty. Deano got enveloped by the supporting All Blacks and got caught in the ruck, his huge frame trapped on the wrong side. Referee Brian Kinsey blew for the penalty – to New Zealand.

'If ever Grant Fox needed to land a penalty, this is it,' said Grant Nisbet in commentary. 'He's scored 580 points in Test rugby, but the next three – if he gets them – will be the most important.'

It was forty metres out, but bang in front of the posts and there was a strong wind behind him. Grant Fox, my old Auckland Uni teammate. One of the deadliest marksmen in the game. I knew exactly how this was going to go. He nailed it and with it sealed the first Test, 20–18. It was a hammer blow. But we had showed what a good side we were and felt confident that we could come back and win the series. 1–0 down? Not a problem; we'd come back from that four years earlier. Why couldn't we do it again?

Rather unusually, we had two weeks and three more provincial games before the second Test. Taranaki, Auckland and Hawke's Bay were all chances for us to right the ship, just as we had done against ACT in 1989, and give us a boost going into the second Test. The signs looked promising in New Plymouth as we dispatched Taranaki 49–25, but they weren't the strongest of sides. What stood out about that game was that it marked the Lions debut for Martin Johnson – not that Johnno's appearance on tour was without controversy, albeit nothing to do with him.

Wade Dooley, that tower of strength for us in 1989 and throughout his magnificent England career, had returned home following the tragic death of his father and Johnson had been summoned in his place, on the understanding that Wade would be allowed to return to the tour party after the funeral – but that didn't happen. The New Zealand Rugby Union offered to fly him back out, but the Four Home Unions Committee who ran the Lions said that Wade had been replaced and would have to remain in England. It was appalling. We felt enormously let down and devastated for Wade; as senior players, we had been promised that he would be allowed to return and the committee had backtracked on that. Johnno came out and he was fantastic and he played his way into the starting line-up for the second Test at the expense of Andy Reed, but the situation didn't exactly do wonders for the mood in the camp.

Johnno is ensconced in his home office for our Zoom chat about his life with the Lions. 'I was incredibly nervous,' he says about his arrival on tour. 'But in many ways, I had hardly any time to think about it. I turned up, got told the lineout codes and pretty much went straight into it against Taranaki. It was very, very tough on Wade, but I didn't really have time to think about that either until later. You've just got to put all the peripheral stuff to one side and concentrate on playing.'

And boy did he play. Andy Reed had done well in the first Test – so much so that the All Blacks ended up dropping Ian Jones for the second Test – but Johnno had a physicality that Andy didn't have and we felt we needed that in Wellington if we were going to level the series.

But while Johnno was stamping his mark on the tour, other guys were drifting away. While it only really became obvious later on, in retrospect, this was when the wheels started to come off the tour for some of the dirt-trackers.

Trust is a massive part of leadership, particularly in a team environment. For me, trust is everything: as a leader you have to know that you have the trust of all the individual members of the team, and in turn you have to trust the people around you to do their jobs. And if you're not able to trust that person, why not? Are they not quite good enough? Is their attention span not there? Is something else going on in their life?

As I've said before, touring can be very, very tough and it's not an environment that suits everyone. The pressure is intense and so it's hugely important to balance training, playing and the seemingly endless travel with fun and moments to let off steam. Traditionally – although of course not exclusively – this revolves around nights out together drinking. It is a truism of many Lions tours that some of the most important bonding between players occurred thanks to nights out on the piss. Looking back through my diary from 1989, there seldom seemed to be a night (other than before a game) when I wasn't out having at least a few beers – and often a lot more than a few. From a sports science point of view, it's not great for the body, but holistically it's huge. It's a release from that treadmill of training and playing and dealing with the pressure of the tour. It breaks down barriers between players. Geech and the other members of the management in '89 came out with us as well. What also bound you together as a group of players was hauling yourselves out of bed the next day to go through a gruelling training session together, even though you felt like shit. The collective effort to turn up for one another and complete the training come what may is crucial in building a team – and trust in one another.

But there's a fine line between giving people the freedom to blow off steam and guys losing control and compromising the wider group. And therein lay the flaw that undermined the 1993 Lions. Some of the dirt-trackers tipped just on the wrong side of that line and never recovered from it. Their minds were gone. Their focus was compromised. Instead of being part of the greatest sporting adventure of their lives, they went into holiday mode. I still can't believe that I'm writing that about a Lions tour to New Zealand. This book is intended to show examples of great leadership, of tremendous teamwork and remarkable decision-making under pressure. But it is important to include chapters such as this that show what happens when the diametric opposite occurs.

I have to hold my hand up and recognise that as captain I was at fault for not identifying the problem and trying to sort it out. Maybe I was too focussed on the Tests at that stage. I remember, for example, going out for beers one night with Will Carling, just the two of us, and we had a great night. We talked and we laughed and I think we managed to iron out some of the underlying issues that had existed between us before then. We addressed the issue of the captaincy of the tour and at the end of the night we knew that we had each other's full support. Will had been a bit out of sorts on tour and his form hadn't been great, but his focus was much better in the days that followed and he trained with much greater intensity and intent. He still wasn't back to his very best, but he was improving and we still had several weeks of the tour left. But then his girlfriend arrived in New Zealand and I think her presence gave him some kind of perspective on the tour, how he was playing and how he was enjoying it. And the truth was that he wasn't playing as well and he wasn't enjoying it as much as he might have. Should I have stepped in to try to help him? Probably. In fact, definitely. But as I have said, touring with the Lions is an incredibly intense experience. You barely have time to think before you move on to another hotel and another training pitch and another reception and another press conference and prepare for another game, all the while trying to keep your own body and form in a good place. And so I didn't, Will's form and enjoyment continued to drift and he lost his place in the Test side. Eventually, it was Peter Winterbottom who took him aside and called him out on it. And in fairness to Will, he stuck in there and put in some very strong performances for the midweek side in the final weeks while many around him had given up. His captaincy and play in those games showed what a very good player he was.

The next match was Auckland at Eden Park and we put out a very strong side, but they did too, their ranks peppered with All Blacks like Grant Fox, Michael Jones, Zinzan Brooke, Sean Fitzpatrick, Olo Brown and Craig Dowd, who had all played in the first Test, while centre Eroni Clarke and wing John Kirwan would join them for the second. It was a hell of a match at a packed Eden Park, which they edged 23–18, Foxy's boot making the telling difference with three late penalties to snatch it – a sickeningly familiar feeling. I remember sitting in the changing room afterwards and being pissed off that we'd lost, but still comforted that all that really mattered was putting in our best performance the following week in the second Test.

On the Tuesday we headed to Napier to play Hawke's Bay. Jesus, that was a tough watch.

Jerry grimaces when I remind him of that day. We both remember sitting together in the stands, barely able to understand some of the performances we were witnessing from our teammates as we fell to a 29–17 loss. 'It was a weird one, wasn't it?' he says. 'There were some guys clearly trying as hard as they could, but others looked like they couldn't be bothered. Couldn't be bothered playing for the Lions – what the hell is this about? I remember feeling so angry about it; it still makes me angry. No one should ever take the honour of wearing the Lions jersey for granted. You think of how hard we'd all worked to get on that tour – and what the guys sitting at home would have given to have just one chance to be out there in that jersey – and then you had guys walking around, half-heartedly tackling and hitting rucks. It was a fucking disgrace. Embarrassing.'

'Martin Bayfield once described the tour as being like a stag do,' I say.

'Bayfs isn't a million miles away, we had a lot of big nights out, but the boozing we did – it was normal for that time. We had some massive nights out, but we had massive nights out in '89 and '97 as well, so that wasn't the problem on its own. The problem was that certain people stopped caring about the jersey. And that's unforgivable.'

'Apathy has an effect on morale, even if it's not all that obvious,' remarks Geech. 'If a player, or a group of players, are apathetic, it affects their attitude in training, around the hotels, on the buses. It means that when we went and had a few beers, they went at it in a slightly different way. And it's infectious, it worms its way into the minds of other players because it stops them from preparing as well as they might otherwise prepare.'

Over the course of the remaining two weeks on tour, that apathy may well have begun to take its toll, but we shouldn't forget that the Test team was still full of stone-cold winners, determined to make history. We had lost the first Test but we were still in the fight. This was survival time now, though, and we knew we had to deliver in Wellington.

We also knew that the All Blacks would be looking to improve in the second Test, so we had to as well – and as such the management decided to mix things up with the team. Kenny Milne, Paul Burnell, Andy Reed and Will Carling dropped out, replaced by Mooro, Jason Leonard, Johnno and Scott Gibbs.

I felt that these were good, positive changes – but much of the week was also spent in considerable anxiety as I had a problem with my hamstring. I'd pulled it against Auckland and it was still giving me real problems as Saturday approached. I went to see Geech about it and he listened to my complaints and my doubts about whether I could play or not. He sat quietly for a moment and then said, 'I don't care if you only last five minutes; you're leading the team on to the field tomorrow.'

'Psychologically it was huge that you led the team out,' reflects Geech all these years later. 'The Lions captain has a symbolic power when he runs out that tunnel and on to the field, his players steaming out behind him. You were our captain, our leader and one of our best players. The New Zealanders not only respected you but they also feared what you could do to them. You were a powerful runner and tackler, you orchestrated things from the backfield and you could kick goals from anywhere. If they knew you weren't fit and we had to change captains, that would have been a huge boost to them. And even if you only lasted five minutes, we were prepared for that scenario; meanwhile, they would have spent a week worrying about you – and if we'd called it early and not played you, they'd have had an edge.'

A smile plays on Jerry's lips when I mention the hamstring. 'It's interesting on a tour because the dynamic between the captain and the team changes over time,' he says. 'It's different from a Five or Six Nations campaign or the autumn Tests. In those other matches, you get to go home in between games and after training, you're not with each other all the time and so I think it's easier for the captain to come in and gee everyone up and be a leader and be constantly positive because it's in short bursts. But on tour there's no let-up and it's tiring and difficult and at times the senior players have to get the captain geed up rather than the other way around. That's natural, it's human nature – you can't be up the whole time, especially on such a gruelling tour. I remember you struggling with your hamstring before the second Test and the fucking talks we had to have to get you to play . . . I remember a few of us sitting with Geech, and he said, "Look lads, we've got to get Gav right, we need him out there on the field leading us." We started off in agreement, but we had to work so fucking hard to get you on that pitch that we thought, "We'd be better off without him, it's taking too much bloody mental effort to get him out there!"' He cackles loudly – that throaty, wide-mouthed laugh of his that's impossible not to laugh along with.

'Nah, nah,' I say, 'I just wanted all the English boys coming by my room to tell me how good they thought I was.'

He cackles again and throws some more choice expletives my way.

'I didn't want to let the team down,' I say when we've both calmed down. 'It was all about the team; I didn't want to let you down.'

'In some way you had to come to terms with it,' he says. 'You were probably going to be in some discomfort, but Robbo wouldn't have sent you out there if you couldn't run.'

Robbo – Dr James Robson – was on his first tour with the Lions. Having toured with Scotland in 1990, he quickly became a vital cog for both teams, going on to tour six times with the Lions between 1993 and 2013 and to notch up more than 250 Tests with Scotland by the 2021 Six Nations. More than just a person there to treat aches, pains and illnesses, Robbo was an amateur psychologist, a mental rock for the team; his room – open at any hour to anyone on tour – was a safe haven where players, management and back-room staff would go to talk about some physical distress troubling them and end up spilling their hearts out. A wonderful confidant to me on that tour, he also worked wonders with my hamstring that week.

'There are obviously some occasions where you've just got to say, "I'm sorry, that's game over, you can't play,"' he says when I relay Jerry's comment to him. 'But most of the time, ninety per cent of the time, it's about weighing up the balance of risks. So with your hamstring, I could say to Geech, "The worst that can happen is that he only lasts five minutes and he rips his hamstring. The best that can happen is he's just got a bit of discomfort, but he'll be able to manage that himself and he'll gets through the whole game." And that's what we did.'

'I remember training that week,' adds Jerry. 'The senior players made sure we bigged you up, it was all positivity towards you, and it worked! Until you dropped that first high ball under our posts.'

'Thank you very much. How could I forget?'

It was the same tactic that Grant Fox had used in the first Test for Frank Bunce's try – and it paid dividends again. The All Blacks won a lineout just outside our twenty-two and Foxy hoisted an up-and-under. It came down right on the try line. I'd positioned myself well, with a foot planted either side of the line so that I could dot it down for a twenty-two drop-out. But I lost sight of the ball in the piercing Wellington sun and it dropped right through my hands. Eroni Clarke had chased well and he dived on the loose ball to score. Foxy added the conversion. 7–0 down, barely two minutes on the clock. *Fuck me, great start, Gav.*

'No, it wasn't a great start,' says Guscott, with a cat-like grin. 'But we got ourselves back into it. Rob Andrew got a drop-goal and you got a couple of penalties. Your hamstring was holding up fine.'

'Adrenaline,' I reply. 'It's an amazing thing. After conceding the early try, I don't recall thinking about my hamstring once.'

'As a young player on that tour, I was so pleased that you were out there,' says Johnno. 'Tony Clement was the back-up full back and he was a good player, but he didn't have anywhere near the same aura for us or for the opposition. And even though I was young, I was able to appreciate that by playing with a dodgy hamstring you were putting your own reputation at risk, but you were doing that for the team so that we had the best chance of success, and that was really galvanising.'

'I'm not sure if I'll put that in the book, it blows too much smoke up my arse,' I say.

'Well you should, because it's true,' says Johnno. 'This is a book focussing on leadership, isn't it? Well that was good leadership. We needed you and you put your balls on the line for us – and then you delivered. Even if you did gift them a try!'

That's kind of Johnno, but I'm not sure if the lesson to take from this is that a player should take the field with an injury. We got lucky with mine; it was minor enough for me to overcome it and, as Jerry intimated when talking about the Tests in '89, I had fourteen world-class players around me to help take the pressure off. We showed admirable game management playing into the sun, our attack was slick, the forwards were thundering around the breakdown and Bayfs and Johnno dominated the lineout

– so completely, in fact, that it forced the All Blacks into some skulduggery. We were leading 9–7 at half-time and in those days we stayed out on the pitch for the break. During the following week, Geech showed us a video clip from half-time which focussed in on the All Blacks' huddle. Back in 1993, you could only make substitutions if a player was injured. Well, with Bayfs and Johnno ruling the roost no matter who had the throw, Laurie Mains, the All Black coach, had to try and level the playing field.

'I remember watching the video,' said Johnno. 'They cheated at half-time, didn't they? A guy ran on the field with a wee note from Mains which he gave to Fitzpatrick. Fitzy read it then looked up at Mark Cooksley, had a quick word, and all of a sudden Cooksley is on the ground with a leg injury. Off he goes and on comes Ian Jones.'

Not that it made a huge amount of difference. Ours was one of the best lineout performances I've ever seen – and crucially, not only did it give us a steady supply of ball, it put the shits up the All Blacks. Even more crucially, it put the shits up Fitzpatrick, their totemic leader – and it was his error that led to one of the great Lions tries for Rory Underwood.

The All Blacks set up a maul on halfway and as they began to roll around the edge, Fitzpatrick lost control and knocked the ball on. Dewi Morris was the first to it and darted blind, fixed Bunce and passed to Guscott. Jerry straightened the line and managed to force Kirwan into two minds about where to defend before slipping the ball to Rory. That half-second of hesitation in Kirwan's mind was all that Rory needed and he burnt him on the outside and scorched down the touchline. John Timu was covering across at full back but he didn't get near him. Rory was in at the corner.

I couldn't manage the touchline conversion, but I added a fourth penalty to take the score to 20–7, which is where it remained until full time. It was only the Lions' sixth ever victory on New Zealand soil and the biggest winning margin – which it remains to this day.

It was one of the greatest feelings of my life walking off that pitch. I found Geech and gave him a big kiss and said, 'Thanks for having faith in me,' I said, and he replied, 'No, no, that's all right. I knew you could do it.'

I saw Fitzy after the game and had a wee chat. 'Just wait until you read the papers,' he said, looking a little ashen. 'They're going to crucify us for this.' He was right, they tore them to pieces. But that wasn't unusual in New Zealand when the All Blacks suffered a loss. What was also not unusual was for that criticism to add motivation to an already hugely motivated team to make amends. I knew that a big backlash would be coming our way the following week. But we had momentum now – all we had to do was somehow find the strength to keep it up.

And that's why the final midweek game of the tour, against Waikato, was such a body blow. Just as against Hawke's Bay, the dirt-trackers took a pasting. And but for the efforts of a few players, like Carling and Stuart Barnes, it looked like most of the team were already mentally on the plane home. Future Lions coach Warren Gatland wore the number two jersey for the home team and he was magnificent, at the vanguard of a huge Waikato performance. They thumped us 38–10.

'You felt for some of the boys in the midweek side, because they were still playing their hearts out while the rest had just given up,' reflected Peter Winterbottom many years later. 'They didn't do the shirt justice. The key to any successful Lions tour is having a focus on success throughout the whole squad, not just the Test team. The dirt-trackers have to drive the performance levels because if they play well, the Saturday side has to play even better to keep their shirts. It makes training more intense, more

60

accurate, more worthwhile and it just adds and adds and builds the team spirit. Whether you're in the Test side or not, everyone has to pull in the same direction. On the two tours I went on, in 1983 and 1993, we didn't do that, and the Waikato and Hawke's Bay matches in 1993 were embarrassing.'

When I reflect on this, do I feel let down? No, I don't feel let down. Is there anything I could have done differently to prevent the schism? Am I any less a leader or a person because some teammates of mine went off-tour for a while? Perhaps I'm not the one to pass judgement on this, but I don't think so. What I realised after a while on that tour was that you couldn't be all things to all men, and it was physically and mentally impossible to try and be in control of every situation. I don't think you can ever be in total control in any case – and if you tried to be, you would make even bigger errors. All that you can do in scenarios like this is to try and set some standards, both for yourself and for the team. As a captain you can lead by example in training, you can lead by example on the field of play, and you then do your damnedest to try and get everyone else to follow you. But there is only so much the captain can do. After that, it's down to the individual and, unfortunately, not every individual followed that lead in 1993. I suppose those are the lessons, as painful as they were, that we learned from that tour.

Despite the setback in Waikato, we were still in the series. Our backs had been against the wall ahead of the second Test and we'd produced one of the finest Lions performances of all time to win. Now we had a chance to finish the job and go down in history.

We had a brilliant start. Scott Gibbs crashed over after fifteen minutes and I added the conversion to an earlier penalty and we were looking good at 10–0. But the All Blacks at Eden Park are a different beast. The ferocity increased and they began to play with greater harmony, roared on by the crowd. Lee Stensness chipped over our defensive line to put away his fellow centre Frank Bunce, before Fitzy got on the end of the rolling maul to score. Foxy kicked both conversions for a 14–10 half-time lead. Nobody in a red jersey gave up that afternoon, but we ran out of steam in the second half and the All Blacks punished us. Foxy kicked us to death and then Jon Preston dug the final knife into the ribs with a late run-in. The final score was 30–13 and the series was settled 2–1 to New Zealand.

Afterwards, Fitzy and I shared a photo in swapped jerseys with a massive shield that had been created for the series. I have a bit of a rigor smile, but it's a nice photo of us together. You see how much it means to Fitzy, understandably.

'Playing the Lions is a massive, massive thing for the home team,' he says. 'We only get the opportunity to play you every twelve years, so in rugby terms it's not even a once-in-a-generation thing, it's probably a once-in-every-two-generations thing. The Lions have always been a huge thing for me personally. I was eight years old in 1971 when the Lions came to New Zealand and ripped us to pieces. They won every provincial match and then took the series. Those guys were my heroes. So to play the Lions myself was incredible. They are the last of the great tourists; no one does tours like that anymore. Winning that series was incredibly important for so many reasons – it helped us recover from the disappointment of the 1991 World Cup, it helped us on the road to the successes we enjoyed over the next few years, and it marked our place in history.'

For all that the 1993 tour ended in defeat for the Lions, I think the leadership lessons learned from it were stark and they had a significant impact on Geech, Johnno, Jerry, Ieuan and the other boys that went on the next tour. It might seem simplistic, but it became clear that for a Lions tour to have success, every member of the party and every team that takes the field has to have enormous pride in playing for the jersey and for each other, have a desire to never let standards slip and to do justice to the legacy of those who have worn the jersey before them. And the simple truth is, in 1993, we didn't have enough players that were committed to that ethos, and the squad had been further weakened from the outset by the horse-trading that had occurred in the final selection meeting before the tour.

THREE

ALL FOR ONE

1997

MARTIN JOHNSON'S LIONS career started with a brutal hangover.

It was 13 June 1993 and he was in Canada on an England B tour. 'I woke up that morning, feeling absolutely horrific,' he tells me. 'We'd played the final game of our tour the day before and had a massive night out. We were about to get back on the piss again pretty early on the Sunday with a court session when I got pulled aside to be told that Wade Dooley's dad had sadly passed away and he was leaving the Lions tour in New Zealand – and I'd been called up.

'Now, obviously, the England boys weren't going to let me get away with that one, so I had to down a load of drinks and I ended up getting absolutely plastered again. I can't really remember getting home to the UK. You know when you pile the bags up outside the check-in desk? I can remember lying on those, but that's about it.

'I slept it off on the way home, then drove up to Leicester and went into work to see my boss. He was obviously delighted that I was back because I'd been away for three weeks, but I had to say, "Bob, I've been called up for the Lions tour." You could see the contrasting emotions on his face because he was very happy for me but also realised that he now had to find cover for me and it was summer and everyone else was going off on holiday.

'He said, "How long are you going to be gone?" And I had to tell him it was going to be five more weeks. He just said, "Oh," and held his head in his hands for a little while. Anyway, he was brilliant about it and I drove back down to London that night. I met up with Bob Weighill [from the Four Home Unions Committee] at Twickenham and he took me to a room that was full of all the kit the Lions had left behind for the replacements. It was like an Aladdin's cave of Lions stash. Absolutely incredible. In those days you could just about buy a replica jersey, but nothing else, so I was like a kid at Christmas seeing all this kit. You don't really feel worthy of it . . . it didn't even seem real.

'Anyway, once I had all the kit I headed to the airport and met up with Vinny Cunningham, the Irish centre, who'd also been called up – for your brother. I slept virtually the whole way; he must have thought I was some sort of complete weirdo because I barely spoke, just slept. But it had been a hell of a few days.

'I made my debut against Taranaki in New Plymouth. It was almost too big to describe the moment. I remember running out with my Lions shirt on and just feeling all these different emotions – excitement, nerves, a question of "are you worthy" in the back of my mind. It was the same when making my debut for England, but this was now the Lions, the red jersey. I'll always love that badge, and Geech would always go on about that badge, as well. It was just emotive.

'It was a tough game – a typical midweek game. They were all full of spirit and the crowd were all up for it, but we eventually got on top of them, we were a little bit too good, and won by a scoreline that probably doesn't quite reflect how tough the game was at times.'

'You did bloody well,' I tell him. 'From the moment you arrived, you made an impression. It was awful for Wade, but you showed immediately that you deserved to be there. They didn't give you much time to acclimatise though, did they? About three minutes. Then they threw you in against Auckland in the next game as well.'

'That was a hard, hard game.' He shakes his head at the memory. 'I remember Zinzan Brooke calling it the fourth Test afterwards – and he was right, it felt like a Test match. More than half the All Blacks were in that team and Eden Park was bouncing. It was nip and tuck and they just edged it. A tough game. A brilliant game.'

'And then you were playing a Test match for real a week later,' I note. 'Geech asked me what I thought about playing you and I didn't think twice. You looked very comfortable; I was never worried about putting you in the side.'

He barks a laugh. 'Well, I was very worried, I'm glad you weren't! I think, whenever you play, unless you're born with some sort of massive self-confidence, whenever you go up a level, it's always "am I good enough?" I just wanted to be worthy of being there, of being in the shirt. There were a lot of very experienced players on that tour, who I'd watched as a schoolboy, including you, so there was this sense of "is this really happening to me?"

'I remember Deano grabbed me quite early after I'd arrived and said, "Look, if you get stuck in and just get on with it and do what you do, you've got a chance here to make the Test team." That gives you a bit of confidence, but you've got to go and do it.

'So I played that Taranaki game midweek, and a good thing for me was I'd played some of these teams when I'd been in New Zealand three or four years before, so they held no fear for me.

I'd played Taranaki and beaten them, and I'd played against Auckland and been beaten. So it wasn't totally unknown.'

Indeed it wasn't. And if it hadn't been for a shoulder injury that required an operation in the UK, Johnno might well have been lining up in black in that Test series instead of red.

Born in Solihull in the West Midlands in 1970, Johnno had been a schoolboy star and despite playing No.8, the England age-grade coaches spotted his obvious potential and converted him into a second-row. In 1988, England Schools travelled to Australia to play a three-team tournament with Australia and New Zealand. England won both their games and reports about the quality of the side soon filtered back to New Zealand, where John Albert, who was head coach at Tihoi, a tiny club near Taupo in King Country, was on the lookout for new players. Tihoi were bottom of their league and were struggling for playing numbers. Albert wrote to the RFU and asked them to forward his letter to each member of the schoolboys' side, advertising a season of playing club rugby in New Zealand. 'I figured the New Zealand schoolboys would be spoken for,' Albert recalls, 'and the Australians were probably being sought by rugby league clubs with lots of cash. So I went for the Poms.'

Johnno, only nineteen at the time and playing in the Leicester Tigers' youth team, jumped at the chance. He paid for his flights out to New Zealand in exchange for board and lodging. He moved into the spare room at John Albert's house and the day after his arrival he was pulling on his boots for his first game for Tihoi.

'He arrived on the Friday, we had him playing on Saturday, and then we tried to get him drunk on Saturday night so he could get a good night's sleep,' recalls Albert. 'It was easy for me to pick him because we didn't have many players and anyone over six foot was a bloody good asset to us. The opposition players all wanted to show him how tough they were, to welcome him to

New Zealand the old-fashioned way, but he could handle it. He took what was given. By the end, he was dishing it back, too.'

'Most of the players were either farmers or bushmen who felled trees for a living,' remembers Johnno. 'It was pretty rough. Some guy would turn up that you hadn't seen before and he'd put his kit on and go out and smash people for eighty minutes.

'We had guys who would play prop one week and in the centre the next. They would get stuck into each other. It was physical work.'

After just a few games, he received an invitation from the great Colin Meads, chairman of King Country, to train with the provincial side – and within ten days he had forced his way into the team. He played throughout the season for King Country and was then selected to train with the New Zealand Under-21s. Although he didn't make it into the Under-21 team that year, he joined College Old Boys Marist in Taupo the following season and John Hart, who would later coach the All Blacks, selected him for the Under-21s at the end of the year, where Johnno would line up alongside several future All Blacks who would all play against the Lions in 1993: the fearsome wing Va'aiga Tuigamala, full back John Timu, flanker Blair Larsen and prop Craig Dowd. The Junior All Blacks went on an undefeated three-match tour of Australia, where Johnno got the better of another player with whom he would have a long international rivalry: John Eales.

'I didn't realise he was English until after the game,' recalls Eales. 'I went up to him at full time and said, "Oh, thanks for the game," and in this thick English accent, he responded, "Yeah, well played, mate." Over the years we had some good battles. I have the highest regard for him; we were very different players and he was a lot harder than I was, a lot better at all that tough stuff and whatnot – but I think what you could say about him is that every team that he played in played better because he was there. And I reckon only a little bit of that would have been what he said, and much of it would have been what he did. Because he was the sort of guy that led by his deeds, and if there was a hard job to be done, he was the one doing it. He was athletic and tough; I reckon he would have been among the hardest trainers and certainly, if there was a physical contact session in training, I don't reckon he'd have been a guy you'd want to be around too much!'

'I was all set to stay in New Zealand and who knows what might have happened,' reflects Johnno. 'But I needed a shoulder operation. There was a specialist recommended to me back at home, so that's who I went to see. Once the op was done and I was recovering at home, I was back in the Leicester set-up and the New Zealand side of things felt like it was done.'

Once recovered from surgery, Johnson worked his way into the Tigers' first team, where he would become a permanent fixture for the next fourteen years.

Johnno won his first cap for England in the 1993 Five Nations against France at Twickenham; his next two caps were won during his stunning late appearance for the Lions that summer. Although the All Blacks won the series 2–1, it must have been bittersweet for the New Zealand selectors to watch how well their one-time future prospect went in the colours of the opposition.

'There's nothing surer than he would have been an All Black,' remarked Colin Meads. 'Martin was a quiet, nice young fella when he arrived. He was a workhorse and I was supposed to be his tutor. After he had played two or three games for King Country I thought I'd better say something to him. This was up at North Harbour. I said to him: "Martin, you've got to get more aggressive. You're allowed to hurt the opposition when you've got the ball. People don't realise that. You're a big unit. When you get the ball you're in charge of the whole game. You're allowed to knock someone over. You've got to get more aggressive." He listened to me and he changed. It was all part of his development. He became the enforcer, England's strong man.'

By the time the next Lions tour came around, Geech was once again at the helm and knew what he wanted from my successor as captain. Geech was head coach at Northampton at the time and he knew what effect Johnno had on his Leicester teammates and the opposition every time the Tigers took the field. He had also become central to a hugely powerful English pack that had won a Grand Slam in 1995, claimed the Five Nations title again in 1996 and been pipped 23–20 in what turned out to be a Grand Slam decider against France in 1997. He wasn't on many other people's shortlist to lead the Lions as he was captain for neither Leicester nor England, but that didn't bother Geech.

'People are probably fed up of me using the term "Test match animal",' says Geech with a grin, 'but that is exactly what Johnno was. And more than that, he was a Lions Test match animal. He'd been dropped in at the last minute in 1993, right into the cauldron of the Test series in a must-win game and he took to the whole thing as if he had seventy caps, not one.

'Each country we tour with the Lions has its unique style of rugby, its unique quirks and unique identity. South Africa is a country of big men and they respect big men. Physical intimidation and dominance are the hallmarks of rugby out there. They have always had talented backs, but they want to break you physically before they give the ball any air. You need a certain type of character and a certain type of player to stand up to that. Johnno ticked every box for me. It didn't matter that he wasn't captaining Leicester or England; he was a leader for them – and he would be surrounded by great leaders, who would help him.'

'That, for me, was the key,' says Johnno. 'Every time a Lions tour comes around, I get asked about leadership and people want to talk to you and get the secrets. "Oh, Johnno, you were a good captain, blah, blah, blah," and I say, "Well, the first thing you need to be a good captain is to have a good team with you and a great group of leaders." In 1997, that's exactly what I had. Ieuan Evans: captain of Wales, Lions legend. Jerry Guscott: probably England's greatest-ever back, Lions legend. Jason Leonard: battle-hardened, experienced, a Test Lion in '93. Scott Gibbs: been there, done it, seen it all, a Test Lion in '93 and then a pro rugby league player. Rob Wainwright: captain of Scotland, a shrewd operator. Lawrence Dallaglio: captain of Wasps, hugely charismatic. Keith Wood: captain of Ireland, also hugely charismatic. Tim Rodber: hugely experienced, an Army captain, a warrior. All these guys could talk the talk and walk the walk. There was no need for Churchillian speeches from me – these guys could do that all for me. Then you add in Geech and his right-hand man, Jim Telfer, who are two of the greatest speech-makers in sporting history, plus the manager, Fran Cotton, who was also a Lions legend, and you didn't need me to write inspiring speeches. So that is the secret. These guys are totems. All I had to do was say a few words now and again and take the lead by training my balls off and playing as hard and as well as I could.'

It sounds simple, doesn't it? But Johnno has a special ability to assess situations on and off the field and break them down into their simplest form, drilling to the nub with laser-like accuracy and understanding. My admiration for him, which has always been sky-high, has only grown over the years as we talk more often.

Fin Calder has a story about Johnno which illustrates his charisma as well as the regard in which he is held by his peers. 'In 2017,' says Fin, 'there was a special dinner for all the living

Lions captains. Sam Warburton couldn't make it, but there was you and me, Paul O'Connell, Brian O'Driscoll, Johnno, Ciaran Fitzgerald, Billy Beaumont, Phil Bennett, Willie John McBride, John Dawes, Tom Kiernan, even Ronnie Dawson was there. Now this is a room of big, big names – characters, leaders. And Johnno got up to speak and you could have heard a pin drop. We all deferred to him. Among that group, he was the lion king.'

'Johnno was never flashy,' says Geech. 'He did the hard work and he did it brilliantly and that's what inspired people to follow him. That's who we wanted to lead us in South Africa. I spoke to Jim Telfer about the fact that I wanted to give the captaincy to Johnno and he said, "Are you sure?" and I said, "I've never been more sure of anything in my life." That was good enough for Jim, and it was the same with Fran. They backed my judgement and then they backed Johnno.'

The Lions had a fearsome schedule in front of them. After a couple of lower-key opponents to begin the tour they then had to take on some of the most iconic teams in rugby history – Western Province, Northern Transvaal, Transvaal and Natal before facing the Emerging Springboks and then begin a three-week crusade against the Springboks, the team that had been crowned world champions two years earlier, had won a first-ever series against France in France at the end of 1996 and contained some of the greatest players ever to play the game.

'Touring South Africa is always incredibly difficult,' says Geech. 'Every team is filled with huge men, as I say, and like New Zealand, the whole country buys into a Lions tour. They love it – but that doesn't mean they will make it easy for you. I went on a reconnaissance trip the year before when the All Blacks were on tour in South Africa and their head coach, John Hart, was good enough to let me join their camp for a few days so that I could see how they took on the challenge. It was both fascinating and enlightening. I wrote a twenty-page report on my findings when I got back and presented it to the Lions committee.'

'What were your key findings?' I ask.

'The first was to take a bigger squad than the Lions had ever taken before. He said to take three players in certain key positions like scrum-half and hooker because with a tour like that if you only have two players they will both be either starting or sitting on the bench for every game and they'll be exhausted by the time we reach the Test series.

'He also said, "South Africa will try and mess up as much of your organisation as they can, because it's in their interest for you to be on edge the whole time. You'll turn up for training and the scrum machine you were promised won't be there; the training ground you booked will already have someone on it; rucking shields and tackle bags will be mysteriously missing. So take control of as much as you can." So we copied the All Blacks and brought all our training gear with us, we even shipped out our own scrummage machine and had Nigel Horton, who invented it, driving it around the country in a lorry. Everything we did, we were in control of. There was nothing they could do to mess us up.

'That advice from John Hart was all really good, and then just watching them train and hearing them talk about how they planned to take on the Springboks, I started to get a game in my head that I knew we had to look to play.'

'That was a hell of a series,' I say. 'I remember it well. The All Blacks won 2–1.'

'Yes, for the first time in their history they beat the Boks in the series in South Africa. In the first meeting I had with the squad in '97, I showed them a video clip of the last ninety seconds of the second Test that the All Blacks won, and it's ninety seconds of rugby within five metres of their try line. They're just defending and defending as the Springboks batter their line trying to score in the dying seconds of the match to win and keep the series alive. And when the final whistle goes, I think there's a knock-on, you look at Sean Fitzpatrick, Zinzan Brooke, some of the great All Blacks, and not one of them is on their feet! They are all absolutely flat-out on the ground, exhausted, they have nothing left. And I showed that to the Lions players, and I just said, "That is what you're going to have to be prepared to do to win a Test series in South Africa."'

The Lions met up at Weybridge in Surrey for a week's training and bonding before flying to South Africa. They brought in a team-building company to run some fun exercises for the players, but a more basic form of team bonding also worked the magic of breaking down barriers, just as it has done on every previous Lions tour: a few good old-fashioned piss-ups.

'Those sessions are as important as anything else you might do,' says Johnno. 'It's a bit agricultural, but having drinks together really does help to break the ice and forge bonds. We made it a rule that we would go out as a full squad at least once a week on tour. Not everyone had to have a skinful of booze, but we would go out for dinner all together. It was a really important factor in keeping the group tight.'

'Those rules – ones we made ourselves – were key,' adds Jerry Guscott. 'The management said to the players, "You write your own code of conduct," and that was a great leadership moment from them because that empowered us and made us responsible for our own behaviour. So if we fucked up, we hadn't just let down a coach who had set a series of rules, we'd have let down all the guys we played with and we'd have let down ourselves, broken our own standards. That was clever of them. It meant we kept ourselves in check. That's not to say we didn't have some massive nights out on tour, and some guys got super loose at times, but we policed ourselves one way or another. The All Blacks have a saying about "crossing the whitewash". On the outside of the whitewash – i.e. away from the training field or a match – you can do what you like, within reason, but when you cross the whitewash to train or play, it's business time and you don't fuck around, you deliver. In 1997 – and in 1989 – guys would turn up for training in pieces, but they would cross the whitewash and no matter how rough they felt, they would do the business. For whatever reason, that didn't happen in 1993; but it did in 1997.'

'You've got to have a kind of a framework,' agrees Lawrence Dallaglio, when I mention the Lions Laws, as they became known. 'I don't like to use the word culture, because it's over-used, but you need a modus operandi of how you're going to work as a group, and the law can't be laid down by the coach or the manager, it's got to be a framework and a set of principles agreed by the players.

'It was an open forum; we spent a lot of time with Impact, the training group, and we discussed what kind of framework we were all comfortable operating within. What's our view on timekeeping? If you're going to get picked for the team, when should you be told? If you're going to get dropped from the team, when should you be told? We dealt with absolutely everything and then we presented it to each other, distilled it down to what we felt was the right sort of MO for us all, and then we agreed it and signed it off. Then, if there was ever an issue on the trip, we had this framework to come back to, which we'd all signed up to. I think it was a really, really good thing – probably ahead of its time; it was really important to do.'

'I had this big thing about week five,' says Geech, 'because I think week five is the pressure week. If there's something not right in the tour party, it will raise its head in week five. If there's somebody that irritates you, then it'll go over the top in week five. And week five is generally the first Test week. So if things are going to be difficult, it's going to be during that week. So we talked a lot about week five and week-five behaviour and how the players would manage themselves if they weren't picked in the Test team.

'Once they had the laws agreed, Impact put them on a little yellow laminated card and gave them to each player. And the thing was, if a player ever started to step over the line, all somebody had to do was to start bringing the card out, and then there'd be an acknowledgement, and the card would go back. So, all the discipline and organisation of that was purely within the group; they respected what they were doing with each other as a group.'

'We were lucky that the tour was just full of very, very good people who all wanted to be successful,' says Johnno. 'I remember the first time we sat down at a senior players' meeting at the start of the tour, my worry was that I'd not captained England and had only captained Leicester a handful of times and that people could be thinking, "Why is he captain? Why isn't someone else captain? Why isn't Ieuan captain, why isn't Keith Wood captain, why isn't Rob Wainwright captain, why isn't Jason Leonard captain?" But the moment I sat down with those guys, you could tell the mood was: "This is about us winning, not me winning or me playing or me leading, it's about us." That was exceptional. And we all worked together to keep an eye on the rest of the players, making sure everyone fitted in and was happy. It was shared responsibility and shared leadership – an incredibly important dynamic.'

'The only way you're ever going to be successful is if you create that kind of philosophy and mindset where you're prepared to share everything that you've ever learned as a person and as a player with everyone,' says Dallaglio. 'You've got to put it all out there on the table; you've got to download your rugby and your life experiences and just share it with everyone. There are not many organisations where you go into bat with your three biggest competitors and tell them everything you've ever learned! But equally, it's about giving and sharing, so the more you give, the more you learn. But it takes something quite unique and quite special to have the trust in those around you to be able to do that – but we knew that it was the only way that the team was going to be successful.'

When I mention this to Keith Wood, he nods his head vigorously. 'That's exactly it,' he says. 'It's hard to learn a new way of playing in two months. It's hard to follow what a coach says every fifteen minutes in a training session. You're limited to the amount of time you have. But if you can get people to buy into a philosophy, a culture, then everything becomes an awful lot easier. So our culture was trust in the player beside you. That's sort of indirect leadership, but that's incredible leadership, and incredibly forceful and repeatable. And the idea that you had to trust the people around you meant you had to understand the people around you. That's a piece of leadership that's incredible: that suddenly, you're looking at how the guy next to you does something. I now understand his nuance. I now understand what makes him tick. And a lot of that is done off the field, not on the field. I think that's what I loved most about that tour: the players each knew their job but they also focussed on trying to understand each other a little bit better. And that then helped us play better.'

'There were no egos,' concurs Geech. 'And that fed into the way we wanted to play as well. I wanted us to be fluid and dynamic, to play on the edge as often as possible, and involving every player on the pitch. The southern hemisphere teams tended to think of northern hemisphere teams as predictable, cautious and one-dimensional. That was the opposite of how we wanted to play. We wanted players who were good enough – and felt empowered enough – to play the game as they saw it in front of them. They had to make decisions on the move and had to get in and out of contact quickly to keep the ball alive.

'In the selection of any large group, there are invariably choices which turn out to be mistakes. But Jim and I could put our hands on our hearts to this day and say that there wasn't one individual we would change if we could have our time again.'

'There were some very brave calls you made,' I say. 'Will Greenwood was uncapped. Barry Williams was third-choice hooker for Wales. Matt Dawson was third- or fourth-choice scrum-half for England. Additionally, you brought in all these guys who had recently been in rugby league and were still finding their feet in union. You had Tom Smith and Richard Hill who only had four caps each. Neil Back only had five caps and hadn't played for England for two years. Jerry Guscott wasn't starting for England. There were five guys playing for Newcastle that season, who weren't even in the top league in England at the time. Both your stand-offs came from the same club and Gregor wasn't even playing in that position that season for Scotland. You played Neil Jenkins out of position at full back. Huge, huge calls.'

'Yeah, but we saw something in each of those guys that would fit with the way we wanted to play in South Africa. And, unlike in 1993, they were *our* calls – no one was forced on us, and I think that added confidence in what we were doing. If we were going to go down against the Springboks, we weren't going to go down wondering. And if we got it right, we felt we might just spring a trap on them.'

The Lions flew into Johannesburg to a disparaging welcome from the hosts. Guscott remembers it well. 'Louis Luyt, who was the president of the South African Rugby Union, gave this awful speech where he basically said, "Thanks for coming, but we're going to smash you 3–0." It really pissed people off. I looked around at the squad and thought, "Mate, you have no idea what you're talking about. Look at the calibre of this squad, the coaches and the management; we've got a serious chance here. But write us off if you want to – there's a shock coming your way."'

There's no doubt that Luyt's speech was disrespectful in its tone, but he wasn't the only one predicting a Springbok massacre of the Lions. Every newspaper in South Africa – and most in the UK and Ireland as well – predicted either a 3–0 or 2–1 victory for the world champions. Some even suggested that the Lions would suffer at least four losses in the provincial games as well.

'The 1997 Five Nations had been poor,' recalls Geech, 'and accounts of some of the games were really scathing. We were about to embark on the first Lions tour to South Africa in seventeen years and you could see that their media felt that British and Irish rugby wasn't constructive or dangerous in an attacking sense. You could look at it two ways from our side of things: either we were in trouble, or we were going to be able to come in under the radar, written off. We took the stance that this was all to our advantage. France winning the Grand Slam hid the fact that England were extremely good and among the other nations there were some real gems playing, even if the matches themselves had been a bit underwhelming.'

'It's easy to take the sledging we got in the press and elsewhere and use it as fuel,' reflects Johnno. 'And that's exactly what we did. You might talk a big game to the media and say that you don't read newspapers or those kinds of things don't bother you – but you're lying. Any player who has ever said that is lying. But if you don't let it demoralise you, then it can be a great driver. And I don't think any player who makes it as far as the Lions is ever going to be demoralised by something like that. There is too much of the winner in each one, too much of the competitor. They wouldn't be there otherwise.'

'I think that's something that helped galvanise us as a group,' says Richard Hill. 'We were going to go and play against the world champions, the domestic game in South Africa was deemed to be very strong, very powerful, forward-orientated, and we were going on a tour where no one gave us a hope in hell of winning. That pulled us together, helped focus our minds. There were going to be no easy games.'

The Lions burst into action against Eastern Province and scored thirty-nine points in a performance full of power and dynamism. It wasn't perfect by any stretch of the imagination – the defence was breached on a few occasions and the set piece creaked – but as an opening statement, it was impressive.

The second game against Border was a stodgier affair but that was largely down to appalling conditions, and the Lions battled to another win. The warm-ups now over, game three was where the tour started for real: Western Province at Newlands, the stadium where the first Test would also be played.

'Western Province was a huge game,' says Johnno. 'They had a massive pack and a lot of Test quality – they had current Boks in James Small and Fritz van Heerden and guys who had a load of caps behind them like Garry Pagel, Keith Andrews and Robbie Brink, and then they had guys who would come through to have big international careers in the years afterwards, like Corné Krige and Bobby Skinstad, while Percy Montgomery was going to make his Test debut against us in the series. So this was our first big test. It was also my first game because I'd been struggling with a groin injury; it required an op but James Robson knew that I could make it through the tour if we managed it carefully.'

'Again, that was an important aspect of management on that tour – keeping a close eye on the injuries guys were carrying and monitoring their playing loads,' remarks Geech. 'James Robson was outstanding at it.'

'It was hard watching the first two games and also not being involved much in training,' says Johnno, 'so I was absolutely champing at the bit to get out there.'

He wasn't the only one. James Small, playing on the wing for Western Province, was desperate to show the Springbok management that he was still good enough to play Test rugby despite his team not playing in the Super 12 that season (Western Province had failed to finish in the top four of the previous season's Currie Cup, on which Super 12 participation was set) and the press attention around the match was huge.

'That week was when the press coverage really went up a gear,' notes Hill. 'Johnno was playing, James Small was playing, it was perhaps the first indication from our side about who the coaches were thinking might play in the Test matches. There had been a lot of press before, but it suddenly went to a new level. Geech and Fran, in particular, were very good about managing the team through that.'

'It can be a minefield,' says Geech. 'You have to tread your way through it very, very carefully. The press are trying to create a narrative, they're trying to find angles, they're looking to rile you into saying something. You also get the press in South Africa trying to psych you out and get under your skin. Western Province was a classic example of that. In the build-up, it was all about them knocking us off our stride and James Small making a statement. Afterwards, when we'd beaten them comfortably and played some superb rugby, they concentrated on the weakness of our scrum and the claims that Small had been gouged by John Bentley – which was a piece of nonsense that even the South African Rugby Union didn't rise to.'

'They were right about one thing, though,' says Johnno. 'Our scrum was struggling.'

'That was bad news for the forwards,' says Geech with a wry smile. 'Jim was fizzing. He'd held back a bit at the start of the tour so that the players could bed in and get to know one another, but he knew it was now time to start getting to work properly with them.'

'I still get cold sweats thinking about some of the forwards sessions we did on that tour,' says Hill, a thousand-yard stare in his eyes. 'They were brutal – yet they were also pivotal moments on the tour. In another environment or with another squad, the training we did might have been too much for the players; they might have rebelled, starting complaining, split into factions, spiralled into negativity around Jim. But it didn't happen.'

On the Monday after Western Province, Jim Telfer inflicted a training session on the pack of such savagery that it has gone down in rugby folklore. They went through forty-six scrums in forty-two minutes.

'I've taken a back seat up to now,' said Telfer to the press following the session. 'But I thought we were very docile up front last week, tiptoeing through everything. They needed a lead. I use very simple, up-front language to get through to the players. It was tough, but you have to hurt yourself before you can hurt the opposition. I'm a great believer that, if you're in the comfort zone, then you're deluding yourself that it will all work out. This is a harsh country and they won't be beaten easily. When the Springboks pull on that jersey there's a whole aura surrounding it. They have to match the reputation of their past. This is a rugby culture; a hard, alien environment. There's a danger that a few of the younger players might think we've cracked it after our opening games, but we haven't at all. The difficult games are in front of us, not behind us.'

Two days later, Telfer was at it again, this time with the frontline forwards selected for the match against Northern Transvaal. Simon Shaw and Mark Regan had played off the bench against Mpumalanga that afternoon, but as soon as they'd showered they were driven back to the team hotel in Pretoria where they were told to change into their training kit and get out on to the paddock for another beasting.

Across the chill evening air, Telfer's voice could be heard berating one of his charges. 'Get lower, you big bastard!'

The forwards were scrummaging against Nigel Horton's Powerhouse machine, which was fitted with hydraulics to push back against them.

'That thing was a torture device,' says Hill.

'Oh, did Hilly say that?' asks Woody. 'He should have tried being in the fucking front row with those hydraulics coming back at ye. It was savage.'

'We'd always known that there would be a point when we had to work on the scrum,' says Geech. 'Before that we'd concentrated more on running patterns, defensive patterns, handling – but this was now the time for the scrum. It wasn't an issue of size or technique, it was about timing and coordination. All those players from different packs had to learn how to scrummage together, and that took repetition. A lot of repetition.'

'We'd all heard about Jim before the tour,' says Hill, 'but nothing prepares you for the actual person you meet. The passion of the man, his desire to make us physically compete with a side that were bigger and stronger by outwitting them tactically and technically was phenomenal. It was clear from the outset, playing the provincial games, that they wanted to try to bully us at the set piece; they wanted to physically take us on at the break-down, and we had some pretty daunting scrummaging sessions, particularly after we lost to Northern Transvaal. That was a pretty intense week of attacking that pneumatic scrummage machine.'

'Those scrummaging sessions have rightly gone down in rugby legend,' says Woody. 'They drove you to the edge. Beyond the edge. It was about timing and technique and working together, but it was also about mental toughness that Jim knew was going to be crucial in the Test series. Knowing that you could go to the darkest places and survive. He drove us and drove us and drove us. Guys were throwing up, nearly passing out, being carried by their teammates as we did sprints between sessions on the machine – which pushed back at you on these hydraulic gears. It was horrific. But do you know what? We also loved it because we were there doing it together and it was making us better.'

'There was total buy-in from the players and Jim was helped by the senior players driving the standards with him,' says Hill. 'It can't just be the coach driving it, it has to come from the players as well. Everyone accepted that if we didn't match or come close to matching South Africa in the scrum, we stood no chance of winning the Test series. And the one thing that any coach does have over you, particularly for driven players, is selection, and when there's a first Test date dangling over your head, you have to show every reason why you can be picked, not why you can't be picked.'

'Touring is a complex thing,' says Geech. 'You have to constantly gauge when to put the hammer down on the players and when to ease off. Jim had to do those scrummaging sessions for the good of the party because we were struggling up front against these massive provincial packs – and we knew that we were going to face an even bigger pack in the Test series. But there are also times when you have to put the brakes on a little with training and let the guys enjoy themselves, and you also have to be acutely aware of how hard and intense the tour is mentally. We'd also learned from 1993 how important it was to make sure that no player felt sidelined and everyone had a genuine chance to play their way into the Test team.'

'We had a number of meetings throughout about keeping everybody connected,' remembers Dai Young, who played three Tests in 1989 yet none in 1997. 'A Lions tour is so different to a normal tour. If you go on a national tour, the guys who are not in the team tend to be guys that are making their way, the youngsters, the fringe players on a low number of caps, but when you go on the Lions, you've got players in the midweek team on sixty, seventy, eighty caps. It's an unusual situation for them, so they need to feel like they're part of it. So we had meetings, a senior players' sort of group to make sure everybody felt connected and that they were important. The Test team was one team representing a squad, but everybody played a part. Everybody wanted to do what they could to support each other.

'The Lions is a unique concept,' he continues. 'The first thing everybody wants to do is get on the plane, get out there. Everybody wants to be given an opportunity early doors in the first couple of games, and everybody wants to try and play Tests. Not everybody does, but as long as people feel they're being given an opportunity, everybody's happy.'

'We fought so hard for each other and that went right back to the very start of the tour,' remembers Gregor Townsend. 'We realised that in 1993 there had been a split between the midweek team and the Saturday team, and that was why the tour went off the rails in the last few weeks – so it was a reaction to that. There was a real togetherness, and it was genuine. I remember training sessions when you felt somebody had turned up not that interested, maybe they'd just had a hard game, then somebody would say to him, "You need to sort yourself out. This is a team session – not just your session." That to me epitomised all the good things about that tour. The team sheet would be put under the door first thing in the morning or the night before in preparation for the team announcement so you could gather your thoughts and if you were not picked it was your job to go up and shake the hand of the guy who had got in ahead of you. If you played on the Saturday you would be out training on the Sunday holding a pad. Not that the players thought about it much, but the payments were for the whole tour, so you shared the exact same bonus money regardless of how many games and Tests you played in. All these little things were vital to making the tour – and not just the three Test matches – a success.'

The all-for-one-and-one-for-all attitude is the bedrock on which any successful Lions tour is built, which makes it all the more difficult when players succumb to injury and are forced out of the tour – an inevitability with a schedule that features so many intensely physical matches. Every Lions tour has suffered these injuries and it can have a major effect on morale, and 1997 was no different.

After just the second game on tour, Paul Grayson was forced home with a groin injury. Scott Quinnell also suffered from a groin injury and had to leave. Ieuan Evans tore his hamstring off the bone at training after the first Test. These injuries were all personal tragedies that these players had to endure, but perhaps the worst – partly because they were captured for posterity by the documentary film makers of *Living with Lions* and partly because of the consequences – were suffered by Doddie Weir, Rob Howley and Will Greenwood. Weir and Howley looked as if they were destined for greatness in the Test side, only for that dream to shatter around them. Doddie had his tour ended by a horrific karate kick to his knee against Mpumalanga that ruptured his ACL; Howley broke his collar bone when running into Ollie le Roux against Natal.

'I can replay each of those injuries in slow motion in my mind,' says James Robson, grimly. 'For Doddie, there was a ruck on our side of the field and Marius Bosman comes around the side and literally stamps down on Doddie's standing knee. It was horrific.

'Against Natal, Rob went around the side of a ruck and clattered into Le Roux. He went down but played on for a few minutes, but found that he couldn't pass off one hand and had to come off. Having to tell both those guys their tours were over . . . it still brings tears to my eyes.

'Will's . . . God, it was awful. I thought he was going to die on the field. He got swung into the ground in a tackle against the Free State and banged his head off the hard ground up in Bloemfontein. He swallowed his tongue, his pupils weren't responding. I genuinely thought that we might lose him.'

'How do you deal with these things?' Johnno looks thoughtful for a moment. 'You go and see these guys in private and you mourn the fact that they're leaving. They don't go home immediately, they're usually there for a night or two more while flights are sorted for them, so you then get a chance to go for a few beers and commiserate with them, but the thing about touring is that you're up and off to the next game very quickly and you have to refocus on the task in hand. It might sound harsh, but you have to move on very quickly. A replacement comes in for the injured player and you have to welcome them in and get them up to speed, all the while concentrating on your own preparation, your own game and what the next opposition have in store for you.'

'It's hard, but you're exactly right,' I say. 'There's no time to look backwards on these tours, you have to keep looking forward. There's always the next big game and there are always difficulties that need to be negotiated. You were hitting a stage of the tour when it was just one big game after another.'

'Exactly. We lost Doddie but then had to concentrate on Northern Transvaal. We were under the pump in terms of the scrum and how the forwards were performing and then we go up to the high veldt and suffer our first loss of the tour.'

'So how did you recover from that? Did it ever feel like the wheels might be starting to come off?'

'A little. That was the fear, anyway. We had to sort out the scrum, so Jim gave us another hiding on the machine. It was a similar challenge to the ACT game you boys played in 1989. We had Transvaal next – or Gauteng as they were called at the time – at Ellis Park. That was a huge, huge game for the tour. We had to win it, just like you guys had to win against ACT.'

'That Ellis Park game was the game where John Bentley scored that incredible try from within his own half,' I note.

'It was. And Austin Healey scored a great try before that. Those two scores plus some outstanding defence saw us through. I was in the stand watching and, do you know what, that's one of my favourite Lions memories – and I wasn't even playing! All the non-playing squad went down at full time and clapped and cheered the players in off the field. We had a big party in the changing room. The whole tour was back on track then and the feel-good factor was back. It was a huge, huge moment. Tour-defining. Just like ACT.'

And like ACT, it came at the perfect time for the '97 Lions. From Ellis Park they went to Durban to play the Sharks, the leading provincial side in South Africa at the venue for the second Test – Kings Park. They may have lost Rob Howley to injury during the game, but they won the match handsomely and Howley's replacement, Matt Dawson, fitted seamlessly into the team. The midweek side then thrashed the Emerging Springboks 51–22 four days before the first Test.

The team that was selected to face the Boks at Newlands perhaps defines all that was so wonderful about the '97 Lions. No one could have predicted the starting line-up when the squad was announced. The perceived wisdom was that the English pack plus, perhaps, Keith Wood would line up against the Boks, with an English-heavy backline outside them. As it was, the English forwards Johnson, Dallaglio, Hill and Rodber were joined by Tom Smith from Scotland and Keith Wood, Paul Wallace and Jeremy Davidson from Ireland, while the combination of Matt Dawson (England), Gregor Townsend (Scotland), Scott Gibbs (Wales), Jeremy Guscott (England), Ieuan Evans (Wales), Alan Tait (Scotland) and Neil Jenkins (Wales) wasn't one that any pundit would have picked before the squad left the UK.

'There was an element of surprise in the selection, but we were the form players,' says Guscott. 'Well, to be fair, I think all the players on tour were in form, but the combinations Geech and Jim picked were working very well together. I didn't see South Africa as a huge threat – I had a belief and an ultimate confidence in our side. I looked at our pack of forwards – our pack of forwards were fucking brilliant. I didn't think the Boks could bully us, I didn't think they could run us off the park. I didn't think there was anything they could do that we couldn't match or surpass. We had good reason to believe we could win.'

'Classic Jerry,' says Johnno with a grin. 'I can tell you now, I have never been more nervous in my life than before the first two Tests of that series. Running on to the pitch as captain for the first Test was a very big moment for me. The stands were packed and there were huge pockets of Lions supporters, which was great – but I didn't really notice too much about it, to be honest. There's so much pressure built up beforehand that by that stage you just want to get on and play.'

I was pitchside working for Sky when the teams ran out. The noise was immense for the Lions; but when the Springboks ran out, it was something else entirely.

'The noise from the crowd when they came down the tunnel,' says Keith Wood, a look of wonder in his eyes as he remembers. 'Fuck me. Thundering. The whole stadium was shaking.'

'South Africa are a team, like France, that can come out and blitz you for twenty minutes on raw emotion,' says Johnno. 'We knew that they were going to come after us at a hundred miles an hour and try to break us early.'

'That's their way,' says Geech. 'That's their psychology.'

'It's one thing knowing that's going to happen,' says Dallaglio. 'It's quite another finding a way to stop it.'

'There was a fear that they might do damage to the front row,' says Wood. 'Neil Jenkins put the kick-off straight out so we immediately had a scrum on halfway. We engaged – and they knocked us back five yards.'

'They detected a weakness in our scrummaging and the South African forwards, it's in their DNA that they want to physically destroy you, to scrummage and attack you in that area of the game,' says Johnno. 'And for us to pick a relatively small front row, they were licking their lips and they came out to try and destroy us.'

'We were just a little bit too high in that first scrum,' says Woody. 'Six inches too high. We could use their weight against them by being lower, and we eventually did that. It was frightening and daunting to have all your fears come home immediately. But then you just have to rest your mind and get some clarity – we realised that we just had to get lower and we'd be fine.'

The Lions dug in and although they leaked a couple of early penalties to go 6–0 down, they clung on.

'Playing at the level of intensity that the Springboks hit us with is unsustainable,' observes Johnno. 'We knew that if we could stay in the game then they would burn themselves out and it would be a more even contest. But as Lawrence says, it's one thing to say that's all you have to do and it's something else actually managing to do it.'

In a magnificent performance that recalled Muhammad Ali's rope-a-dope tactic against George Foreman in the Rumble in the Jungle, the Lions absorbed a colossal Springbok onslaught in the early stages of the game, but by the middle of the second half the Boks, like Foreman, had virtually punched themselves out.

'It was 16–15 and we were just surviving,' says Johnno. 'But you could feel that the momentum was maybe beginning to shift our way slightly. The boys in the front row were beginning to turn the screw a little, using their lower height against the big South African front row, starting to manipulate them. It was Paul Wallace getting his right shoulder up on Os du Randt that created the space for Matt Dawson to make his break to score with twenty minutes to go.'

It was one of the most famous tries in Lions history. With Wallace pushing up on Du Randt, Rodber controlled the ball with his right foot at the back of the scrum. After a little look to his left – as if he was about to pass to Gregor Townsend – Dawson snatched up the ball and broke to his right. He was closed down by three defenders and shaped to pass the ball inside on a switch with Ieuan Evans – but chose to hold on to the ball. The chasing Springboks all bought the dummy and before they could correct their mistake, Dawson had scorched away to score in the corner.

'To see Matt having the confidence to do that was fantastic,' says Geech. 'We'd chosen him because we knew what he was capable of when others thought he was our third choice.'

'That's trust in your squad and trust in your players,' says Woody. 'That's great leadership from Geech and Jim and Fran and Johnno. No one felt like a wildcard, everyone felt like they deserved to be there and were therefore empowered to play their best rugby. Matt Dawson was a classic example. He came in for Rob Howley, who was rubber-stamped to start the Tests until he got injured, and he played with such confidence. Jeremy Davidson, Tom Smith, Paul Wallace – they were all the same. No one had expected anything of them when the tour began, but they grew and grew over the weeks we were out there and by the end they were magnificent. Test Lions. Lions legends.'

The Lions were ahead for the first time in the match and they then delivered the Ali knockout blow with a couple of minutes left on the clock. After being destroyed in the early scrums, it was astounding to see the Lions pack almost win a pushover try on the Springbok line. Referee Colin Hawke couldn't see the grounding, so he reset the scrum. This time the Lions punched through midfield and then sent the ball wide to the far touchline, where Neil Jenkins released Alan Tait with a neat pass to send the winger in for the clincher. At full time the Lions had achieved the seemingly impossible. Their 25–16 win had put them 1–0 up in the series.

'It was an amazing win, a true team effort,' reflects Geech, 'but do you know what sums up that group of players to me and the leadership that they showed? It was the fact that the Test team wanted to help the midweek team prepare for their match on the Tuesday, so they all agreed to get up the following morning and hold pads at training. An incredible gesture. A priceless moment that galvanised an already very tight-knit group.'

'Well, Gav, you've been part of successful Lions tours and successful teams, and I think the adage of "none of us is as good as all of us" would probably have been at the heart of all of them too, no?' asks Dallaglio.

'I think you're probably right,' I say.

'I think we all understood that in '97. On the bus that night, we were on our way back to the hotel and I remember being at the back of the bus, having a chat with Johnno and one or two other players in that sort of senior playing group, and we were saying, "I think we should be on the training field tomorrow with the boys; maybe just have a couple of beers tonight, because we've got another Test in Durban next week and, also, the right thing to do is to be out training with the boys tomorrow, for those who can still walk," and that's exactly what we did. I think that kind of told you everything you needed to know about the group, that we made that decision ourselves, collectively, that we were prepared to support the guys who weren't going to play in the second Test, to hold the bags and be out there, working hard with the boys. And that kind of epitomised what the group was all about, really.'

'It's well known that prior to the first Test, the guys who'd played midweek had to crawl out of bed and train the next day to prepare a Test team to be ready for the first Test,' adds Hill. 'So it was felt that the right thing to do would be for the Test team to get out of bed and get ready for the midweek team, because it was about momentum. We'd found that early on, when we lost against Northern Transvaal: the pressure starts coming on you and South Africa were starting to bay for blood; they wanted more of it. We could sense within South Africa that they still felt that they were going to dominate us in the second and third Tests, so it was a good way of focussing the mind, a good way of bringing everyone together again; we'd had a good night out after the first Test but then you carried on. And whilst preparing a midweek team, we knew that with the boldness of selection of the first Test team, a lot of players probably felt that we could easily be replaced so we had to show we were willing to work no matter what.'

'And actually,' observes Dallaglio, 'the best performance of the whole tour was by that group who played against Free State that week. They played some breathtaking rugby, and beat them off the park, and I think that helped to build the momentum into the second Test, and the respect, the mutual respect that we had as a group – it didn't matter who was in the Test side, who was in the non-Test side – was huge. Everyone on that trip was a Lion, and I think that's the way we all regarded it. Some of us were just lucky enough to go out and play in the Test matches.'

'So coming into the second Test, what were you expecting from the Boks?' I ask.

'Ferocity,' says Johnno simply. 'Geech made a great speech about an injured Springbok fighting for its life and that was exactly what it was like. The speeches from that tour are famous and for a good reason. You had one from Geech before the first game that tapped into the idea of us coming together as four countries playing as one. You had Telfer talking to the forwards before one of the mega scrummaging sessions about us looking ourselves in the mirror and getting better and better. You had Telfer and his 'Everest' speech before the first Test – that winning for the Lions in a Test match is like reaching the top of Everest. And then you had Geech before the second Test saying that we were on the verge of something special – that we would meet each other in the street in thirty years' time and there would just be a look. He had that relationship with the Lions from his era, with guys like Dick Milliken who played in the centre with him in '74 when they defeated the Boks. He wanted us to have the same experience. But first we had to get past this wounded beast that was a Springbok side 1–0 down in a series, that was going to be fighting for its life. And he was right. They came at us even harder than in the first Test. We kicked off, they caught it and then they rolled us back in a maul about thirty yards. I remember lying in a heap on the ground and catching Lawrence's eye and the two of us just having this unspoken understanding: "Jesus, we have to hang on here."'

'And, like the first Test, that's exactly what you did,' I say.

'Yes, but God it was hard,' says Hill.

'Brutal,' says Woody.

'The size, the sheer size of them: man for man, they were enormous beasts,' says Dallaglio, with an almost awestruck shake of his head. 'They were big, big boys, and really, really tough. I often say that the South Africans are a bit like that film, *The Terminator*, you know? Whatever you do to them, they just get up and come back again. You smash them to pieces and then they sort of rebuild themselves and they're back on their feet, and you just think to yourself, "Wow, what are you made of?" It is literally like that against them. They will run over the top of you, and if that doesn't work, they'll run over the top of you, and then, if that doesn't work, they'll have another go at running over the top of you.'

'We just had to put our bodies on the line,' says Johnno. 'Survive, fight, stay in the game, just like we'd done in the first Test, and take any chances that came our way. We rode our luck as well. They missed six kicks for goal. We had Neil Jenkins, who was a machine. Lawrence called the Boks Terminators? Neil Jenkins was a Terminator.'

'Jenks in that series, he was better than Jonny Wilkinson at his peak,' remarks Guscott. 'It was just metronomic to watch. Boom, boom, boom: between the posts, between the posts, between the posts. Incredible. He kicked five penalties in that game to keep us in it. The last one was an absolute monster, right on the edge of his range, to bring us to 15–15. They'd scored three tries but had failed to convert a single one. The pressure of the last few minutes of that game was enormous on both sides.'

'What does it mean to lead and be a great leader?' asks Woody. 'It's a hard one to articulate. But certain guys have this thing that means you would follow them anywhere. Johnno had that. You knew that he would lay down and get the shit kicked out of him to protect you. He would never shy away from anything. So that emboldens you and you fight to repay that. In the same way, other guys set standards that you want to meet. Scotty Gibbs was a fantastic player and he was incredible in that series. A rock in defence, he also had this huge carry into Os du Randt that put the big man on his arse. It was iconic and it lifted our players and made the Springboks think twice about going anywhere near him.

'But Gibbsy was also one of the great guys for recognising weaknesses in his own players, and he'd glower at you. If he thought you were chickening out, he would go at you and make you stick in there. Now here's a story about that. I tore my ankle ligaments in the first Test, and I was heavily strapped for the second Test and I kept rolling over on it, and it really hurt. It was fucking agony. With about fifteen, twenty minutes to go in the second Test, I was down on the ground getting some treatment from the physio, who's digging his thumbs into the torn ligament in my ankle and I'm screaming like a child. And I'm thinking, "I could go off now. I've actually played pretty well, I've given everything I can," and I doubted myself. I was in a lot of pain and I doubted myself for a minute. And then I looked up and I caught Gibbsy's eye. And I knew he knew I was thinking of chickening out. And I couldn't have that. I bounced back up off the ground and got back into the line: I was there in no time.

'We were at a dinner in London about ten years later and I mentioned it to him. And he said, "I remember it." He said, "You were going to chicken out, weren't you?" And I said, "That's what I was thinking!" And he said, "I knew it. But I was never going to let you."

'Now, that's leadership. It's a very hard thing to define, but it's because of the effort he was able to put in, it's because when he spoke, he spoke in incredibly simple terminology, and he was just incredibly easy to follow, there was nothing conceptual about anything he said. Practical, efficient, this was what he expected – and then he went and did it. So you'd follow him because of what he was willing to do to win.'

For those who watched that famous Test series, the dying minutes of that second Test will never be forgotten. Locked at 15-all, the Springboks launch an attack around halfway. Three Springbok forwards clear out the ruck and the Lions defence spread out, giving up on a potential turnover. All except one. Neil Back, fresh on the field for Richard Hill, burrows into the breakdown and emerges with the ball.

'The ball popped out at my feet,' says Woody, his famous grin widening on his face. 'I didn't really think about what I was doing and the next thing I knew, I'd hoofed it downfield. And then I went, "Jesus, I have to run after it now." I ran up and Percy Montgomery ran it into touch. I was running on fumes then – absolutely fucked, my ankle killing me. I could barely see. But now I have to throw the ball into the lineout. This is pretty much our last hope in the game. You have to try and get your breathing under control and then slip into automatic pilot and go through your routines. Luckily Jeremy Davidson reached up a big paw and was able to collect it safely.

'And here's a whole sequence of leadership moments. We drive the maul and Gregor spots a gap at the back of the line and charges into it. That sets the Boks defensive line back another ten yards or so. A great decision. Then Tim Rodber gets hit with a swinging punch from Fritz van Heerden, that splits him over the eye. Rodber is about to punch him back, but he stops himself and goes to clear out the ruck. That was incredible. The discipline not to hit back, not to risk a penalty and instead go to work to win us the ball. He must have been as tired as me at that stage and then he manages to fight the instinct to lash out and just do the right thing. Amazing. And then of course, there's Jerry. Gregor is at the bottom of the ruck and so Jerry goes into first-receiver. He gets the ball from Matt Dawson and just does the right thing – and does it perfectly. He's actually had very little involvement in the game up to that point, mainly just defending. But when the ball comes to him his class tells and he bangs over this perfect drop-goal to win the game and win the series.'

There it is again – a demonstration of the pure class of Jerry Guscott. Two Lions Test series clinched by his brilliance – a grubber to score a try in 1989, a drop-goal to seal glory in 1997. What a player. What a leader in the most pressurised moments imaginable on a rugby field.

'What was going through my mind?' he asks, repeating my question. 'I don't know. It was instinctive, really. I just knew that going for a drop-goal was the right option.'

'I think this chapter will illustrate to your readers just how lucky we were in 1997,' says Geech. 'We had leaders everywhere. And I suppose it shows that the greatest teams are always filled with leaders who are prepared to stand up at the toughest moments and take control of their little part of the game. When all those elements come together you have something very powerful. We couldn't go on and complete the whitewash in the third Test, but we'd done what we'd come to do and won the series. And every player who pulled on a red jersey that summer had played their part. It was a true squad achievement.'

'I remember speaking to Martin Johnson shortly before I led the Lions back to South Africa in 2009 and he told me that the 1997 tour was his greatest rugby experience,' says Geech. 'He said winning that Test series meant more to him than winning the World Cup. That had a profound impact and made me understand again the magnitude of the Lions in South Africa. Most of the great memories embedded into Lions history seem to come against the Springboks.'

'I agree,' says Dallaglio, another famous World Cup winner in 2003. 'For those of us who were lucky enough to be at Newlands and then in Durban, we experienced something that has bound us together to this day. It was the greatest rugby tour I ever went on and probably the greatest rugby experience of all of our lives. To share that as a group was incredible. Geech made that speech about seeing each other in the street in thirty years' time and there would just being a look – and it's true. It's absolutely true. We shared something very special and every time we see one another, there's that look. It's all that's needed, and we're right back there together again. It's magic. It's what it's all about.'

FOUR

MORALE IS EVERYTHING

2001

SATURDAY, 17 JUNE 1989.

It was a balmy night in Brisbane as the Lions lined up against Queensland at Ballymore. Opposite me was the Wallaby full back Greg Martin. There were Australian internationals dotted throughout the team – from Michael Lynagh at No.10 to Anthony Herbert in the centre, Julian Gardner and Jeff Miller on the flanks, Bill Campbell in the second row, Cameron Lillicrap at loose head and Mark McBain at hooker, as well as future Wallabies in the shape of Dominic Maguire, Herbert's centre partner, and Dan Crowley at tight head – who would both make their Test debuts against us in the series – plus Peter Slattery at scrum-half, Brendan Nasser at No.8, Rod McCall in the second row and Paul Carozza on the wing.

It was a brutal, violent game punctuated by moments of sublime skill and determination from the Lions not to be turned over. We won 19–15.

On we went to the next game, happy with the result but thinking little more about it other than it represented a marker in the sand that we would stand up to any attempts to physically intimidate us in future games.

Watching in the stands was a nineteen-year-old Queensland fan. He was sitting with his mates from the Brothers' under-19 rugby team, a gangly beanpole with a mop of thick dark hair. He had been disappointed to see his local heroes defeated by the tourists, but he had also been mesmerised by the red Lions jersey and what it represented. His name was John Eales.

'The Lions bookended my career,' he tells me from his home in Brisbane more than thirty years later. 'In those days you would get a short rugby highlights programme at the weekend and you'd see clips of the Five Nations and it had this kind of mystery about it. Then suddenly you had a team come over to Australia that was a combination of the very best of those teams and it was magical to see them in action at your home ground.

'I remember going round to a mate's house to watch the first Test and it was a real moment for me – I can remember it so, so clearly – watching the Lions come out the tunnel in Sydney and then the Wallabies coming out and the anticipation for the match was enormous. Then I remember watching our guys singing the national anthem and Nick Farr-Jones was crying with the emotion of it all and I just sat there thinking, "How good would it be to be out there one day doing the same thing, singing the national anthem before a Test?" So that's really where the flame started for me to want to be a Wallaby.

'I went to watch the second Test at Ballymore and it was an incredible match. The Lions were on the rack after the first Test but you came back, took no shit and beat us well. The whole occasion was incredible and suddenly the series is on a knife-edge. Just pure theatre.'

'Theatre that you were able to repeat twelve years later,' I say.

'Well, as I say, the Lions bookended my career,' he says, smiling broadly. 'It had some nice symmetry for me, that's for sure. Like a mirror image.'

*

'And so, 2001 . . .' I say.

There's a distant look in Martin Johnson's eyes and I can see him sinking back through time. 'Talent-wise,' he says softly, '2001 was a better team than 1997. A really strong team. Incredible, actually.'

'The team in 2001,' says Brian O'Driscoll, a similar look in his eyes, 'has to be one of the best groups of players the Lions have ever assembled.'

The 2001 British & Irish Lions tour to Australia was an event of huge promise. With England in the vanguard, northern hemisphere rugby seemed at last to be catching up with its rivals in the south when it came to professional standards around fitness, conditioning, nutrition and playing an exciting, expansive style of rugby that was also infused with power. And yet, similarly to 1993 and 2005, it is perhaps easier to look for leadership learnings in where things went wrong instead of right. However, doing so exclusively would prove a disservice to the positive aspects of the tour, particularly around the quality of the rugby played – so we will examine both, while also going inside the Wallaby camp to see how their success was engineered.

Of all the areas to examine, the choice of the 2001 Lions captain was one that can never be called into question. After proving his leadership credentials were as good as his playing ability in South Africa in 1997, Martin Johnson had gone from strength to strength in both capacities in the years since. He had assumed the captaincy of England from Lawrence Dallaglio in

1999, had captained Leicester to European Cup success and to three consecutive domestic titles and was without doubt one of the finest rugby players on the planet. It was a no-brainer that he should be given the Lions captaincy for a second tour – and in the process, he became the first player to be given the honour twice.

Of more controversy was the appointment of the head coach. After three successive tours in charge, Ian McGeechan declined the offer to take on the role again. The Lions committee looked elsewhere and gave serious thought to offering the job to Clive Woodward before settling on Graham Henry, the coach of Wales who had earned the moniker of 'The Great Redeemer' after transforming the fortunes of the men from the Principality.

Although tour manager Donal Lenihan had been instructed to find the best coach available regardless of nationality, Henry, a native of Auckland, came in for some serious criticism from a number of former Lions and sections of the media simply for being a Kiwi; these critics felt that he would be unable to understand the special magic of the Lions having never experienced the environment before. While Warren Gatland would later prove that being born outside the UK and Ireland shouldn't preclude a coach from enjoying success with the Lions, certain incidents on tour would lend credence to this view.

'The Lions go back for me to 1959,' says Henry from his home on Waiheke Island in the Hauraki Gulf, just off Auckland. It is early winter there, but the view from his kitchen window is still lush and green and Henry smiles enigmatically as we discuss his appointment. 'I remember that team coming out to New Zealand and they were the most fantastic rugby side, perhaps the best team I saw play. Bev Risman, Dickie Jeeps, Ken Scotland, Tony O'Reilly and Peter Jackson. Then I saw Carwyn James' team in 1971, and they were also fantastic. They brought out a book afterwards called *The Lions Speak*, and all the Test match players wrote a chapter on an aspect of their game. That book was my coaching bible for many years. So the Lions have always played a big part in my rugby life.

'I then left New Zealand in the middle of the year in 1998, started coaching Wales for the autumn internationals, and then two years later I was asked to coach the Lions tour to Australia. It was a huge privilege but in hindsight it was ridiculous, really, because I'd coached probably less than twenty Test matches by that stage. Hindsight is a wonderful thing, but I know now that I wasn't ready. But that's all part of life, isn't it? All part of learning and all part of the fabric of rugby, I guess. You get asked and it's a huge honour and it was probably very selfish for me to say yes, but it's a difficult thing to say no to. New Zealand Rugby virtually said to me when I announced I was going to Wales, "Well, we don't think you're an international coach," so it was an opportunity to stick it up at 'em. But that's your ego driving you and that's the wrong reason to take the job.'

'A lot of stuff came out about Graham not really understanding the Lions,' says Keith Wood. 'And in many ways, you could counter that by saying he was an excellent coach and we were professional players, many of whom had been on Lions tours before, so did that really matter? But winning a Test series for the Lions is very, very hard to do and you need every little extra per cent you can find to help you get there – there's a lot of emotional buy-in needed if you're going to be successful as a Lions team. And to be honest, if you don't have that, you're sunk. Geech understood that and he used his own personal experiences from being a Lion in his speeches to us in '97 and as a result he managed to get us to totally buy into the one-team concept. Graham Henry, for all his undoubted skills as a coach, hadn't been immersed in that idea of it. Or it maybe would have been something that he could take for granted, because that would be a given in New Zealand: that everybody would have this ideal of playing for the black jersey – that it was something special that you would give your all to do. But the blending of four different types of people, that's a very difficult facet of leadership for a Lions head coach to manage, and Graham maybe didn't give it the amount of weight it required. I think he may have weighted it seventy per cent training, thirty per cent philosophy; I would have said McGeechan had the flip of that.

'The Lions is a strange, unique thing and you can't run a Lions team or a Lions squad the way you run a national team. Everyone wants to win for the Lions, but you don't immediately have that thing of wanting to win for the guys around you because you're so used to knocking the shit out of each other the rest of the time. So a lot of effort needs to be put into the team bonding aspect throughout the whole tour to get that oneness philosophy. Geech understood that. Graham didn't because he hadn't experienced that environment before, not because he wasn't an outstanding coach.'

While the tour schedule was a mixed affair of some extraordinarily weak semi-pro teams and strong Super 12 sides (albeit the strongest, the Brumbies, were denuded of their Australian internationals), there was no doubting the strength of the Wallabies. Having won their second World Cup in 1999, the team led by the talismanic John Eales and coached by the shrewd Rod Macqueen were at their peak, with the majority of their World Cup winners still in place and some outstanding talent, such as tyro flanker George Smith, coming through. The Brumbies were top dogs in the Super 12 and Australia held sway over every rugby-playing country on the planet, including their old rivals, the All Blacks. Not many sides in rugby history have been so dominant as this Wallaby vintage.

'I was ready to finish at the end of 2000,' recalls John Eales, when I catch up with him over Zoom at his home in Sydney. 'The only reason I played one more year was to play against the British and Irish Lions. We'd had a lot of success as a team in the few years before that and it might have been a good idea to bow out after winning the Tri Nations in 2000, but as a nation we'd never beaten the Lions in a series so I desperately wanted to play. That Lions series was just so important to us as a country.'

Meanwhile, in the northern hemisphere, England and France were dominating the newly formed Six Nations, while Ireland were a burgeoning power. Scotland and Wales, while still grappling to get a handle on professional rugby, had also enjoyed recent success – Scotland winning the Five Nations two years earlier, Wales enjoying a thrilling run of ten consecutive victories under Henry from 1999 to 2000, which had included some big scalps in England, France and South Africa. It was off the back of these results that Henry was given the Lions job.

Donal Lenihan, that great Lions stalwart from 1983 and, in particular, 1989, was installed as manager for the tour and he has subsequently talked about the lead that the English players had over their Celtic cousins at the time. 'England were way ahead in 2001,' he said. 'I would say comfortably two years ahead of Ireland, Scotland and Wales in terms of professionalism and the environment they operated in. Clive Woodward was in the middle of his great revolution at the RFU and they had resources that the other countries could only dream of. It sounds a bit mad looking back, but six years into professionalism they were still the only Home Nations team to have a defence coach – Phil Larder. We appointed him for the Lions tour, but he was basically working from scratch with the Celtic boys when it came to the defensive systems he wanted to run. They had no clue before that tour, while the English boys all knew exactly what he wanted.'

And here we come to one of the primary learnings from this tour: training loads. The 2001 expedition came at the end of a gruelling season that stretched to eleven months for the players who featured in the third Test. Indeed, because of the foot-and-mouth outbreak that year, which delayed the completion of the Six Nations, the final game of the season was technically played fifteen months after it began. When the players first met up at Tylney Hall in Rotherwick, many of them were exhausted and carrying niggly injuries; some of these injuries were successfully managed – thanks to the expertise of James Robson, on his fourth tour – but some could not be and players began to drop like flies. This was in part due to bad luck, but the players were not helped by the huge amount of training that Henry and his fellow coaches demanded of them.

'Even though the game had been pro for six years by this stage, people were still very much finding their feet with it, particularly when it came to the sports science side and managing player loads,' says Johnno. 'We came into camp at the start of the tour and right from the off we were training really hard for long periods of time – and it didn't let up for weeks.'

'I think the problem stemmed, again, from the fact that England were so far ahead,' said Lenihan. 'Phil Larder needed time with the players to bed in the systems that he wanted. Then, of course, Andy Robinson as forwards coach needed time with the players to get lineouts and scrums and so on sorted. Dave Alred wanted to work with the kickers. Steve Black wanted to do fitness sessions. And Graham wanted to run attack sessions.'

'In all my previous coaching, I'd only ever really had one assistant coach before,' reflects Henry. 'That meant that I was always in control of training sessions, pretty much always the main voice. Suddenly I had to give training time to the other coaches and I don't think I adapted well to it – I still wanted a lot of time with the players and I gave the other coaches a lot of time as well. We were all really excited by the challenge and wanted to impart as much of our coaching knowledge to the players as we could so that they would be in the best place possible – technically and tactically – come the Test series, but it was all too much. I overloaded them with too much information, too much complexity and way too much physical work. That was a failure on my behalf and it was down to my ego – I was so desperate to be a successful head coach of the Lions that I pushed the players too hard. It was one of the biggest lessons I learned from that tour.'

'We were at the end of a long, long rugby season and we were just training and training and training, and it almost became oppressive,' says Johnno. 'In '97, we actually did hardly any rugby training before we left. I remember someone asking me before we left for South Africa, "What do you think about Jim Telfer?" I said, "Well, I don't know, to be honest, we've hardly done any rugby so far." That first week in '97, we mainly did team-building stuff, some canoeing, going for drinks together – all of which was a really good idea, because we didn't need to do the amount of organisational rugby that they do now; we just needed a week of bonding. But it was a different game in 2001 and we had a lot more to organise game-wise.'

'I think it was okay in 2001, actually,' counters Lawrence Dallaglio. 'We were professional athletes and professional athletes should be able to train hard – that's what we were paid for.'

'But it was unrelenting,' argues Keith Wood. 'I blame myself for not standing up and talking more to Johnno and the coaches about it. I remember Johnno and I went and saw Graham about halfway through the tour and we said, "Look, the boys are fucked, we can't keep training like this," and he said, "No, I know, but we just have to do a couple more weeks like this and then we can tail off." But by the time we tailed off, everyone was even more fucked and we couldn't recover the freshness we needed.'

'Then you throw in the vast distances we had to travel between games,' added Lenihan. 'Australia is so vast and not all the travel was the most comfortable – the Lions committee learned from this tour that the players had to travel in business class so that they had appropriate leg room and space – and without that space you can see why guys were aggravating existing niggles.'

'It makes you sound like a prima donna,' says Johnno, 'but you can't cram professional athletes into economy seats on a plane for three hours and not expect there to be some physical repercussions. I remember flying from Townsville to Brisbane after playing the Queensland President's XV and Scott Quinnell had a knee knock. He could barely fit in the seat and had all sorts of issues with his knee as a result. Now, that may not sound like a big deal in many ways, but if professional sport is about the one-per-centers, we were giving away several per cent in our preparation in situations like that.

'Looking back, I just remember the whole tour flying by so quickly,' Johnno continues. 'There didn't seem to be time to do anything. If we ever wanted to have a meeting – like a coaches/captain/senior players meeting – it was always done in an airport departure lounge.'

These were all setbacks and annoyances, yet the talent in the squad was incredible. Of the nineteen Englishmen originally selected (which would swell to twenty-one after injury call-ups), eighteen would be part of the team that would win the World Cup two years later. Indeed, many analysts would cite 2001 as the year Woodward's England played their best rugby in the Six Nations. Martin Johnson, Lawrence Dallaglio, Richard Hill and Neil Back were at their peak. Phil Vickery was carving a reputation for himself as the best tight head in the game. Jonny Wilkinson, still just twenty-three, was clearly a talent for the ages. Then you add into the mix some truly outstanding players from the other nations. Tom Smith, a hero of '97, was playing the best rugby of his career, as was Keith Wood beside him. Both Scott Quinnell and Rob Howley had battled back from the disappointment of leaving the '97 tour with injury and were in prime position for the Test jerseys. And a young talent by the name of Brian O'Driscoll had burst on to the international scene a year earlier, scoring a hat-trick of tries in a rare Irish victory in Paris, and hadn't missed a step since. Then, out wide, you had the wild card to end all wild cards: Jason Robinson, recently returned to union after a glittering career in rugby league. Robinson had yet to complete a full Test for England, but had X-factor dripping out of his ears. If ever there was a side that could break down the most steadfast and powerful defence on the planet – which was exactly what this Australian team possessed – then it was surely going to be this Lions side.

'I'd fallen in love with the Lions in '97,' says O'Driscoll, one of a tiny band of exceptional players to tour with the Lions four times. 'I'd watched *Living with Lions* countless times but to actually get into that environment, you don't really know what it's going to be like. And it's miles better than you think it's going to be, and that's really saying something. It surpassed all my expectations. As a young player, you're suddenly hanging out with people that you've put on a pedestal and people you've admired for years, and all of a sudden, you're training with them and they're your teammates and they're sharing their rugby IP [intellectual property], and you're stealing different components. It's just such an incredible experience.

'You come back from Lions tours an infinitely different player, because you realise what it takes to actually go to the next level. And from a player's perspective, I think there's nothing that matches it. National camps are great, but the standard and quality of the Lions tours in every regard is a level above, the rugby intellect is superior across the board and it's exciting to play in that environment, where you feel as though different people's rugby IQs are on a similar level, because they're the best players in their national set-ups. It's exciting to feel that every time you play or train, the standard around you is just so much higher and it pushes you up a level. More than a level, several levels.'

Woody agrees. 'Take Tom Smith, for example. The second he turned up to training, he was one of the guys who always trained unbelievably well. His standard set a standard, and you had to race to keep up with him at different times. And that's the joy of the Lions – if he does one thing better than you, you want to be able to learn how to do it better than him. You try and do that with thirty players, your game just gets better and better and better, because they all do things in a slightly different way.

'The standard is just so, so good. You could run a line and get tackled and as you went to ground you just knew that someone like Lawrence Dallaglio or Richard Hill or Neil Back or whoever was going to be there, running the perfect support line so that you could offload it to them. It wasn't a preordained move, but at that level those players were so good at reading the game and reacting to it that they would be able to reposition themselves to run the perfect support line. You can't throw an offload like that in a club game because the players aren't there to receive it. You can offload a little bit more in an international, if you have the type of players who will run that line and know that they're able to read you that well. But when you get to the Lions, everybody is up at that standard where they're reading the reactions of everybody else.'

'We're talking high-performance rugby knowledge, reading the game, understanding space, understanding the movement of other people, that sort of stuff,' says Dallaglio. 'When that happens at its best, it's unstoppable.'

'The sharing of IP is also huge,' continues Woody. 'I remember we had a really interesting thing in 2001, where a couple of English lineouts were just brilliant at the time. We couldn't get our head around them when we played against England. And the English guys were happy to put them into the mix; they explained how they worked and the rest of us said, "Okay, that's great, got that, brilliant." And I feel a bit bad about this even now, but we then played them in Dublin in the final game of the delayed Six Nations at the end of 2001 and Malcolm O'Kelly came up to me after ten minutes and he said, "They're using the same calls we used with the Lions in the summer!" He then picked off all their lineouts and we went on to win the game and deny them a Grand Slam. Maybe I don't feel that bad about it, actually! But that shows you how invested you need to be to make the Lions work – you just have to throw all your IP in so that the Lions have the best chance for success. But it's a good idea to remember to change your calls when you go back to playing for your country again!'

The squad of thirty-seven players flew into Perth for their opening match against Western Australia at the WACA. It was a strange start to the tour as it pitched a Lions side full of high-class internationals against a team of amateurs and it was only the humid night air that made them break sweat as they cantered to an easy victory. They put a hundred and sixteen points on Western Australia, then racked up eighty-three points against a Queensland President's XV three days later, which included five tries for the electric Robinson. Their first real test came in game three: the Reds at Ballymore in Brisbane, a team packed full of Wallabies – but the Lions dealt with that challenge by putting forty-two points on them and conceding just eight.

'By this stage, you would look at the results and say, "So far, so good, we're really building something here," but even by then there were some pretty major cracks forming in the squad,' says Johnno. You can't help but notice the tinge of sadness and regret to his voice when he says this. 'We were overtraining, which was putting a lot of stress on the players, but perhaps more significant was the fact that many guys didn't think they were getting a fair crack of the whip when it came to game time; even though we were only three games in, a lot of guys felt that it didn't really matter how well they played, Graham had already pencilled in a Test team in his mind before we left the UK and Ireland and it was going to be virtually impossible to get him to change his mind.'

'And do you think that's true?' I ask.

'I don't know,' he says with a deep sigh. 'You'd have to ask Graham.'

'There were certainly guys who I had in my mind as nailed-on Test players, yes,' says Henry. 'Johnson, Dallaglio, Wilkinson, O'Driscoll – those guys were dead certs in my mind. But I was still open-minded on selection. I hadn't written anyone off. It was important to train combinations together, though, so that they got used to playing with each other and that's maybe where some players thought I'd already made up my mind about things.'

'Despite some growing friction in the squad, we were going along really well,' remarks Dallaglio. 'Then we took a bit of a kick in the guts against Australia A.'

Australia A were coached by Brumbies head honcho and future head coach of Australia, Japan and England: the wily Eddie Jones.

'It was a beautiful warm evening in Gosford,' remembers Jones, 'and the Lions were expected to romp to another victory. They'd scored 241 points in their first three games. I'd been given just five days to prepare Australia A with Scott Johnson. Scott and I came up with a game plan of playing wide so we could stretch the Lions. Many of our players weren't good enough to become full internationals but they were committed to doing something special in a game which would be a career highlight for them. They executed our plan almost perfectly. Against a very good Lions team, led by Lawrence Dallaglio and featuring Jason Robinson, Mike Catt, Will Greenwood and Austin Healey, we ran them off their feet and hit the lead early. We'd been relaxed but concentrated in our preparations and it paid off.'

'They played very well and starved us of a lot of possession,' remembers Dallaglio. 'They won 28–25.'

'They outplayed us,' says Johnno. 'They had more passion than we did. It's as simple as that, really. We just had to hope that it was going to be a wake-up call, just like Northern Transvaal had been in '97.'

In the aftermath of the loss to the shadow Wallaby side, Henry declared in a press conference that he would need to start concentrating his efforts on preparing the Test team for the series. For a squad that was creaking under the perception that the head coach had already identified his Test team, it was a grave error to voice this objective as there were still fixtures to be played against the Waratahs and New South Wales Country before the first Test. Did Henry's proclamation mean that, no matter how well the fringe players performed in those two games, they would be unable to break into the Test side? It seemed so – and, as a result, the dirt-trackers felt cut adrift and the divisions within the squad grew deeper. I look back on this and hold my head in my hands. Wasn't this the exact lesson that Geech had learned in 1993 and corrected so brilliantly in 1997? Where the 1997 Lions management got things right, it seemed that the 2001 management were getting things wrong. Yes, the 1997 team had straddled both the amateur and professional era and so had a greater focus on leisure and enjoyment than later iterations, but the balance had swung too far the other way in 2001 with too much training and a perception of favouritism splitting the squad in two – failures which would be repeated in 2005. It seemed as if the Lions were causing more issues for themselves than the opposition.

As the successful Lions of 1989 and 1997 had proved, the midweek team is the lifeblood of a successful tour. Harmony, good team spirit and support for the Test team comes from everyone feeling they are playing an important part and that if they can show some form they will be rewarded for it. Think of the guys who came from left-field to play huge roles on those two tours: Jerry Guscott in 1989, Tom Smith, Paul Wallace and Jeremy Davidson in 1997. It is crucial that this kind of player can come through for the Test series by proving his worth in the build-up games. Without that element, you might as well just have a Test squad train for six weeks in the UK and Ireland and then fly in for the three Test matches. It also ignores the stats that show the huge turnover in players during a series due to form and injury. If you have already discarded a player and made him feel second-rate, how can you expect him to step up to the plate when you need him in the second or third game of a series?

'It was hard for those guys in the midweek team,' says Woody. 'And Graham and the other coaches will, I'm sure, put their hands up and say they should have helped make them feel more included.'

'That's a regret,' concedes Henry. 'I should have been more sensitive to how the players were feeling. I could have communicated selections more tactfully, helped the midweek guys feel more included. That's something I certainly look back on and would change if I could.'

The next match, against the New South Wales Waratahs in Sydney, was a brutal affair that ended with the Lions winning 41–24, but the result was largely overshadowed by the rough-housing which led to five yellow cards and one red being dished out by referee Scott Young. Lions Danny Grewcock and Phil Vickery and Waratahs Tom Bowman, Brendan Cannon and Cameron Blades all spent time in the bin, but the most shocking incident of the night earned Waratahs full back Duncan McRae a red after he pinned Lions fly-half Ronan O'Gara to the ground and pummelled him so severely that the Irishman needed eight stitches to a bloody left eye.

'It was a joke,' remembered Lenihan. 'It was like Canterbury in 1971 – all those stories about Lions players being taken out by cheap shots before the Test series. They definitely went out with an agenda to rough us up. It wasn't all down to violence, but we lost a lot of players that day.'

With O'Gara's face in pieces, the Lions also lost Dan Luger – who had been in incredible form on the tour up to that point – Robin McBryde, Will Greenwood, Neil Back and Lawrence Dallaglio to go with the already injured Mike Catt, Simon Taylor and Phil Greening. O'Gara would recover to play again on tour – but the others were all flying home.

'About two weeks before the tour, I partially tore my ACL in the last club game of the season,' remembers Dallaglio. 'I didn't think I was going to be able to go on the tour, but they put me through a horrendous fitness test and somehow I passed it and they took me on the trip. Now, did I think I was a hundred per cent in the right shape to go? Probably not. But I was passed fit, Graham Henry wanted to take me; they said, "We'll give you every opportunity," and then some Australian did me a favour and snapped the other half of my cruciate in the Waratahs game. And that was it, tour over.'

'I'll always remember going into the medical room after the game and Johnno was getting some stitches,' remembers Lenihan. 'He was lying there getting stitched up and he asked me, "What's the story with the other guys? Dallaglio, Greenwood, Back?" And I said, 'They're out. They're all out." He kind of gazed at me for a second and then said, "Okay, we'll deal with it."

'These were guys that he had spent a lot of time with, played some major games with, knew really well, but he was just like, "Okay, we'll deal with it." I've always said, if I'd told him he was the only lock left standing in the squad and he had to play in there on his own, he'd have said, "Okay, I'll deal with it." My admiration for him went through the roof.'

Johnno shrugs when I mention this story to him. 'It's the nature of the beast. Touring is hard: very, very hard. It's attritional and you always get bad injuries. You just have to try and deal with it. You can't turn back time, you can't do anything else. There's no point dwelling on what might have been. You still have a squad full of international players, you just have to trust in them to step up.'

'It was a hammer blow to lose Dallaglio,' says Henry. 'He was at the peak of his powers in 2001 and was a guy who we were going to build a lot of the play around in the Test team. He was a huge leader in the squad as well, spoke excellently, was passionate. We were going to miss all the injured players, but him in particular.'

'It's another thing that makes winning a Test series for the Lions such a rare, beautiful thing,' says Woody. 'So many things can go against you winning – so many things can go against you even going on a tour! We all get injured; twenty-five per cent of rugby union players are injured at any one time. So there's always a good chance that a great player won't go on a Lions tour. There are situations where guys experience a drop of form for two months which means they don't go on a Lions tour, or a series of wins in the Six Nations might give a country a bigger proportion of players than they might otherwise have. All those things happen, and it comes down to the opinion of different people. Then, once you make the tour, you have to hope you're in form or find form and can maintain that form. And you have to hope you don't get injured. But every time you take the field in one of the build-up games, you're going up against guys who are probably playing the biggest game of their lives and they're going after you. And that's before you get into the attrition of the three-match Test series at the end of a bloody long season. The players are being held together with tape by that stage and you have to raise your game to its absolute peak to win.'

'But that's all part of the magic of it,' I say. 'It's why we love it so much.'

'You're right,' says Woody. 'It's so rare, it's so precious, it's so fucking hard. There's a magic to it all; it's absolutely exceptional.'

New South Wales County down in Coffs Harbour was the final run-out before the first Test and the dirt-trackers swept past them 46–3. As an exercise in showing that they were good enough to play in the Test team, it revealed little as the opposition were so poor, but there was nothing the players or coaches could do about that. All focus now turned to the first Test at the Gabba in Brisbane.

'In the weeks prior to the Test series,' says John Eales, 'I remember watching the Lions and just thinking, "These guys are having a great build-up to the series. They have all the momentum." We'd had great success in the few years before, but we were coming into this big game and were probably a bit underdone. We'd played the New Zealand Maori three weeks before as a warm-up and we were feeling reasonably confident, but I'll never forget walking out at the Gabba. We came up the steps from the changing room and on to the ground and all you could see was this sea of red. The whole grandstand was full of Lions fans. You could hardly see a gold jersey anywhere. Hardly anyone wore gold jerseys in those days; you'd get the odd Wallaby jersey, but there was no other gold, whereas every Lions supporter was in red. And that stunned our guys. It was a huge psychological blow for us because we just hadn't expected it. The Lions had obviously always been a big deal but suddenly the travelling support exploded, the numbers at the Test matches just went through the roof from 2001 onwards.'

'And did that have a big impact on your performance?' I ask.

'It was a perfect storm, I think, because we were just terrible in the first half but they were also very good. Jason Robinson scored after just a couple of minutes and we were stunned. Somehow, though, we weren't losing by much at half-time. We were still in it. It was 12–3, I think. So we went into the changing room and you'd know this scenario really well, Gavin: you're in the changing room and you're talking to people, and they're either on or they're off. And usually, they're on – you're talking and they're looking you in the eyes, everyone's got intent. But that day, I remember talking in the changing room at half-time, and the guys' eyes were up here, there, all over the place, and actually the room was stunned, because things weren't working. You could just sort of feel: "This isn't going to be our night."

'And then we went out in the second half and I think Brian O'Driscoll scored a try pretty well straight away and we were done, and we got beaten badly. Scott Quinnell got a try, Jonny Wilkinson kicked his kicks. We were never in it. So yeah, it was a really disappointing start to the series.'

For the Lions, it had been an exquisite performance of power, speed and skill. The final score was 29–13 and the gap could have been even wider. They had just ripped the best defensive team on the planet to shreds.

As the Lions trooped off the field, one of the all-time great Test performances in their back pocket, they weren't to know that they were about to walk into a media storm. Just hours before the Test kicked off, an article by Matt Dawson was published in the *Daily Telegraph* with the headline 'Harsh regime tears us apart'. It went after the coaches' 'mindless' training regime and spoke of some players threatening to go 'off-tour'. Despite the impressive on-field performance at the Gabba, it was Dawson's article that dogged the press conference after the match and in the days that followed. A similarly sensational article would be written by Austin Healey in *The Guardian* ahead of the third Test, in which he castigated the Australian second-row Justin Harrison, labelling him a 'plank' and a 'plod', and attacking the local media, telling them to 'spin this, you Aussies, up yours'. Both articles were as unedifying as they were unnecessary.

'We came off the field feeling euphoric,' says Henry, 'only to have a huge dampener put on all our efforts by that article. It was bloody annoying. Matt had his tits in a twist because Rob Howley was the number one scrum-half. And, you know, we'd had long discussions about taking Austin Healey on tour in the first place. Everybody thought Healey was good enough, but should we take him, because he was a troublemaker? And I said to them, "Look, if he's good enough, we'll take him and get him right." So there was some misplaced arrogance from me again! They knew him better than I did and they thought he would be a problem on tour, but we took him because he was a good enough player; we thought he might make a difference. If you had your time over again . . .'

Woody leans back in his chair, a contemplative look on his face when I mention the newspaper pieces. 'I think one of the

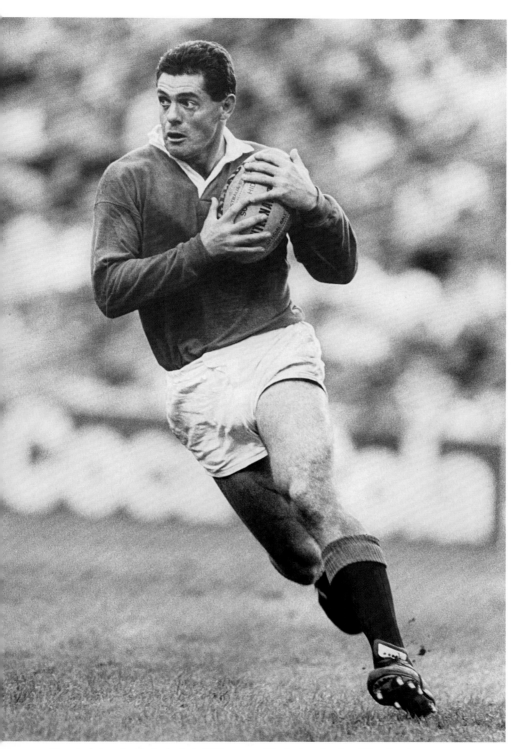

Yours truly in action in Australia in 1989 – some of the best weeks of my life and rugby career.

The great Donal Lenihan, one of the most important players on the '89 tour as leader of Donal's Donuts. *Inphophotography*

Brian Moore and David Sole in action during the Test series against the Wallabies. *Inphophotography*

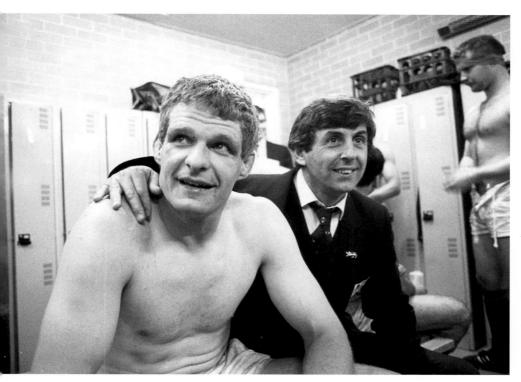

Fin and Geech celebrate winning the third Test in Sydney. 1–0 down? No problem, we'll win it 2–1. *Inphophotography*

Facing down the Haka in 1993. *Inphophotography*

Celebrating one of the great Lions achievements: putting up a record score against the All Blacks in the second Test in Wellington. *Inphophotography*

With my old Auckland University teammate: Fitzy gets ready to lift the series shield after clinching a 2–1 result at Eden Park. *Inphophotography*

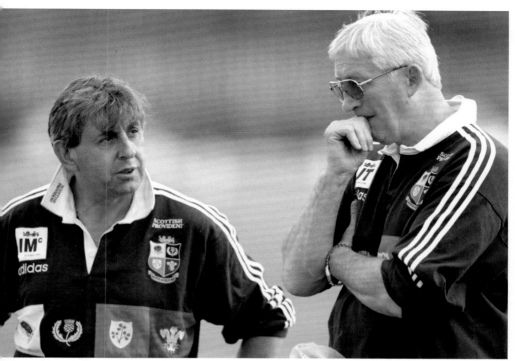

Geech and Telfer: the masterminds behind the Lions' triumph in 1997. *Inphophotography*

(*From left to right*) Jason Leonard, Keith Wood and Tom Smith are put through their paces by Jim Telfer on Nigel Horton's Powerhouse scrummaging machine. *Inphophotography*

Matt Dawson breaks down the blindside during the first Test in 1997 – he is moments away from throwing a dummy that fools each of the Springbok defenders pictured, before scoring a try that turns the game in the Lions' favour. *Fotosport*

Lawrence Dallaglio is adamant that having an emotional edge can prove the difference in achieving victory in elite level sport. Here he shows what it means to play for the Lions before the second Test in 1997 – one of the proudest days of his life. *Fotosport*

Woody chases his punt ahead at the end of the second Test. It's this kick that gives the Lions the vital field position they need to go on to win the match. *Inphophotography*

The ultimate Test match animal: Jerry Guscott sweeps over his series-winning drop-goal. *Inphophotography*

Martin Johnson became the first player in history to captain two Lions tours when he led the team to Australia in 2001. He would learn a huge amount from this latter experience in particular, using the lessons to positive effect two years later to help steer England to World Cup success. *Alamy*

Drico breaks through the Wallaby line to score one of the great individual tries for the Lions in the first Test at the Gabba, Brisbane. *Inphophotography*

Wallaby second row Justin Harrison, making his Test debut, makes the crucial decision to compete for the ball on the Lions' throw in the dying minutes of the third Test. His gamble pays off and Australia hold on to win the match and take the series. *Alamy*

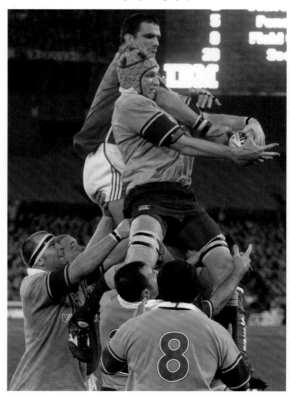

Wallaby captain John Eales embraces head coach Rod Macqueen after masterminding the series victory over the Lions. Having failed to execute their game plan in the first Test, they doubled down on their strategy and produced the goods over the following two matches. *Alamy*

Dan Carter thrived within the player-driven environment created by Graham Henry – a key lesson learned from leading the 2001 Lions – and produced what was arguably the greatest individual performance in the history of Test rugby. *Alamy*

Clive Woodward and Graham Henry shake hands at the conclusion to the 2005 series. Henry finished with four wins from the six Tests he was involved in with and against the Lions. *Fotosport*

Back for one last rodeo – Geech had originally put his name forward as manager of the 2009 tour to South Africa, but was persuaded to take on the head coach role for a final time. *Fotosport*

Paul O'Connell in action in the first Test. He and Geech had learned valuable lessons from the disaster of 2005 and were determined to put them right four years later. *Inphophotography*

John Smit, who first played the Lions in 1997, is able to help lay the ghosts of that tour to rest after leading his team superbly in the 2009 series. *Fotosport*

Ugo Monye scores the try that clinches the third Test at Ellis Park. In terms of the series, it may have been only a consolation win, but it helped keep the Lions concept alive and put the jersey in a good place ahead of the next tour to Australia in 2013. *Inphophotography*

Andy Farrell delivers his 'Hurt Arena' speech ahead of the third Test in 2013. *Inphophotography*

Jamie Roberts is mobbed by George North, Owen Farrell and Conor Murray
after scoring his match-clinching try in the third Test in Sydney. *Inphophotography*

After a sixteen-year wait, the Lions claim a series win. *Inphophotography*

An insight into the toll that the even 'easiest' of the 2017 New Zealand fixtures took on the Lions – here Alun Wyn Jones, Iain Henderson, Ross Moriarty and Sam Warburton ice their battered bodies after the Provincial Barbarians game. *Inphophotography*

Gats had romantic notions about returning the New Zealand with the Lions, but many of these were dashed by the domestic media's attitude towards him. His management of this aspect of the tour would prove to be as vital as any other as the Lions chased a place in rugby history with a series win over the All Blacks. *Inphophotography*

Choosing their words carefully: Sam Warburton and Kieran Read appeal to referee Romain Poite moments after the controversial penalty/scrum decision at the end of the third Test in Auckland. *Inphophotography*

Inseparable: the Lions and the All Blacks mix in together for the trophy lift after an unforgettable drawn series. *Inphophotography*

problems from that tour,' he says, 'is that a lot of guys had been on the previous tour and maybe presumed they'd be playing in the Test team because of their past achievements – and you just can't make that presumption. One Lions tour doesn't automatically lead to another Lions tour. I went to Australia in the box seat but I never made a presumption on any day that I was an automatic number one choice.

'Look, I was not the best athlete, but once it came to a rugby training session, my goal was to be the best guy on the training field. Always. That's what I wanted. I failed, of course, and failed often, but that's not the point. That was my target: my target was to out-train everybody that was there. So the higher the level, the higher you have to out-train them. I was there to work my bollocks off. But I have to question whether some guys thought they were entitled to be picked because of things they'd done in the past and, when they weren't, they thought it was because the coach was just playing favourites. I don't know if that's true or not – all I know is that we never gelled together in 2001 like we did in '97. We never got it. Which is a tragedy because it was a better squad.'

The sense of entitlement – and thus the greater sense of being cut adrift by the coaches – is perhaps at the heart of some of the problems that emerged on the tour. The practice of players writing columns for newspapers was stopped after 2001. On the whole, these articles were harmless. Until they weren't.

'In terms of harmony, I never felt like we were disharmonious as a group,' says Richard Hill, 'but clearly when you come out after having one of the greatest Lions results ever in the first Test, you don't expect to be briefed with the message: "Oh, this has been said in a newspaper article." Matt and Austin had their say and that was their individual opinions, but clearly it wasn't canvassing how we all necessarily felt – but once someone's done an article like that, you're all being lumped into the same bracket with them and it caused distractions.'

'I don't know if it caused too many distractions,' counters Johnno. 'The management made Matt apologise to the squad and we just made a bit of a joke of it, as players do. It was a bigger storm outside the squad. Those two guys played their hearts out in the midweek game that followed to beat ACT. For us, or for me certainly, that's all that mattered. The media in Australia is very planned and orchestrated. They're there to do a job on you from the first minute you arrive there and it doesn't matter what the truth of the matter is: you're a northern hemisphere rugby team, you're big, you're brutal, you're into fighting, you can't play rugby, your rugby's boring, and you're arrogant, full stop. That's the story. It was the same at the 2003 World Cup – and actually, 2001 did us a lot of good because when we went back in '03 we knew what to expect. It was the same story, different team name. Exactly the same story. *You're arrogant, you think you're superior, your rugby's boring, forward-dominated, you're old blah, blah.* Same story.

'Daws was apologetic about causing people a problem with his article; he wasn't apologetic about what he'd said, but he was apologetic because it had just given everyone a bit of grief. But those articles showed their frustration of having been there in '97 and 2001 wasn't living up to those experiences. They were like, "Ah, it's not what it could be or should be."'

'It's funny,' says Woody, 'people say: "Everybody loved each other in '97." No, they didn't. But everybody respected each other in '97; that's the thing, I think, that actually had to happen. You don't have to like them all, but my God, do you have to put it all on the table. That's the . . . for the want of a phrase, that's the leadership side of it. You give yourself to the team completely and you leave nothing out. If you all do that, then you all respect each other deeply and you can achieve things in the most difficult of circumstances. If you don't have that . . . well, that's when you can fall on your face.'

'We had a coach who was dictatorial compared to what a lot of our guys were used to: "You will play this way,"' adds Johnno. 'On previous tours, we'd been given a rough structure to play within, but there was freedom to make decisions and react off the cuff to situations in front of you. We now had preordained moves that lasted six, seven phases and everyone had to remember exactly where they had to be for each phase. Now, that was the way the game was at the time, but you have hardly any time to bed those plays in on a Lions tour. So we spent ages in training going through this playbook of moves and I think a lot of guys struggled with it. With England, we were playing really well at the time. Our back line in particular were used to Brian Ashton, who was very much more touchy-feely, more of a Geech type of character than a Graham, where Graham was, "Here's a big sheaf of paper, these are all the moves, this is how we play, crack on with it, that's it, end of." It was very difficult, I didn't know him, I didn't have a relationship with him to sort of be able to say, "Hang on, this is not going to work with this group, you've got some very, very good rugby players, let them go and play." And we saw that in the first Test when we scored tries that were not anything to do with Graham Henry's pattern of play; they were just good players playing rugby.'

'What did you do in the week after the first Test?' I ask Eales. 'How did you prepare for the second Test? I know Aussie Rugby did a whole thing of getting gold scarves and t-shirts and hats and stuff handed out to the fans to try and balance the colours in the stadium – but as a team, what did you guys do?'

'So, there were two elements at play,' he replies. 'There's the off-field and there's the on-field side of things – and that goes for the administration as well as the players. The administration picked up the ball after the first Test and said, "Yeah, we've got to have some gold to counter that sea of red," and they did that and they did that well. They encouraged Wallaby supporters to wear their jerseys and then handed out scarves and t-shirts and hats outside the stadium, which gave us that sense of support when we ran out for the second Test. But I think a really interesting leadership point from inside the team was that when we went down to Melbourne, we had to make a decision about our game plan. We had to analyse the first Test and ask ourselves: "Did we have the right plan and execute it poorly, or did we have the wrong plan altogether?" And in some ways, the braver call was to say, "Yes, we had the right plan but we executed it poorly," because you're saying, "We're doubling down on this. We just got flogged, but we're doubling down on the same thing." And that's what we did.

'We said, "You know what? We were just so poor in our core execution in that game, but if we execute it accurately, it will work." We'd studied the individuals in the Lions team, we'd studied the units, and we'd watched all their games, and we knew we'd have to play compelling rugby to be able to beat them, but we also knew that we didn't do that in the first Test. So we went down there into that second Test, saying, "We're going to try to do exactly the same thing, but execute it better."

'And I remember that was a big week, because we were under a lot of pressure, people were talking about us saying, "This team's gone, they're over the hill. They've had a good run, but some of them shouldn't be there anymore, blah, blah, blah." We were getting that criticism from former players and things like that, and while you try to ignore it, you can't help but take it personally and that's a real driver.

'And then we went into that game, and half-time in that game

– this is the interesting thing – half-time in that game, I think the score was almost identical to the first game: we were down, from an outsider's point of view, probably not looking that good, but we actually felt really good as a team.'

'We were performing comfortably in the first half,' remembers Richard Hill, 'but the difference between the first and the second Test was that we weren't winning comfortably. I think we outplayed them in the first half, to a level that was similar to the week before, but we weren't winning the scoreboard; we weren't capitalising. Whereas Jason Robinson had used his sparkling feet and scored within the first couple of minutes of the first Test and Brian O'Driscoll had made a line break which became a score, in the second Test we were creating similar line breaks and opportunities, but we just weren't scoring the points.'

'I remember going into the changing room at half-time in that game,' says Eales, 'and the team was so awake, they were alert and they felt good, and we said, "Guys, this is coming, this is coming, we're doing a lot of things well, we're just not scoring yet." But we actually felt like we were a lot more in control. Now, I'm not sure if anyone else watching the game felt that! But we did, and it was a very upbeat changing room.'

'I've never been in a game that turned so much at half-time as the second Test,' says Johnno. 'We made a few mistakes and suddenly they were a different team. The first half of the second Test was probably our most dominant half, we should have scored at least two if not three tries, then we come out, we make some mistakes and we give away an interception try and they end up running away with the game.'

'Martin's right, that's pretty much how it went,' adds Eales. 'We went back out after half-time and we got that stroke of luck with Joe Roff's intercept try and it kind of validated how we'd felt in the changing room. We could feel the momentum shifting massively in our favour, and then we ended up winning that game by more than the Lions won the first game.'

'Even when Jonny threw the interception to Joe Roff, we weren't out of the game at that point,' says Hill. 'It was just that our confidence drained away while the confidence in Australia went through the roof and they started playing a game that was suiting them and put pressure on us and we didn't recover. And that's credit to Australia, because they'd worked hard to stay in the game and once they got the interception, they felt the momentum shift their way. And, ultimately, that was poor from us – not to capitalise on our opportunities and then to let the game get away from us. But it was still all to play for in that last game and there was no reason why we shouldn't have got it done.'

'It was series on after that,' says Eales. 'But I think for us, it was a really good lesson about trusting our game plan. What makes it tough for both teams was that we both had a lot of injuries, and that's another thing you have to deal with. We lost Stephen Larkham; Jonny Wilkinson had to go off, they lost Richard Hill to a concussion.'

'There were bodies everywhere,' says Johnno.

'So both teams had to deal with injuries,' continues Eales. 'I think what was important for us was being able to make a conscious choice of how we wanted to play, double down on that strategy, and then go out there and back ourselves to be able to come back and square the series, and then head over to Sydney for the third Test.'

I mentioned to several players my fascination with the impact of emotion in Test rugby – how to manage it, why some players thrive on it, how others like to keep cool and calm, how it can be obvious when one team is dialled in emotionally and one team isn't and how decisive that can be when it comes to performance.

It has always intrigued me how some players can freeze when they play in these huge pressurised occasions, while others can be inspired by them. And this was a huge occasion. Outside a World Cup final, does it get any bigger than a deciding match in a Lions Test series?

'Emotion is a huge driver,' agrees Dallaglio. 'In professional rugby, especially at that elite international level, most players are on an equal footing in terms of their fitness, their strength and conditioning, their skill levels. Obviously you get outliers like a Brian O'Driscoll or a Jason Robinson who can do things that no one else can, but other than that we're all roughly equal. But rugby is a game where emotion plays a huge part in success or failure. If you can tap the right emotional touch-points, then you can add significantly to a player's or a group's performance.'

'The morning of the second Test,' says Eales, 'Rod Macqueen, our coach, came and spoke to me and he said, "Look, I just want to let you know that whatever happens tonight and next week, I'm retiring at the end of this series." He didn't tell anyone else then, but after we played the game and won, he stood up in the changing room and said, "Right, I just wanted to let you all know I've made this decision, I'm retiring after this week." He was a great coach, Rod, he'd led us to the World Cup win in '99 and he had a lot of very strong bonds with that playing group. It added an extra dimension to things because we now knew that he and I were nearing the end of the road with the Wallabies and I think it gave the boys just a little added extra to want to do something special for us, to make sure we didn't just slip off into the night after a series defeat. A Lions tour is career-defining for the host nation players; it's so rare and so unique and so special to get to play them in that once-in-twelve-years window and you want to put your marker down to say that you were good enough to beat them, that you conquered that juggernaut. And

Australia had never won a series against the Lions before. That was a very powerful driver that week.'

'As captain, how did you manage the pressure and the emotion that week?' I ask.

'Number one, you've got to manage yourself,' says Eales. 'A lot of people think you get to be captain and it just comes naturally for you, but I think the first mistake you can make as a captain is to forget about yourself. Now, I'm not talking about being selfish, but if you don't look after yourself, then you're not going to be able to look after others. So I think you've got to make sure you're doing all the right things, so that you're going to be mentally and physically in the right frame of mind come kick-off.

'And once you've done that then you can look at your leadership of other people. Elton Flatley came in to play fly-half, taking over from Stephen Larkham. Now, Stephen Larkham was such a key player for that team through that era, so that was a big change; that was like taking Jonny Wilkinson out of the England team at the time. So then you're saying to yourself, "Okay, what's going to help this guy through?" We all knew Elton really well, he'd been playing Super Rugby for the last five or six years, had played a lot of Test rugby, was a very, very good rugby player, but you knew there'd be a bit of pressure on him. So, you say, "Okay, how do you take the pressure off him?" One of the reasons we'd been such a strong team over the years was because we had very robust systems in place – we knew exactly how we wanted to play the game, and that was clear in everyone's mind. So we just made sure he could slip easily into that system. We also had very strong players around him – we had George Gregan inside him and Nathan Gray and Daniel Herbert outside him in the centres. So we had experienced players around him, and then you just want to reinforce the system. You might tweak it a little and say, "Okay, we're going to play it a little bit tighter, rather than a little bit looser," which you might do when Stephen Larkham was there. "Maybe kicking can come more into our game." We knew that it was going to be a big forward battle, so we had to be able to get on top in the forwards. If we did that, then we could set a platform for Elton to play his best game, to make the right decisions because he'd be going forwards not backwards. You take on a greater burden so that the game is less pressurised for him. That was our plan.'

'I wish I could say we were all pulling in a similar direction in our camp as well,' says O'Driscoll, 'but we weren't. I've come to learn over the years just how important the whole squad is in weeks like that, how big a role the non-playing guys have. It was something I recalled in 2013, which we'll get on to later, because it shocked me in 2001. We were one-all in the series, in the final week together as a squad and had everything still to play for. And I remember one day someone turned around and was like, "Where's such-and-such player?" – I won't name him – and someone else said, "Oh, he's in the Blue Mountains." "What?" "He's gone visiting the Blue Mountains with his girlfriend and her mother." This player wasn't involved in the team for the third Test and was just like, "I'm off-tour, I'm going on holiday." So he didn't even turn up for training – I couldn't believe it.'

'You look back and you can see all the little things that went wrong – some you can help and some you can't,' says Johnno.

'Like what?' I ask.

'Well, take the kick-off times, for example. There was nothing we could do about that because of the time change and the northern hemisphere TV audience wanting to get up and watch the games first thing in the morning as opposed to the middle of the night, but it had a big effect on how the squad gelled. In '97 almost all of our kick-offs were in the afternoon, so after the game we could go out and eat together and socialise together, have a bit of a night out. In '01, every game was the evening, so by the time you've played, you've done the post-match, it's getting on for eleven o'clock/midnight, and then we're travelling, it was very busy, so we never got those same opportunities to bond over dinner and a few relaxed beers.'

'And how about the things you could have controlled better?'

'Again, we come back to the training demands, which were far greater. We were training for three hours at a time sometimes, just ridiculously long sessions. You had specialist coaches who wanted their time. So it just became an all-work, all-travel tour, with very little time to relax, get to know each other and enjoy what you were doing. So it just became hard work, really, that tour, unfortunately.'

'Any other little moments?'

'Of course, there were loads. Some concerned players who had been on fire losing form. I think back, particularly to Iain Balshaw and Ben Cohen, who I think hated that tour. Balshaw had burst on the scene in the 2001 Six Nations and he must have thought Test rugby was easy. We turn up, we pass the ball around, we score forty points, he gets a couple of tries, we go and have a beer, job's a good 'un. And I remember when we beat Queensland, we beat them well but he didn't have a great game and he was carping on about not getting enough ball or getting it at the right time – I should have grabbed him then and said, "Iain, it's not all about you." You know, he was young and relatively immature rugby-wise. But I should have said, "It's not all about you, Balsh. Some days, you won't do anything, but if we win, that's fine. Some days, you'll be the star, and that's fine." But I think he thought if he didn't get the ball and run and score loads of tries, then it wasn't a great day for him – but it's not always like that, is it? I mean, playing full back, as you know, some days, you're just doing your job: catching, kicking and linking, and that's it.'

'For me, the most important thing was being part of a winning team,' I say. 'If I had the worst game in the world, well, I'd take the worst game in the world and playing in a winning team over playing brilliantly as an individual and being on the losing side. Every day of the week I would want to win. It was never about me: it was about the team.'

'Exactly, that's how it goes sometimes. So we had these sort of sub-plots going on with some players. Benny Cohen had made one mistake in a game and he'd been sort of written off, whereas actually he was the best winger, best power winger we had in British rugby, and we should have looked after him better to get his mind right and get him back in the Test frame. And I blame myself for not sorting that out.'

'I can only really speak from an English point of view on this,' adds Richard Hill, 'but I think we as a group – and Johnno in particular – learned a lot from that tour. We realised that we had to take greater control of things if we felt we were being pushed too hard by a coach. Exhaustion really did play a big factor in 2001 and, as lots of people will have told you, we clearly got some bits wrong on that tour when it came to managing the workloads. It was often a bit cloudy about when the downtime was and when work time was. We were often given the opportunity to have a day off but it was up to you whether you wanted to do an extra lineout session and things like that; and that ain't a decision, is it? Not when you're fighting for a Test spot. So you go and do the lineout session, you go and do another heavy gym session and so on. And so you don't actually get any time off to let the body and the mind recover.

'At the 2003 World Cup, at the tournament itself, there would be periods of saying, "Look, I think this is verging on too much, we need to have a break or we need to have a bit of time to ourselves." Johnno would be constantly dialled in to how the players were feeling and from time to time he would go to Clive and say, "We need to tone it down, the boys are knackered and we're losing our edge because of it." And when he did it, Clive's reaction was, "Okay, if Johnno's bringing it to the fore, it must be important, it must be right." That was great leadership from both of them and a hugely important lesson that Johnno took from 2001. We were in pieces by the end of that tour and if we'd managed the players better, who knows how it might have turned out.'

'In the final week, I was one of only six players who could train,' remembers Woody. 'We somehow managed to get a team on the field, but we had to call up Andy Nicol from being on the piss as a tour guide to sitting on the bench – that's how depleted we'd become. Austin's back went the day before – his body was just breaking down, like so many others. If the game had been played two days earlier, I doubt we'd have been able to field a team, it was that bad.'

'It wasn't the best preparation,' says Johnno dryly. 'And it wasn't fair on Andy to come in like that. Imagine if Daws had gone down injured after five minutes and Andy had had to play for seventy-five minutes? It wouldn't have been fair on Andy and it wouldn't have been fair on the Lions. Luckily that didn't happen. But we were right in that game, despite everything. It came down to the last minute, didn't it?'

It was a great Test match, a worthy finale to a fantastic series. Robinson and Wilkinson scored tries for the Lions, while Daniel Herbert picked up a double for the Wallabies. Wilkinson and Matt Burke were both kicking superbly for their teams and as the final minutes ticked down, it was only thanks to two additional Burke penalties that the Wallabies held a six-point lead. Trailing 29–23, the Lions had a lineout close to the Wallaby line and the hosts looked like they were preparing themselves not to contest it so they could defend the driving maul that the Lions pack was sure to unleash.

'How do you manage the lineout, what do you do, how do you think about that?' asks John Eales. 'We lost David Giffin after the second Test, who was a really key player in our team, and Justin Harrison came in to play his first Test match, and that was a big call from Rod to hand a debut to a guy in such a key position, up against the Lions captain, in the deciding Test.

'But then Justin probably did one of the key things in that game, which was to ignore the instruction not to jump. He went for it and he stole that lineout. Justin figured that in such a key moment, Martin Johnson, being the player and leader that he was, would call the ball to himself. So Justin went for the ball and won it. It was a great moment that summed up where we were as a team. We had all these great players who were playing within a great system, but we didn't have one person who was the star all the time. I think in a truly great team with a great system, you'll have a different person star in different moments of the game. We used to talk about really taking the moment: at some point in the game, you're going to get an opportunity to own a moment – you're actually the only one who is going to get that opportunity at that precise point – and that moment might be the one that turns the game. So we always tried to challenge people to be ready for that moment, to have the confidence to take ownership of it, and that's exactly what Justin did that night.

'The elation at full time was just massive,' he reflects. 'Elation and relief that we'd finally done it. We'd won a Test series against the Lions. It was a huge thing for us in Australia in so many ways – the result, the quality of the Test matches, the huge travelling support that kind of blew us away. There'll never be doubt again in Australia about how big the Lions are. We got caught a little bit by surprise in 2001, but by 2013 the anticipation for the Lions arriving was just massive – it had been building and building for years beforehand. People are already talking about the Lions coming in 2025. The significance of it will never be underestimated again. And we're desperate to win it again so that 2001 doesn't stand in isolation.'

And what of the Lions at full time?

'Fucking desolate,' says Woody bluntly.

'It was very tough to take,' says Brian O'Driscoll. 'And it only got tougher over the years. I was just a kid in 2001 and I thought I'd get plenty more opportunities to win a Lions series or two. Well, I got the opportunities and we kept blowing them. We finally managed to do it in 2013, but before that I wondered if I'd ever manage it – and with every loss we subsequently took, it made the 2001 all the more painful to look back on.'

'We were so close,' says Johnno. 'So close. And because we were so close, it makes you analyse every little aspect of that tour. There are a number of reasons why we didn't manage to win the series, but the main one I think is that we never really had that togetherness that we had in '97. We very quickly became the midweek and the Saturday sides and there was a very big difference in performance between the two, just like in '93. The gulf in morale between the two was so stark – and morale is everything. If you have the morale, you have a chance: if you don't, everything becomes so difficult. And if people lose that, then it's very hard to get back. I blame myself for that as captain – not seeing the comparisons to '93 – when I was bloody well there – and not sorting it out.'

'Well the captain from '93 knows what you're talking about and feels the same about that tour,' I say.

'It's so hard on tour, as we've said, but we should have sorted it out,' continues Johnno. 'The senior players on both tours could have done more, couldn't they? We should have done more. It's a collective effort to bring guys with you who are maybe wobbling and going off the rails. If you don't do it, two or three guys can derail a whole squad. I've seen it at club level, Test level and with the Lions. When the pressure comes on, if you've got any cracks, they will show. But if you have lots of people making sure no one gets too down then you can all pull through it. When you're winning, everyone's great, fantastic; when there's a bit of pressure, or you're losing, or there's criticism, that's when you find out what you're about, that's when the team has got to come together. So morale really is everything. We had it in '97 and we edged the series. We didn't have it in 2001 and eventually, when we got a crack, we weren't strong enough to come through it.'

Johnno and I are at the end of our marathon chat that has taken us from the Lions tours of the 1970s through to the 2021 iteration and down dozens of highways and byways along the way. It has been fascinating and enlightening and we could have carried on for hours more. Johnno is a man who should be listened to in every rugby outpost on the planet.

'So how do you look back on 2001 now?' I ask.

'The Tests from 1997 and 2001 were played on Sky during the first Covid lockdown,' he says. 'I flicked through them a bit and I showed my little boy – he occasionally wants to watch some of it . . . occasionally . . . I hold his head! But I tell you what, the regret around 2001 is more now than ever. We were so good. We had such a good team. We should have won that Test series comfortably. And for all the successes you enjoy in the game, it's the losses that really stay with you, don't they?'

I nod. 'But you learned from it,' I say. 'As a leader.'

'Yes,' he agrees. 'I learned a lot and I was able to use those lessons positively with England. But it still hurts. It still really hurts.'

And what of Graham Henry?

'There were so many lessons learned – for both me and the Lions,' he says. 'I had taken on far too much by thinking that I could coach Wales and the Lions at the same time and it was a great burden to try and do both – and it also affected some of the relationships I had with the Welsh players. There hasn't been a coach since who did a job with their national team at the same time as the Lions, and I think that's absolutely right. When Warren Gatland was with Wales he took a sabbatical for the year he was Lions coach and I'm sure he'll agree that that was vital.

'I had a tough time after that tour. I went back to coach Wales but I had some mental wellbeing challenges and the WRU were very good and they let me out of my contract and I returned home. It took a while, but I got myself right, got back into coaching and it was the making of me, to be honest. I was then lucky enough to be handed the head coach role with the All Blacks in 2004.

'When I took that job, I reflected on my time with both Wales and the Lions and I realised that I had always created a very coach-driven environment, but the Lions were full of leaders and I should have handed over more responsibility to them and cut back on the coaching hours. So that was my aim with the All Blacks: to create a player-driven environment – and we enjoyed huge success as a result. Over a period of three or four years we had a ninety per cent win rate and that was down to the players driving standards and controlling their environment. We had an unfortunate blip against France in the quarter-final of the 2007 World Cup, but the NZRFU kept faith with me and my coaching team and we got another crack at the job. Luckily, we were able to get back to winning ways and went on to win the World Cup in 2011. But all through that period I applied lessons I'd learned from 2001 about keeping our back-up players involved in games and supported in the environment, letting the players lead and drive what we did, making sure there were no dickheads who might poison the environment. As a result we cut some players over those years who had a negative effect and we created a squad that set its own high standards and lived up to them, who could think their way through problems; and when we lost three No.10s in the build-up to the 2011 final, we had the depth – and the understanding within the squad of how we wanted to play – to sub players in and still win the tournament.'

'It was a wonderful period of All Black rugby,' I say. 'And within that, of course, was another Lions tour.'

A small smile alights upon Henry's face. 'Yes, four years after 2001 I was involved in another Lions tour – this time on the other side. That was interesting as well.'

FIVE

WHEN MORE, MORE, MORE EQUALS LESS, LESS, LESS

2005

'DO WE HAVE to talk about 2005?' asks Brian O'Driscoll.

'Would you rather we didn't?'

'I think I could probably go the rest of my life not talking about 2005 again. There aren't too many great memories from that.'

The hurt is etched on every aspect of Drico's face. 2005. A Lions tour to New Zealand. O'Driscoll as captain. The core of his squad World Cup-winners with England just two years earlier. An ultra-modern head coach promising that no stone would be left unturned in pursuit of victory. It should have been a fairy tale. A dream. But it turned into a nightmare.

John Eales described the Lions tour as a juggernaut in 2001. By 2005, it was a behemoth. There was more fan interest, more media attention, more travelling support, more shirt sales, more corporate backing, more players, more coaches, more back-room staff, more, more, more . . . Too much.

Having led England to the pinnacle of the game at the 2003 World Cup, Clive Woodward (now Sir Clive) had fallen out with his RFU employers and resigned – but not before he had been appointed as head coach of the 2005 Lions tour to New Zealand.

He would later say his appointment was mistimed, believing that he should have been given the job in 2001 when he and his first-choice players were at their peak. But that was only one of myriad reasons for the failure of the class of 2005.

In fairness to Woodward, he analysed the reports from previous head coaches, examined the playing schedule in New Zealand and looked at the state of play in northern hemisphere domestic and international rugby. He realised that any player he selected would be on the verge of exhaustion after yet another long season, that the arduous travel to and around New Zealand would only add to this, that the rugby challenge would be mighty, and that of all the places that the Lions tour, New Zealand is the hardest country to fly replacements out to should there be any injuries. As such, he concluded that the best way to deal with all these challenges was to take a larger squad of players than ever before so that every position was covered and the players wouldn't be overplayed.

Woodward's success with England had been based on a no-excuses environment: if he provided his players with the best facilities, the best coaches, the best medical staff and the best back-room support, then they had no excuses for not performing on the field. And it worked – England became the best team on the planet. Surely this approach would also work for the Lions? Consequently, Woodward took almost as many support staff as he took players. There were two sets of coaches (one for the Saturday team and one for the midweek team), a vast medical department, a squad of media gurus led by former Labour spin doctor Alastair Campbell, a chef, a lawyer, a referee . . . it went on and on. In order to avoid snoring roommates, the players were given their own rooms. To cut down on travel fatigue, they would have three central bases in Auckland, Wellington and Christchurch from which the match-day squads would strike out for the games, often flying on the Lions' own private jet. To overcome the aura surrounding their opponents, the Lions would only refer to them as 'New Zealand' rather than 'the All Blacks'. To ensure unity, the Lions would have their own anthem, specially written for the tour. Almost every aspect of touring with the Lions had been examined and reimagined for the modern-day player. And yet one crucial ingredient seemed to have been overlooked: soul.

'You've nailed it,' says Paul O'Connell, of his first tour. 'It was soulless.'

'The theory was great,' says Richard Hill, 'and all those types of things worked with England, but it all fell flat on its face with the Lions.'

'Why?' I ask. 'Tell me more. Why did it work for England and not the Lions?'

'There are so many things to look at . . .' sighs Hill. 'I'll give you a few examples. Sharing rooms: it was great having your own room at Pennyhill Park with England, but that was because we spent so much time together. We knew each other so well and we would have weeks and weeks in the same place, so it was good to have your own space. With the Lions, you need the experience of having a roommate and that roommate changing every few days so that you get to know the other guys in the squad. Even if the guy you're sharing with is a nightmare – messy, smelly, snores, has a sly cigarette out the window, is up all night playing cards, all that kind of stuff – you end up having a great laugh about it. You have stories to share with the other players and you have this bond with that guy, even if it was a hellish few days. But we didn't get any of those stories in 2005.'

'What else?'

'Having two separate coaching teams and also having so many players meant that the squad split down the middle very, very quickly. You had Clive, Eddie O'Sullivan, Andy Robinson and Phil Larder taking the Saturday team, and Geech, Gareth Jenkins and Mike Ford taking the midweek team – or the Midweek Massive as they became known. Nobody wanted to be in the midweek team at first because it meant that you had very little chance of breaking into the Saturday team and therefore the Test team; with so many players and such a limited number of games, there were very few opportunities to play your way up the ladder. But the Midweek Massive ended up playing the more enjoyable rugby and they finished the tour unbeaten, so by the last couple of weeks people were looking pretty enviously at their set-up.'

'I wasn't on tour for very long because I broke my ankle,' says Lawrence Dallaglio. 'But I think it's fair to say that there wasn't a lot of fun had while I was there. We did the usual team-building stuff before we left the UK but it was all a bit hollow and corporate. What we needed to do – which is what Geech brought back in 2009 – was to have a massive piss-up or two. But we never got that. Then, once we were out in New Zealand, the pressure was so huge that we never really broke loose and had fun either. And that wasn't helped by the fact the squad was so big. There were guys on that tour that pretty much never trained together let alone played together. There were guys that I barely said two words to.'

'We were basically two teams on two different tours,' says O'Connell.

'The theory of having such a big squad made a lot of sense on paper,' I say, 'but in practice it was clearly unworkable.'

'Clive looked at past tours,' says Dallaglio, 'and realised that an average of eight players go down injured and need to be replaced. Because New Zealand is so far away and has such a significant time difference, it's very hard to get replacements in quickly and have them recovered enough from the journey to play at once – so he enlarged the squad by that number.'

'Which, as I say, makes perfect sense on paper,' I cut in. 'But that means that if a player gets injured, as you did, you already have your replacement there on tour. Which made it completely ridiculous when he flew out other replacements anyway.'

'In fairness to the guys who came out – particularly Ryan Jones and Simon Easterby – they played very well and got into the Test team on merit,' says Dallaglio.

'They did,' I concede, 'but their arrival meant that they had to get game time, which meant that the other guys scrapping around for those positions had to make way for them. That must have pissed off a lot of people?'

'It did,' says Hill. 'And that added to the sense of division within the squad.'

'And for all the planning that went into the tour,' I say, 'wasn't that one of the main lessons that was learned from both 1993 and 2001?'

'You'd have thought so,' says Hill, with a grimace. 'You'd have thought so. It very quickly felt like 2001 again – but without the silver lining of the nice rugby and how close the Tests were.'

Forty-five players were initially selected by Woodward and, of that, the vast majority were the men who had helped him lift the World Cup two years earlier. Again, this was fine in theory: that England squad was full of winners who knew how to go down to New Zealand and defeat the All Blacks, having done so in the summer of 2003. However, the gaping flaw in this logic was that since that famous night in Wellington, which was followed by a win against Australia in Melbourne and, a few months later, by a victorious World Cup campaign in Australia, England's form had dropped off a cliff. They had finished third in the 2004 Six Nations before touring New Zealand and Australia again in the summer of 2004 – and this time they'd been humiliated, losing 36–3 and 36–12 in the two Tests in New Zealand before shipping fifty-one points to Australia in Brisbane. Things continued to spiral down the following year as they finished fourth in the 2005 Six Nations. And yet twenty-one English players were selected for the Lions, while Grand Slam-winning Wales had only ten players, Ireland had eleven and Scotland had three. A third of the squad were over thirty and Neil Back became the oldest Lion on record at thirty-six.

'Too much trust was placed in those England guys to produce the goods out of nowhere,' says O'Connell. 'They'd achieved greatness with their World Cup win – they were one of the best teams of all time – but that England side was in serious decline by 2005 and a lot of guys went who should have been nowhere near a Lions shirt.'

'That's maybe true,' says Dallaglio, 'but do you know what? We never really had the quality across the board that year. I mean, you talk about Clive, and there's a lot of things he would have done differently if he was given the chance again, but if you look at the rugby that was played in the lead-up to that tour, England had won the World Cup in '03 – so the Kiwis were pretty pissed off about that and were coming after us – but the quality of the rugby in the northern hemisphere after that wasn't great. Wales won a Grand Slam in 2005, but they weren't a brilliant side. Ireland had had a poor Six Nations that year, England had had a really poor Six Nations, Scotland had only just beaten Italy at home to avoid the wooden spoon, so you can talk about the quality of the coaching and you can talk about doing things differently, but at the end of the day, we were playing the best side in the world, who had a point to prove, and we just didn't have the quality of players on that trip to overcome that.'

It's a very fair point. While northern hemisphere rugby was in the doldrums at the time, the quality in the south was soaring. New Zealand had some of the greatest players the game has ever seen coming into their own – Richie McCaw and Dan Carter were the stand-outs, but figures such as Tana Umaga, Keven Mealamu, Doug Howlett, Justin Marshall, Tony Woodcock, Carl Hayman and Mils Muliaina are also in the pantheon of greats. And, as we've discussed before, a Lions tour is a huge deal for the host nation. They were determined to prove a point after a disappointing World Cup in 2003 and they wanted to maintain their country's excellent record against the Lions. And opposite Woodward in the coaching box was a man who knew all about the Lions and what a tour meant for both sides. Graham Henry had been appointed as All Black head coach in 2004 and was about to take on the side he had led to Australia in 2001.

'I look back on 2001 and think what a marvellous learning experience and a privilege it had been,' says Henry. 'It was a bit strange to be on the other side of the fence four years later, but I was hugely excited by the challenge. And all of New Zealand was excited about welcoming them. The Lions are part of the rugby fabric, they're probably the most important brand in the game. The boys who get selected for the Lions feel hugely elated and it's the peak of their rugby career, and the teams they play against also feel very privileged to be playing against the Lions, because of the history and what it all means. I think professionalism has taken away a lot from rugby, a lot of passion . . . but I think the Lions connect us back to the amateur days. And if you just look purely financially, for South Africa, Australia and New Zealand, it's a windfall every twelve years and it keeps them afloat; it's very important for the community game, as well as the professional game, in each country because that money falls back into clubs and schools and keeps the game alive – and that's even more important today than it's ever been.

'So, for me, you only have to count on two fingers what the most important things in rugby are: the Lions would be one of them.' He grins. 'And the All Blacks would be the other.'

'And how were you shaping up as a team ahead of the tour?' I ask.

'That was the second year that I was involved with the All Blacks,' says Henry, 'and we could see that the team was starting to gel really well after a big change in coaching personnel and management after the 2003 World Cup. Dan Carter had broken through into Test rugby as a centre but moved to fly-half on our end-of-year tour in 2004, playing against Italy, Wales and France, and was beginning to get comfortable in the position. We beat the French in Paris by a big score, 45–6, so it was a very defining moment in the development of that rugby team. They left Europe feeling really good about themselves and with this huge incentive of a Lions tour waiting for them. For the All Blacks, to play against the Lions is one of the two biggest highlights of their careers: probably a Rugby World Cup first and a Lions tour a close second. It's the rarity of the tour that makes it so special because, as a player, you probably only get one opportunity to face the Lions; very rarely do All Black players get two opportunities, so it's massive for them. And so mentally and physically, they were at the peak of their powers. I guess the Lions boys probably realise how motivated the opposition are to beat them, but when you've been on both sides of the fence, you really come to realise how important it is to both teams.'

After a warm-up match against Argentina at the Millennium Stadium in Cardiff, which was drawn 25-all after Jonny Wilkinson (playing his first Test since the World Cup final) kicked a late equaliser, the Lions flew into Auckland at the end of May. Their first match on New Zealand soil was against Bay of Plenty in Rotorua, which they won 34–20 – but they also lost Dallaglio to a broken ankle after just twenty-five minutes.

They put thirty-six points on Taranaki in New Plymouth in game two before playing what was referred to as 'the fourth Test' against a very strong New Zealand Maori side at the Waikato Stadium in Hamilton. Woodward selected the heaviest front row in Lions history at fifty-four stone, ten pounds, but despite playing on an almost equally heavy pitch, his team was unable to overpower their opposition.

Turning around 6–6 at the break, the Maori brought on Carlos Spencer at stand-off and upped the pace of the game, the speed with which they won the ball at the breakdown befuddling the Lions' defence. The Maori scored a penalty through Luke McAlister before Leon MacDonald burst through for a try, which McAlister converted for a 16–6 lead. O'Driscoll managed to pull a try back for the Lions, but it was too little, too late and McAlister added a late penalty to round things off at 19–13 to give the Maori their first-ever victory over the Lions.

It had been the first real test of the tour and the Lions had come up short. The press were scathing in their assessment and the blanket media coverage across New Zealand was soon crowing about a potential All Black whitewash of the Lions in the series.

'I was only twenty-six at the time and pretty new to captaincy, so it was a pretty intense time,' says Drico. 'In fact, it was suffocating. I enjoyed it the least of all the Lions tours I went on because I felt a huge pressure all the time. In New Zealand, the Lions' focus is something else, it really is. It's everywhere you go, the people are very knowledgeable about the players and because you're always wearing kit, there's really no escaping from the attention. And as soon as you sustain a loss, the pressure just ramps up another level again. Losing to the Maori was a major psychological blow.'

'I still maintain New Zealand is the hardest place to go on tour,' I say. 'I think New Zealanders are absolutely ruthless when you play against them, and it doesn't matter which team they represent, they're in the same mould and they play rugby the same way and they're absolutely committed to winning and doing everything they can to achieve that – and they're bloody good footballers as well.'

'And it goes beyond their rugby,' says Hill. 'I think just as a country, they're great at how they support their national team. It's the national sport and therefore were were all recognisable as rugby players. We were probably more recognisable out there than we were back in the UK. So when you walked into a coffee shop anywhere, they knew who you are. And they knew how to rattle your cage. As a team, a squad, we never really got it going. It felt like we were always on the back foot and didn't handle the attention very well.'

Drico nods at this assessment. 'I found it difficult from that perspective, that there was a definite pressure and onus on you as captain and as a leader to always be front and centre and in the spotlight, but also the rugby was very, very hard. We didn't have the strongest of teams, to be honest. It was nothing like the 2001 team in terms of quality and of guys playing in their prime.'

'It looked to me,' I say, 'like the plan was essentially to pick the 2003 World Cup team plus you and Paul O'Connell tagged on.'

Drico gives a tight, humourless smile. 'I think that was pretty much the plan, yeah. And what was that famous quote of Mike Tyson's? "Everyone has a plan until they get punched in the mouth."'

'So at what stage did you get punched in the mouth?'

'I think we took several punches in the mouth! But you look back and you probably identify the Maori game as a big marker for them. We should have won that one. We needed to win that one.'

'The challenge in South Africa and New Zealand,' says Dallaglio, 'is that every game is a fucking tough game of rugby. Not quite so much in Australia, because their strength in depth isn't quite the same, but, you know, Jesus, the midweek games in New Zealand and in South Africa can be as hard as the Test matches. That's why you need to be absolutely on the money every game. You can't be taking any passengers on a Lions tour, because it's bloody tough.'

The Lions got the show back on the road by beating Wellington, Otago and Southland, but none of those wins were especially convincing, particularly in light of the fact that none of those sides had any of their All Blacks playing.

The record still showed, however, that the Lions had momentum going into the first Test in Christchurch. They had played seven games, won five, drawn one and lost by only six points to the Maori. And all of Woodward's preparation had been focussed on this moment: the Test series.

Even with the distance of all these years, it's a difficult thing to go back and watch the first few minutes of this game.

It begins with the anthems. The Lions play 'The Power of Four', a vacuous dirge that the players are visibly reluctant to sing and none of their supporters know. This is followed by a passionate and powerful rendition of 'God Defend New Zealand'. Then comes the haka. Woodward had taken advice from Maori elders and experts about the best way to respond to the challenge. The Lions formed an arrowhead in their half, with O'Driscoll at its tip. When the haka was over, Drico bent down and picked a clump of grass which he then tossed into the air – to symbolise pulling the rug from under his opponents' feet. The whole scenario was nicely choreographed, was culturally sensitive and was designed to show that the Lions wouldn't be intimidated. As with much of Woodward's planning in 2005, the theory was sound. In practice, however, the response seemed only to inspire the All Blacks to even greater levels of ferocity.

Just sixty seconds later, Drico went to clear out a ruck. He was hit by Umaga and Mealamu on the counter-ruck, had a leg lifted by each and was then dumped head-first into the ground. To protect his head and neck, Drico flung out a hand to break his fall – and the impact dislocated his shoulder.

One minute into the Test series and the Lions' leader – and one of their most important players – was out of the tour. It was a sickening blow and one that the Lions never recovered from. In pouring rain and howling wind, the All Blacks played some astonishingly skilful rugby and tore the tourists to shreds, scoring two tries through wing Sitiveni Sivivatu and lock Ali Williams, while Carter added a conversion and two penalties for a 21–3 victory.

'Losing Brian in that first minute or two was . . . it's not great to lose your tour captain at any time,' says Hill, 'but especially not under those circumstances.'

'How did it affect you?' I ask.

'It fairly takes the wind out of your sails,' says Hill. 'But it was our responsibility as players to pick up the pieces, reset and get on with the job – but we never did.'

The media attention in the aftermath of the Test centred almost exclusively around the O'Driscoll injury. There was uproar in the British and Irish press – and from the Lions' camp – when neither Umaga nor Mealamu were cited. The matter was then inflamed when they issued the most feeble of apologies.

'To be brutally honest,' says Dallaglio, 'when Brian O'Driscoll got stretchered off, the next guy who should have been stretchered off was their captain. I'm not saying that Umaga should have been taken out illegally, but every player should have gone after him and hit him so hard he had to go off. But we didn't really have the cavalry to do that. Instead, he played a sublime game and had a big part in both their tries.

'After the game, the All Black PR machine swung into action very rapidly, and all of a sudden, it seemed as if what had happened with Brian was all our fault not theirs. But the reality is that we should have reacted a bit differently to that. It riled us in the wrong way and they got another win there. We were made to look like whinging Poms and all the rest of it. Made to look soft.'

'What was the reaction to the incident from your side?' I ask Henry.

'Tana Umaga and Keven Mealamu were involved, and they themselves thought they were squeaky clean, to them it was an unfortunate rugby incident. Obviously, the media had different opinions, depending on what hemisphere they lived in! But one of our criteria to try and be successful was to control our own environment, and if you get involved in situations that are not going to make any difference to the result and cause you to get distracted, that's a negative. So, we just supported Tana – who was the main person who got targeted by the Brian thing because he was captain. It was just bloody unfortunate, that's how we viewed it. We thought it was a bloody shame that it happened and we obviously felt sorry for Brian, but we needed to get on, and so we supported Tana, and probably Kevvy, to some extent, and just got on and focussed on the second Test.'

'And you were able to park the distraction of the media circus and Alastair Campbell's involvement and so on?'

'When you're coaching the opposition, you don't get into that,' reflects Henry. 'You're so busy focussing on what you can do to try and get a result, if you get distracted by what's happening over the fence, that's counterproductive. So from our point of view, we just got on with it, and didn't get involved. Obviously, we looked at the Lions as the tour went on and looked at strengths and weaknesses, as you do, and that's part and parcel of rugby coaching, but as far as the number of players and the media circus, if that's what you want to call it, and all those things, we didn't even dwell on that.'

With O'Driscoll out, the captaincy was handed to Welsh full back/wing/centre Gareth Thomas. O'Driscoll, however, was torn about whether he should stay on tour and support his squad, or take his leave and let the guys who were still able to take the field focus on the job in front of them.

'Do I wish I'd gone home?' he asks. 'One hundred per cent. There's no place for an injured player out on the tour, captain or otherwise. So they're all things that you wish you could go back and change – but the only thing that you can ultimately do is make sure that they don't happen a second time. When I got injured in the second Test in 2009, I knew I wasn't hanging around for that third Test that week. I knew I was going to get the earliest plane out because of the experience of feeling at a loose end four years previously.

'When you're injured, there's an immediate disconnect; that's partly in your own head, but also in other people's heads, because you can't do anything on the pitch, be it in training or in the Test matches, to help the team, so you're just a spare part.

'Also, with me still being in the country, the news story around my injury kept going. I think it would have been parked an awful lot earlier if I'd just gone home. So that should have happened, and less probably would have been made of the whole thing.'

'But I can see why you still felt a responsibility to the other players to stay,' I say. 'As a captain and a leader, you wanted to keep contributing if you could.'

'I also didn't want to feel as though I was jumping ship after the first Test loss. But you're right, I thought, "Hang in there and we can genuinely turn this around." But then after the second Test, I should probably have gone home after that, when the series was done. But it almost exacerbated that initial feeling that I didn't want to be seen to be leaving the country when things were getting tough and we need to hang in there.

'I was kind of off on my own tour, though, particularly in the final week. I barely saw the team and I might as well have been at home because I just felt disconnected and sort of lost. I should have bitten my pride and just gone, "Listen, it's time to go home, I'm of no value here anymore so let's call it quits; I'll head back and try and get started on rehab."'

The Midweek Massive had an almost meaningless run-out against Manawatu in Palmerston North, scoring 109 points to six, before the second Test in Wellington. Woodward had rolled the dice by playing Jonny Wilkinson in the centre alongside O'Driscoll (for sixty seconds) in the first Test and he rolled it again for Wellington, hoping that Wilkinson would rediscover the imperious form at stand-off that had made him the best player in the world two years earlier, despite a lack of any evidence on tour suggesting that he would. Gavin Henson, the star of that year's Six Nations, was drafted into the centre alongside Thomas, who shifted in from the wing, and Shane Williams took the No.11 shirt, while late call-ups Ryan Jones and Simon Easterby came into the back row to replace the injured Richard Hill and the overpowered Neil Back. In many regards, Woodward's selection looked like the Dutch boy trying to plug holes in the dam. Graham Henry also shuffled his selection, but his changes only made his side look stronger. And so it proved.

Dan Carter would put in a display that many pundits would describe as the greatest individual performance by any rugby player ever. It was masterful; close to flawless. But so, too, were the performances of those around him. The Lions scored an early try through their new captain but then came the onslaught. There was no need for violence at the breakdown this week – instead, the All Blacks brutalised the Lions with their speed of thought, hand and foot. The final score was 48–18 but it could have been a whole lot more.

'For all the various mistakes we made and injuries we suffered,' reflects Richard Hill, 'one thing that should never be overlooked is how well New Zealand played. They brought a squad together of outstanding individuals who clicked seamlessly as a team. Tana Umaga was at his peak and guys like Carter and McCaw were starting to come into their own.'

'You know, we weren't a million miles away on that trip from playing very well,' reflects a more philosophical Dallaglio. 'The team that lost narrowly to the Maoris wasn't a million miles away, but that loss robbed us of some confidence. And then we lost one or two players – I was probably one of the more senior players at that time in the forwards, and Brian was the most senior player in the backs. Added to that was that, for whatever reason, the quality of rugby that was being played in the build-up to that tour wasn't anywhere near where it needed to be. So combine all that and we were really struggling.'

'I think it needs to be recognised that the second Test was one of the greatest performances ever produced in rugby history,' says Henry. 'Collectively we played really well and Dan Carter was just outstanding. I don't think any side could have competed with us that day.'

With the series gone, the Lions hoped to restore some pride in the third Test in Auckland. But it wasn't to be. The All Blacks had last lost a Test match at Eden Park in 1994 – a record that still stands to this day – and they wanted to secure a series whitewash at this rugby fortress. Carter was injured and missed the match but the All Blacks barely blinked. Luke McAlister, who had been superb for the Maoris against the Lions, stepped into his shoes and produced a superb performance as he conducted his teammates around the field. When the dust finally settled the scoreboard read 38–19 and all of Woodward's grand plans were in ruins.

'A lot has of course been made about the size of the tour party and what have you,' reflects Dallaglio. 'But to be honest, you could probably have taken 300 players and it still would have been the same result. New Zealand were an outstanding team and they had a point to prove, especially against the English players.'

'How do you look back on the tour?' I ask Drico. 'What lessons did you learn from it?'

He sighs. 'I think that, as painful as it was, sometimes you've got to get things wrong to realise how to do them right. Clive tried to revolutionise the Lions – and fair play to him for trying because the roots of the Lions are based in the amateur era and it shouldn't really work as a concept anymore – but in so doing it allowed us to really see what it is that has worked for the Lions in the past, what makes it so special to the players and what gives it those little sparks of magic that can turn a Test series in your favour. We learned that rooming on our own, like England had been doing for the World Cup, just didn't work on a Lions tour because it created segregation, it stopped there being an investment in one another, which is vitally important. Without it, there's no bonding, there's no one that has your back, making sure you're on time for meetings, wearing the right kit. All those small things, they all add up; they're all little aspects that blend a team together.

'And yeah, listen, as captain, and I'm sure Clive would be the first to say as well, lots of mistakes were made, but mistakes are no good unless you learn from them. They made modifications in 2009 that they have carried through to the subsequent tours that hark back to the old-school way of touring – but they might never have known just how important those aspects were without the experiments made in 2005. So some good has come from it.

'I look back and wish that I'd challenged some of the things Clive implemented, done things differently personally as a captain. But I was still only young and when you're part of a machine like the one Clive created, it's very hard to challenge what's going on until it's too late.'

'I think that was one of the big learnings from 2005,' says Hill, 'and what Geech focussed on in 2009, was around the camaraderie, the interaction between players, spending time together with one another. They reduced the squad size, reduced the back-room staff, they went back to sharing rooms, all that stuff. And they had to because after 2005 – and after 2001 to a degree – if they didn't get it right in 2009 there was a very real chance that the Lions were finished. There had been a similar threat ahead of '97 because a lot of people said that a Lions tour couldn't survive in the professional era, but we managed to revive the concept by winning the series. But with the way everything went in 2005 it looked like it might be the death knell. So the pressure on 2009? It was huge.'

SIX

LOOKING BACK TO GO FORWARD

2009

IT WAS 14 June 1997. Durban, South Africa.

The braais had started early in the car parks and on the rugby pitches around Kings Park. A haze of smoke filled the air and drifted high above the concrete walls, iron girders and spiralling walkways of this great rugby cathedral, known affectionately to the locals as the Shark Tank – the home of the Natal Sharks.

Back in 1997, the Sharks were the undisputed top dogs in South African provincial rugby. They were the Currie Cup holders and had recently played in the Super 12 semi-final, losing to the eventual champions, the outstanding Auckland Blues, at Eden Park. But all that success was in the past. The only focus on 14 June was the present because the British & Irish Lions were in town and their Saturday side were about to play their final match before the first Test of the 1997 series against the Springboks.

Even though Natal were unable to field André Joubert, Henry Honiball, Mark Andrews and Gary Teichmann because they were in the South African team, they were still able to select seven internationalists along with a number of players who would be capped in the near future. Among these was a young tight head who had just made his breakthrough into the senior squad. John Smit was eighteen years old and wasn't long out of Pretoria Boys High School. Despite spending much of his life on the high veldt, he was a dyed-in-the-wool Sharks supporter and was living the dream in his first year as a pro at the province.

Smit had made his Sharks debut off the bench against Western Province a week before the Lions rolled into town. It had not gone particularly well. As he recalled when we chatted over Zoom, 'I had my arse handed to me by Garry Pagel. Robbi Kempson was suspended for the game and Mac [Ian McIntosh, the Natal coach] started Dave Morkel and I got called up to the bench. The following week we played the Lions and Robbi was back in the team – but for some inexplicable reason, Mac dropped Dave from the squad and kept me on the bench.'

It was a hot, humid afternoon in Durban, with a light breeze blowing in off the Indian Ocean. Deep in the bowels of Kings Park, Smit sat on the bench in the Sharks' changing room and looked at the jersey in his hand.

'I couldn't believe I was there,' he says wistfully. 'I was on the bench against the Lions. The Lions! I looked around my changing room and I could see our captain, John Allan, about to play his last game for the province, literarily steaming as he prepared to go out and play. This was such a huge, huge match. We were about to face the team that was pretty much the Lions Test side that was going to face the Boks in Cape Town a week later. We wanted to bloody their noses before the series and make a bit of history by beating them. They wanted to stamp some authority and show they were ready for the Tests. The atmosphere was incredible. I looked at their pack: Tom Smith, Keith Wood, Dai Young, Martin Johnson, Simon Shaw, Lawrence Dallaglio,

Richard Hill, Eric Miller. Jesus, what a team. If I came on, it'd either be scrummaging against Tom Smith or Jason Leonard, who was on the bench. I was absolutely shitting myself.'

It was a game of huge incident. The Lions, who had struggled in the scrum in many of the previous provincial matches, were rock solid, but they also lost one of their most important players when scrum-half Rob Howley darted around the side of the ruck and ran into the twenty-two-stone human bus that was prop Ollie le Roux. Howley broke his collarbone and was out of the tour. It was a devastating blow, but the Lions barely missed a beat as Matt Dawson slipped seamlessly into what was now a very well-oiled attacking machine. By the time the clock ticked into the final quarter, the Lions were 28–12 up. Ian McIntosh signalled to Smit to get ready to go on.

'Oh my God, this was it,' Smit remembers. 'I jog up and down the touchline, trying to stay calm. The play stops and I get the nod. I could hardly breathe because of the nerves. Kings Park was packed, the crowd were going crazy. And I was coming on for a scrum – no messing around, straight into the action. Before I got to the mark, John Allan comes up to me, grabs me by the sleeves and chest bumps me five or six times, screaming in my face to pump me up. I tell you, by the time we packed down, I was more afraid of my own captain than I was of that Lions front row!'

The game would finish 42–12 to the Lions and Smit only has the odd flash of memory of those final few minutes, so fast did they pass. But he still remembers the huge swell of pride that washed through him as he returned to the changing room. 'I remember sitting there in my jersey afterwards and not wanting to take it off. It had been such a special experience. I hadn't been able to keep my first jersey, because you only get your jersey after the season ends, and I hadn't played enough games to earn it. But this jersey was a one-off, with a special Natal Sharks/

British & Irish Lions emblem embroidered on the sleeve and it was mine to keep.

'Then I looked up because Mac was calling my name. He was by the door with Dai Young, who wandered over to speak to me. "Well played," he said. "Do you want to swap shirts?" I remember feeling a little sick. All around me the other Lions were starting to file in to swap shirts, but I was desperate to hold on to mine. "I'm so sorry," I said, "I'd love to swap – but I've been dreaming about playing for the Sharks my whole life and I get to keep this jersey. I'm not sure if I'll ever get another one." He looked at me kind of perplexed, then said, "Hey, no problem," shook my hand and headed back to his changing room.

'About five minutes later, there was another shout from Mac. I look up again and this time it's Jason Leonard at the door. I go over and Jason says, "I heard about what you said to Dai. Listen, I want you to have my shirt – and we don't need to swap. I just want you to remember this day. I'm sure you'll go on to have a great career, but you're right to keep that jersey, it's special. Good luck. I'm sure you're going to go on and play many times for the Boks." And then he left.

'I'd been playing rugby since I was a kid and I had never really realised the power of rugby until that moment. Jason really showed me what rugby is, much more than anything that had ever happened on the field. The Lions smashed us that day and they ended up beating South Africa in the series and I couldn't help but be gutted by those results – but I was also happy for that Lions team because they'd come down to South Africa and played some amazing rugby. The dummy from Dawson and the drop-kick from Guscott . . . those moments haunted South Africa for twelve years, but I was also happy for that team that they achieved that series win. That shirt of Jason's has always been very, very precious to me.'

'Jason's an amazing character,' I say. 'And clearly a pretty good judge of a young player!'

'I was converted to a hooker in the years that followed,' says Smit. 'And I won my first cap for the Boks in 2000. At the end of that year, I was selected for the Springbok tour to the UK and Ireland. After we played England at Twickenham, I went and found Jason and I handed him my jersey. I said, "You probably won't remember this . . ." and I reminded him of the story and thanked him properly because I'd been so stunned in 1997 that I'd barely been able to speak to him. We had a few beers afterwards and have remained good mates ever since.'

Smit would go on to be one of South Africa's all-time great players and leaders. He would win ninety-four caps for the Boks and captain them to World Cup glory in 2007. Just over a decade after that game against the Lions in Durban and with the World Cup winner's medal tucked away in his trophy cabinet, Smit moved to Clermont Auvergne in France and brought the curtain down on his Test career. Or so he thought. Peter de Villiers became Springbok coach in 2008 and lured Smit out of intentional retirement, the carrot of the 2009 Lions tour too tempting to resist.

'The ghosts of '97 were a burden on South Africa,' Smit tells me. 'It was a huge motivating factor for me getting out of my contract at Clermont to come back to the Sharks because I wanted to reverse the result of that series. It was a huge motivator for our whole 2007 World Cup squad, in fact, because we all wanted a chance to play the Lions and get some revenge for '97. That '97 series was a bit of a millstone around our necks, but the Lions were also very important to the culture we established in the team. I'd sensed that as the game was getting more and more professional in the early 2000s, it was also getting too serious. It was becoming more of a job than a passion, and passion is the bedrock of any successful team. I remember realising that we were no longer getting to know the opposition. We'd created a barrier with the Australians and New Zealanders, who we played every year; we wanted to hate them as much as possible, so we didn't feel too guilty when we hurt them, you know? And we became this kind of isolated island where we played rugby and smashed people and then went our separate ways. It was the same with the other countries we played as well.

'I got together with a couple of the senior guys in 2004/05 and said, "I think we need to go back to how I started my career, by mixing with the opposition in the changing room afterwards, and to do that we must send out an invitation to every team that comes to play us and ask them for some beers afterwards. We're not going to be any less hard or less physical in the game, but if we send out an invitation the week before, saying, "Hey, no matter what happens, beers in our changing room afterwards, please come and join us, swap jerseys, have a chat," I think it will only do us good as a team. And so this thing started. The Kiwis jumped on it immediately and the rapport was brilliant within a week. The Aussies took a little bit longer, and some of the other teams also took a bit longer, but eventually it became like the old-school days: we would smash each other up and love doing it, and then joke about it over a beer afterwards. And it was the memory of Jason and his jersey that inspired that decision. It made me realise how important that human element is to rugby union and how crucial it is to keep that kind of thing alive.'

'And the key, of course,' I say, 'is that it doesn't compromise your desire to win. It doesn't distract you from that.'

'Oh no,' he says, his eyes glinting. 'It doesn't distract you. In the build-up to 2009, all we could think about was beating the Lions. It was our sole focus. Our obsession. We'd been waiting for twelve years for you okes to come back to South Africa and we couldn't wait to play the Test series. We'd have beers together after the games, but we wanted to smash you up first. After winning the World Cup, that Lions series was the most important thing any of us would ever do.'

*

The 2009 tour was equally important to the Lions. After the damaging experience of 2001 and then the utter disaster of 2005, the survival of the Lions was once again on the line, just as it had been in 1997. Was the concept still relevant in the modern age? Did the players still see it as the ultimate honour? Could it still justify its place in a crammed sporting calendar?

These were some of the many questions circling the wounded Lion like birds of prey. The Four Home Unions Committee knew that they needed a strong response after Clive Woodward's efforts to ultra-modernise had failed so spectacularly. They needed to rediscover some of the old magic of a Lions tour, needed, as John Smit would say, to make it old-school again. And so they went to two people who understood those aspects best. Gerald Davies, a Lion in South Africa in 1968 and New Zealand in 1971, was appointed manager. And Geech was brought back for his fifth and final tour as a coach.

Geech had seen first-hand where things had gone wrong in 2005 and so set about making some fundamental changes four years later. He reduced the size of the tour squad, the coaching panel and the back-room staff. The players would all get a chance to stake a claim for the Test jersey. They would all train together, eat together, share rooms.

'So I had no intention of being involved in 2009,' he tells me. 'But during the last week of the 2005 tour, Bill Beaumont, who was manager of that tour, and I went for lunch out on Waiheke

Island. We had a couple of bottles of wine and a nice lunch, and we talked about what had happened on the tour. I said to him, "Bill, this must never happen again. In 2009, the players have to share rooms, they have to train together and travel together. There are certain principles that have always been in place on Lions tours and you have to bring them back, because otherwise you'll never get what you want on the rugby field, because you've not got it right off it." That was me passing on my learnings from the tour, but I didn't think at the time that I'd be the one putting them into practice.

'Bill asked if I'd consider being the manager in 2009. I said, "Well, yeah, I might do. It's so important to me that we try and make it as good as it can be for the players, so yes." Anyway, I think Gerald Davies was also on the Lions' committee and he put his name forward as the manager, so the next thing I get is a phone call from Andy Irvine asking if I fancied being head coach – so things changed a little bit! But by that stage I wanted to do 2009 to set the Lions' record straight for the way it should be, the way it should look, and the nicest thing that happened was that Brian O'Driscoll, who had then been on three and captained one, came up to me at the end of the tour and said, "Thank you." He said, "Now I understand what it is to be a Lion." And that meant a hell of a lot to me.'

With his old sidekick Jim Telfer now long retired, Geech brought in the men who had masterminded a Welsh revival the previous year (and which would last for more than a decade) to assist him. He made Warren Gatland his assistant coach while Shaun Edwards ran the defence, Rob Howley took responsibility for the attack and Neil Jenkins ruled the roost with the kickers. Having experienced huge success with a second row captain in South Africa with Willie John McBride in 1974 and Johnno in 1997, he handed the role to Ireland's Paul O'Connell.

'I wanted to make sure we did justice to the Lions jersey,' says O'Connell. 'I don't think we did that in 2005. One of the key things I wanted to focus on in 2009 was living up to the tradition and history of the Lions. A lot of things went against us in 2005 but we didn't do the tradition justice. That was a big motivation for me and for a lot of us who were on that tour. We saw 2009 as a big opportunity to put that right.

'I think one of the problems with 2005 was that we still hadn't yet reached peak professionalism – we were chasing the concept of peak professionalism and trying to find more and more ways for us to be more professional and less and less amateur. But there's a lot of very good, important things in amateurism for rugby, because rugby is a very, very tough game and emotion plays a big part in it if you want to be successful. I believe one of the reasons the Irish provinces are successful is because the players are playing for the team they grew up wanting to play for. We're not like the French clubs, where they have players from all over France and all over the world playing for them; we generally have quite local teams with a few foreign players. There's a lot of heart and a lot of soul that goes into playing for your province in Ireland and that really helps with the performances. When you're on the line with seconds remaining, it's that passion for your team and teammates that gets you through it. And that's the same passion that's needed on a Lions tour. You can't be cold and emotionless about wearing that jersey, which is kind of how it got in 2005.

'Clive's ambition in 2005 was for the tour to be the most professional Lions tour of all time – which was a good idea, a very good idea – but in the pursuit of that I think we left a lot of the really important things of the Lions behind. I think he overlooked the fact that the England team he'd coached had been together for a very long time – a core had been together since

1997, through the 1999 World Cup and then peaked together building up to 2003. And maybe we assumed, because Clive was head coach and because we'd a lot of those England players, that the tightness and togetherness would be there, without actually having to work too hard on it, or having to speak about it. But every Lions tour is a brand-new entity. It has no culture before you start, you have to build it every time.

'So take the single rooms, as an example. The single rooms would have been an English thing at the time, but because they'd been together so long, they didn't need to room together, so there was probably massive value in single rooms for them because it gave them space, it kept their relationships fresh, they weren't in each other's pockets all the time. But on a Lions tour, there's great value in sharing rooms, because it means you spend time with people that you don't know, and their mates call to their room and so you end up catching up with them as well.

'But whenever I say this about that 2005 tour, and that we went almost too professional, there was also a whole group of us senior players there that Clive was very open to discussing and arguing and talking things through with. It's not like a load of us said, "Hang on a minute, this isn't going to work," you know? We went along with what he was saying because he had enjoyed huge success and a lot of it made sense on paper. So I don't blame him for it; I blame us all as a collective for how 2005 worked out.'

'Did you and Geech chat about all of this before the tour?' I ask.

'Yeah, we did. Geech had been there as well, obviously, so he knew all the problems, and we had a good chat.'

'I flew over to Limerick to see Paul,' remembers Geech. 'And we had a really good meeting where we discussed 2005 and what we wanted to change for 2009. It was quite a long list!'

As ever on a Lions tour, there would be a strong leadership group in place to help O'Connell and Geech achieve their goals.

But for the first time ever, there would also be a former captain among the players.

I asked Drico how he learned that he would be going on the tour, but wouldn't be captain for a second time.

'It was simply a case of Geech ringing me up and telling me that he was going with Paulie for this one, and I said, "Fair enough,"' says Drico. 'Of course, you never want to be overlooked for a captaincy role, but I could completely appreciate Geech going with Paulie, who was a great leader and really important to Ireland and to Munster at the time. I think I would probably have been far better equipped to have been captain in '09 than I had been in '05. I was still only twenty-six in '05, still relatively inexperienced, and by 2009 I had two Lions tours under my belt and had a bit more experience captaining Ireland. I would probably have been able to deal with some of the pressures and the expectation a bit more, four years later. But I totally got why they went with Paulie.'

'Captaincy is a real privilege and a real honour,' says O'Connell. 'But there's a lot of pressure that goes with it. Brian had been doing it for a long time with Ireland, and sometimes it's nice to have a break from captaincy, to be honest. I think he probably enjoyed the break and he certainly played some of the best rugby he ever played – the game plan we used gave him a lot of space to play, and he formed a great partnership with Jamie Roberts in the centre. He probably enjoyed not having the pressure of captaincy – even though he was a captain anyway; he spoke like a captain and played like a captain and did all the various leadership things alongside me, except he didn't have to go to the coin toss and he didn't have to go to the media the day before the game.'

'I suppose I can look comparatively at the tours that I went on and Paulie's right,' says Drico. 'That was the best tour from my perspective, because I had the experience of being captain previously, I was a helping hand to him, I was still probably in the prime of my career, probably played the best rugby of my life that year, but I wasn't the new kid on the block any more. So all of those different aspects lent themselves to me being a bit more relaxed and it really helped me to enjoy the tour, which I definitely did. We had a great time and we had a really good team spirit.

'I asked Geech if I could I call Paulie to congratulate him and then I started to focus on what I could bring to the party to support him. All good teams have multiple leaders, and yes, there's the focal point of the captain and there's a huge pressure and onus on them, but if you can take some of that workload off them, or if you can help them by being another voice and watch out for them and just be a helping hand, it's always going to be beneficial to that individual and beneficial to the team.

'I'd like to think that I did that in '09 and then subsequently in 2013, helping to share that leadership workload. All the more so on a Lions tour when you don't know some of the players like you would in your club or your national teams; you need the national leaders and the national captains or ex-captains to speak to their own players and particularly the younger players. It's such a unique environment and it can be quite alien, so it's important to draw on all the skills you've learned over the course of previous tours to make it easier for other guys in the party.'

As Drico says this, it reminds me that Fin did the exact same thing in 1989. The leadership group back then had a member from each country so that their fellow countrymen could speak freely if there was something bothering them. O'Connell's leadership group had players and captains from each country and it kept the channels of communication flowing across the entire squad. Again, it was an old-school concept, but an effective one.

'Geech thought of all these things,' says O'Connell. 'He was also conscious of not having too big a group, he was conscious of not having too many coaches, he was conscious of having a very simple game plan; I always said that we played the Welsh game plan on that tour, which we were able to learn really quickly. It was really simple and allowed everybody to get on the same page really quickly. We had a much smaller group, so we were able to train together and travel together, all the players were able to fit on the same bus, which was a bit of a novelty after 2005.

'There were a lot of very simple things like that done. We were encouraged to go out on the piss. I remember when Craig White, our fitness coach, gave one of his first speeches, he showed us a sachet of Dioralyte and he said, "Look, if you do go out, please drink one of these when you come in; we want you to have a few beers and spend time with one another, but when you come in in the evening, drink one of these so you rehydrate." Just little subtle things like that, whereby you knew things were going to be a little bit more relaxed; you knew there was going to be a big emphasis on people spending time with one another, getting to know one another, building relationships with one another, and we were probably willing to sacrifice a little bit on the professionalism side for that.'

The Lions would have a huge challenge ahead of them, as they always do when travelling to South Africa. A mix of playing at sea level and altitude would test their aerobic capacity, the constant stream of enormous opponents would test their power and their bravery. And if they were to stand any chance of success, they had to be tightly bonded, have each other's back, be prepared to put their bodies on the line and also have the ambition to take on South Africa in attack, just as the great teams of 1974 and 1997 had done.

'You can never underestimate the value of someone that really knows and understands the Lions and Geech was the master,' says O'Connell. 'I think he was brilliant for Warren Gatland and Gats learned so much from him about the Lions. I remember sitting in a meeting and Geech saying, "The most important job we have is selection. We have to get selection right," and you're kind of going, "Of course, isn't that blatantly obvious?" but he took the job of picking the right people – not just the best players, but the right people – so seriously. He wanted to make sure he was getting the right people on the plane, who were going to be able to play a few positions, who weren't particularly injury prone and could train and play for the whole tour, who were going to be able to coach on-field and be leaders in terms of having fun and bringing people together. You know, it sounds like the most obvious thing in the world, but when you hear one of the best coaches in the world saying, "The most important job we have to do is select the right people to go on the plane," you realise that experience has taught him that those selections are what can make or break a Lions tour.'

'The combinations of players who will work well together as well as personalities that will thrive in that environment is key,' says Geech. 'If you get it right, you have a chance to win a Test series and have a successful tour. If you get it wrong, you've got the potential for real disaster.'

One of my favourite aspects about the Lions is the breaking down of preconceived perceptions you might have about a player from another team. More often than not, you find that a player who you couldn't stand on the field in the Five or Six Nations is actually someone you form great bonds of friendship with. In 1989, those outside England had all sorts of preconceptions about Mooro and what he was like as a man. Touring with him broke all those down and we were able to appreciate the man beneath the caricature we had built up around him. The same was true of James Haskell in 2017. In 2009, the player coming into camp that looked set to rub people up the wrong way was Mike Phillips, the Welsh scrum-half.

'You know what,' says Drico, laughing, 'he was someone that everyone outside of Wales hated because of the manner in which he played, because he was antagonistic, because he had an edge to him, because he was physical, confrontational, and all the things that you would admire in a fellow player or a fellow countryman, but everything you hate in an opponent. And then all of a sudden, he becomes a teammate and you get to know the real individual, rooming with one another, and you have a laugh and you kind of break down the barriers that maybe playing on opposite teams and spending minimal time together created. And off the back of that tour, after spending more time together and investing in one another, you create these long-term relationships that last far beyond your playing career. And that's a magical part of these tours.

'You know, I tell a story of how I remember feeling like a Lion for the first time. It was about a week or ten days into my first tour and someone in the team room said, "Who wants to go for a cup of coffee?" Four or five of us went and for the first twenty minutes it didn't register with me at all that I was the only Irish guy there. Then, when I clocked that, all of a sudden, I realised, "Oh, okay, we're just teammates now, we're not actually English or Scottish or Welsh or Irish, we're Lions." And I think it's those eureka moments that make you go, "Wow, this really is spectacular." It's a comforting feeling and it creates a sense of complete buy-in to what you're doing as this new team.'

The initial party for the ten-match tour comprised thirty-seven players, a significant reduction from four years previously, and had a greater balance across the nations. Grand Slam-

LOOKING BACK TO GO FORWARD

winning Ireland (who also provided the Heineken Cup winners from Leinster) just edged the touring numbers with fourteen to Wales' thirteen, England's eight and Scotland's two, although these numbers would shift before the party even left their home training base at Pennyhill Park in Bagshot, Surrey. Jerry Flannery, Tom Shanklin and Tomás O'Leary all had to withdraw with injury, Leigh Halfpenny was in and out with injury concerns and Alan Quinlan was handed a twelve-week ban for a gouge in the Heineken Cup semi-final against Leinster. These were challenges that had to be overcome, but the group managed to achieve this.

'We did the usual team-building exercises that have become part of the norm with a Lions training camp,' says O'Connell, 'but a big thing we did was that we also went out on the piss a lot. It all sounds a bit basic, but it really helps to break down the barriers between players. We carried that on while we were away. Once you played a game you knew it was okay for you to go out and have a good time. One of the big challenges of tours in Australia and New Zealand is that all the games kick off at seven or eight at night because of TV. But because South Africa is more or less the same time zone as us, most of the games were three o'clock kick-offs, which gives you time afterwards to spend together in the evenings – and that's huge for building team spirit and a sense of togetherness. In the context of a Lions tour, that's massive because you've got to become a team, not just fellas wearing the same shirt.'

The tour didn't get off to the most spectacular of starts with a shaky win – albeit at altitude, which many players struggled with – over an invitational Royal XV in Rustenberg, only sealed late on, but the tourists soon got into their stride to show the potency of their new combinations. They put seventy-four points on the Golden Lions, edged the Free State Cheetahs 26–24, put thirty-nine points on the Sharks, twenty-six on Western Province and twenty on the Southern Kings to reach the Test series unbeaten and in high spirits. By this stage, the throngs of Lions fans that had been growing over the preceding weeks were swarming the country in droves. They filled Durban ahead of the first Test as anticipation for the clash against the world champions reached fever pitch.

'The build-up to the series was incredible,' remembers O'Driscoll. 'The Springboks had been held back from playing any of the warm-up games, which was a shame as it diluted the quality of the opposition and also robbed us of the little one-on-one battles you might otherwise get with your opposite man, but the quality of our squad meant that we were driving each other really hard in training. So many guys put their hands up for Test selection that it drove the standard higher and higher each time we trained. The competition was really intense. As a result, there were some great players who didn't get into the starting Test XV. That was great for those of us who made it because you know you don't own the Test jersey, you're only a custodian of it and if you don't perform then you'll lose it. That's a powerful motivator. And that's before you run out at Kings Park and find the whole place is dressed in red.'

It stirs the soul to look back on that hot, clear day in Durban. As Paul O'Connell and John Smit led their sides on to the field they were greeted by the main grandstand awash in red. All around the stadium it was the same, a great wall of red and noise, the roar of 'Li-ons, Li-ons, Li-ons!' absolutely deafening.

Jean de Villiers, the Springbok centre, remembers it vividly. 'A lot of us had based our decision to continue playing in South Africa after the 2007 World Cup on the chance to play against the Lions,' he says. 'Many of us remembered the disappointment when the Boks lost to them back in 1997, when most of us were just kids, and we had also seen how popular a series against the

Lions had become when they toured Australia in 2001 and New Zealand in 2005. We wanted to be part of that, and we knew that not every player gets a chance to play against the Lions, because they visit so rarely.

'It was an unbelievable series. It started as we ran out of the Kings Park tunnel for that first game and were expecting to see a sea of green but were confronted by a sea of red.'

'That sums up the uniqueness of a Lions tour to me,' says Smit. 'That you're at home but when you run out, seventy per cent of the crowd are dressed in red. They're rowdy, they sing and they go crazy. It's the most unbelievable atmosphere imaginable.'

The game started at a hundred miles an hour and barely let up for the following eighty minutes.

'We always knew we had to target the first Test,' remembers Smit, 'because the Lions are always at their most vulnerable then. They've had the least amount of time together, they've probably not figured out all the best combinations – it's almost impossible to get selection a hundred per cent correct in the first Test, so we knew we had to get in early, start fast and make sure that we got the result.'

'It was a real captain's performance,' I tell him. 'You led from the front and scored a try barely four minutes in, then you won a penalty by absolutely demolishing the Lions scrum to go 10–0 up, and you won another scrum penalty a little later. You and Bismarck du Plessis and the Beast [Tendai Mtawarira] were taking the Lions' front row apart – which was an area that I imagined they were targeting as you had only just moved back to playing prop after seventy-two caps at hooker.'

'It was a pretty challenging time for me, to be honest,' he replies. 'I had spent my early career as a tight head and moved to hooker when I was twenty-one/twenty-two. But by the time 2009 came around, Peter de Villiers had this conundrum because he wanted me in the team but Bismarck was playing unbelievable rugby at the time. I think what made the decision easier was that there wasn't another tight head that was crazy good at the time. Jannie du Plessis was still young, he wasn't quite there yet. So we sort of took the risk of moving me to tight head and picking Bismarck at hooker, which I backed as a decision because it meant I could still play and lead the team, but I was shit-scared that I was going to let everyone down.'

I mention the story John Eales had told me about 2001 – that his first priority in readying himself and the team for facing the Lions was to get his own preparation right and then he could concentrate on helping out the other guys in the team.

'I think that was exactly where I was, too,' says Smit. 'Although my preparation was motivated purely by fear of failure. I think I was also helped by the media, who really got into my selection and identified it as our biggest weakness. And the more they did that, the more we focussed on scrumming. We did live sessions against every Super Rugby franchise in South Africa; we put an absolutely huge amount of effort into the scrum. Then, selection-wise, the Lions probably could have done a little better; they could have taken advantage of me and picked a bigger hooker than Lee Mears; they should have picked Andrew Sheridan at loose head to go after me; and picked Adam Jones so that Bismarck couldn't help me. If they'd just gone with an absolute behemoth tight five and tried to exploit me, they might have had better luck. But they didn't, and when that first scrum went so well, it was like a match to a gas fire because it really got our confidence going. It led to us backing the one area which we thought would be our biggest weakness and it became our biggest strength.'

With Smit anchoring the tight head, the Beast and Bismark du Plessis took the Lions' tight head Phil Vickery to pieces. England's World Cup-winning No.3, once considered the best tight head in the game, was subbed off early to chants of 'Beast, Beast, Beast!' echoing around the ground. He still considers it the darkest moment of his career.

Adam Jones came on and things started to improve for the Lions up front. With that stability now in place, the Lions had a platform to play – and they thundered back into the match in the final quarter. With the Springboks 26–7 up, the Lions scored a try through Tom Croft in the sixty-eighth minute and, six minutes later, Mike Phillips darted over from close range. With Stephen Jones kicking brilliantly, the Lions had eaten up the ground between the sides and the score was poised at 26–21 with six minutes to go.

The Boks needed a steady hand to guide them through these final fraught moments of the match, but Smit had been substituted some time earlier.

'I think we'd maybe got ahead of ourselves just after half-time when we were comfortably leading,' he tells me. 'I think Peter thought, "Okay, well, this is much easier than I thought," and he took me off to save me for the next game. He was always very good about managing my game time. But we'd spoken about the fact that the longer the Lions played, the better they'd become – because they were a new unit – and that's exactly what happened. We got ahead of ourselves and we pulled all the subs off and the scrum began to turn around and started to become a vulnerability for us, and that got the Lions' tails up.

'Momentum swings all the time in rugby,' he continues. 'It's very seldom that you have momentum go your way for eighty minutes, unless you're playing against a really poor opposition. Momentum swings, and if you don't know how to manage the downswing, it's very difficult to swing it back up.'

'There were panic stations in the Bok ranks,' I say. 'It was clear that they needed you back out there.'

'Yeah,' he says, a cat-like grin spreading involuntarily across his face. 'So thankfully there was that injury to Deon Carstens . . .'

'Were you in contact with De Villiers, saying, "We've got to make some changes here, I've got to get back out there"? How did that second substitution manifest itself?'

'I got a message through one of the medical staff who was plugged in with a radio link to the coaches, and I just said, "Look, you've got to make a change here, because the momentum's swung, we're no longer on the front foot, and there's not enough leadership on the field to do the small things that change momentum and get it back. Because all we needed was just to stop it from increasing further for the Lions; we needed to pause and do certain things that would disrupt it.'

'What kind of things were you looking to do?'

'The first was to get a stable scrum, then to play a bit more territory. They were enjoying playing quickly, so we needed to send one or two more guys into the ruck to slow the ball down. In the same way, if we were up against a team that was playing slowly, we'd have tried to get the ball wide and move it and make space. So these are the small things that you can do as a captain – you pick up on the momentum swing and make adjustments, getting the message across the team about what we've got to do to get things going in our favour again. At the time, that wasn't being done, so the message went up and it wasn't long before I had to get warm again. Deon went down with an injury, I came on and we managed to arrest their momentum and see out the game. And that was huge because now we had one game in hand and all the pressure was now on the Lions to win the next two, whereas we only had to win one – and both those games would be at altitude, which we knew would be tough for them.'

Although clearly questionable from a sporting integrity point of view, the Springboks had successfully gamed the rules around front row injury substitutions to return Smit to the field where he had delivered a masterclass in game management.

The midweek Lions had their first stumble of the tour by only managing to draw with the Emerging Springboks on a stormy night in Cape Town, then the circus travelled north to Pretoria for the second Test – which would turn out to be one of the all-time great matches in the game's history.

The Lions made some adjustments to their starting line-up, with an all-Welsh front row of Gethin Jenkins, Matthew Rees and Adam Jones, while Simon Shaw was handed his first Test cap for the Lions on his third tour. In the backs, Lee Byrne had succumbed to injury and was replaced by Rob Kearney. The Springboks, meanwhile, only made one change, bringing in Schalk Burger for his fiftieth cap in place of Heinrich Brussow, who dropped to the bench.

'Pretoria . . .' says John Smit wistfully. 'That was, without a doubt, the toughest, most exciting Test match I ever played in my career. Everything about that Test match was remarkable.'

'It was fast, it was loud, it was played by two teams at the very top of their games,' says O'Driscoll, 'it was an unbelievable match. And physically, the toughest game I think any of us ever played.'

'It's the hardest Test match I've ever witnessed live, without doubt,' says Geech. 'And some of the best Test match rugby I've been associated with.'

'It was brutal,' agrees O'Connell. 'Every second of that game was about all-out physicality. That's the stuff that the Springboks lived for, but it was also the very essence of our game plan in both attack and defence. And when you get two teams playing like that, it can be pretty scary at times.'

'Without doubt,' says James Robson, on his sixth tour as doctor, 'that was the most physical game I was ever involved in.

I've never seen collisions like it – and the injuries they caused. It was a bloodbath.'

'I remember in the build-up to that game,' says Smit, 'we talked a lot about the resurrection act the Lions had pulled out in the last twenty-five minutes of the first Test. "We've got to be smart about how we play," was the mantra. And so the whole thinking around that second week's preparation was: "Okay, we've got to use the altitude to our advantage. We want to play extremely quickly, we want to get through the phases, we want to put some spin on the ball, and get the pace of the game as high as possible to get that altitude burn into their throats early."

'So we come out – into another bloody sea of red – and the atmosphere is electric. We kick off and twenty-eight seconds in, Schalk gets yellow-carded for gouging Luke Fitzgerald.'

'I hope you won't mind me saying this,' I cut in. 'But it was an absolute mystery as to how he only got a yellow card for that gouge. It was horrific. You should have been down to fourteen men for the whole game.'

Smit grimaces. 'It was bad. There's no excusing it. We were lucky it was only a yellow.'

Burger is equally embarrassed about the whole scenario. 'It was a huge moment for me to win my fiftieth cap, especially in that game and that environment,' he says. 'We set out with the focus of physically dominating the game as we'd done for the better parts of the first Test, so there was a lot of emotion swirling around. But you look back . . . and you get things wrong. It was so stupid of me. I was overhyped, the moment got too big. Never in your life would you enter a game thinking, "I'm going to eye-gouge someone." But you overstep the mark due to too much build-up, you want to make too big of an impact too soon, and these things happen. But I hope it doesn't detract from the fact it was one of the best Test matches ever.'

'So Schalk goes off,' remembers Smit. 'And now I've got to go to the guys, and say, "All right, forget all our tactics about playing fast, now we've got to stall this game for ten minutes." All our planning from the week was out the window and now I'm saying, "Okay, walk to the lineout, walk to the scrum, slow down, kick for territory," – completely the opposite to what we'd wanted to do. And by half-time, we were flipping really up against it; it wasn't looking good.'

'Do you think that then played into the Lions' hands,' I ask, 'the fact that you did just slow down and you were playing more of a set-piece game, then?'

'It did a hundred per cent,' says Smit, 'because part of slowing the game down was actually giving them the ball, because we didn't want to do too much in our own half, so we kicked a bit more and gave them a few more opportunities to attack, but we were also disjointed because we were in between two game plans. We had practised one way and we just didn't transition to plan B quick enough. So, there were times when we were sort of half-pregnant; we had a go and realised, "Shit, no, we're not supposed to be going fast."

'Half-time was an interesting time, you know? I had to get pretty firm with the guys and just reset the clock and try to take control of the Test match – but we never really got that fast-paced game up there to get the fire into the Lions' throats.'

The Lions led 16–8 at the break, thanks to a try from Rob Kearney and the dependable boot of Stephen Jones, while the Boks had responded with a try from JP Pietersen shortly after Burger had returned from the bin.

The second half started with as much intensity as the first and there were soon casualties lying all over the field. First Gethin Jenkins had his head split open and his eye socket cracked, then Adam Jones dislocated his shoulder after being cleared out at a ruck by Bakkies Botha. Coming into the final quarter, and with the Lions leading 19–8, they then lost both their centres within minutes of each other. Brian O'Driscoll clashed heads with back rower Danie Rossouw and both had to be removed with concussion, then Jamie Roberts followed him to the sidelines. Up in the stands, Pieter de Villiers rolled the dice and made a series of substitutions. On came Brussow for Rossouw, Jacque Fourie came on in the centre for Jean de Villiers and Morné Steyne replaced Ruan Pienaar at stand-off.

The effect of all the changes was almost immediate. Roberts and O'Driscoll had marshalled the midfield superbly, but as soon as they were taken off, the Lions defence was breached. Bryan Habana cut a superb line off an inside ball from a scrum set-play to score by the posts. 19–15 to the Lions, but just two minutes later Brussow won a jackal penalty just inside the Lions' half. Playing on his home ground, Morné Steyne guided the ball with ease between the posts. There was just a point in it. Stephen Jones extended the Lions' lead with a superb penalty of his own, but then another of the Bok substitutes made his mark with a thundering run down the touchline. From fifteen yards out, Jacque Fourie barrelled over Ronan O'Gara and through Mike Phillips and Tommy Bowe to score in the corner.

'How he scored that try,' breathes Smit, 'it barely seemed humanly possible that he managed it. He was so flipping close to the touchline . . . and how he managed to get the ball down, I've no idea.'

'We never saw the camera angle down the touchline, though,' I say, wryly. 'I was certain that he had put a foot out – but mysteriously the TV producer was unable to produce that angle.'

Smit bellows a laugh and then grimaces a little. 'Yeah, tries in the corner were pretty lucky for us at that time. We got some help in the World Cup final in 2007 when the angle showed

Mark Cueto's foot in touch – and we got lucky in 2009 when that same angle wasn't ever shown for Jacque's try.'

'It was a hell of an effort from him to get in there,' I say.

'It was, it was incredible. And it really sparked something for us, we really felt like we had the wind at our backs then.'

Steyne knocked over the conversion from the touchline and the Boks had the lead for the first time, 25–22. But back the Lions roared and another penalty from Jones, in the seventy-sixth minute, tied the game at 25–25. It was nail-biting, incredible viewing.

The clock ticked to eighty minutes and the players were out on their feet. Play stagnated around the midfield and Steyne had a drop-goal attempt that fell well short. Kearney gathered it and sent a long kick down the Boks' five-metre line, but Steyne had worked back and he sent an equally huge punt back into the Lions' twenty-two. Time was up. O'Gara trotted back for the ball, Bowe trailing back on his inside, but there was nothing on from an attacking point of view.

'I still remember my shoulders slumping, because O'Gara was just going to kick it out and end the game,' says Smit. 'I could hear all his teammates calling, "Kick it out for the draw." The draw was exactly what they needed, because they would have been able to come back and have another crack at us in week three.'

But O'Gara didn't kick it out. He signalled to Bowe that he was going to launch an up-and-under and then sent the ball skywards. It came down just inside the Boks' half and scrum-half Fourie du Preez leapt to gather it just as O'Gara arrived, chasing his kick. The Irishman collided with Du Preez and flipped him in the air. Referee Christophe Berdos instantly signalled a penalty to the Boks.

'Initially I was going to ask Frans Steyn to kick it because he had the biggest boot in the team, but I remember Victor Matfield coming to me and saying, "Mate, this is Morné's field, he'll do it," and I couldn't really argue, because he'd been doing it for the Blue Bulls the whole season. And I'll never forget tossing the ball to him: I said, "Rather you than me, mate!" And he sort of smiled back at me, and look, that's the beauty of Morné, he didn't look stressed at all.'

Steyne lined up the kick and, with a beautiful, fluid action, sent it soaring through the thin high-veldt air. It cleared the bar with ease. The Springboks had their revenge for 1997. They had clinched the series 2–0.

'We went absolutely ape-shit,' says Smit. 'It was an incredible achievement. It was what so many of us had come back for, to play the Lions and win the series, and to do it like that was just incredible.'

'I remember the dressing room in Pretoria . . .' says Paul O'Connell quietly. 'It was just total devastation. I was part of Irish teams that underperformed at World Cups, Munster teams that lost European Cup finals; I don't think I ever experienced devastation like I did that day. The dressing room was like a morgue, not because we'd missed out on the big prize; probably because we'd put so much into it. We'd burnt the candle at both ends – we'd trained really hard and we'd socialised really hard on that tour as well because we were encouraged to and because we wanted to be a little bit amateur so that we could be a better team on the big day, so that we had the glue that holds you together on the big occasion. And we did have that, you know, we were a very tight group by the Test matches, playing incredibly hard for one another. But for every player and every member of the coaching staff as well, we'd emptied so much of ourselves into it, to fall short in the way we did, it was a really tough one to take. I'll remember what that dressing room looked like for a long, long time.'

'Everyone had given their absolute all,' I say. 'From both sides. It was just like two heavyweight champions going head-to-head and toe-to-toe, and there was nothing left at the end. In many ways it was cruel that it didn't end in a draw.'

'Listen,' says Drico, 'it's nice to look back on what many people see as the most physical, exciting game of rugby that they've ever watched. Well, it definitely felt like the most physical game I've ever played in! But it's nice to be part of those games, as well. It was gladiatorial, and albeit the concussion protocols and everything in place now look after the players better, and rightly so, it was of a time when that Test arena wasn't a place for shrinking violets. That was rugby at its rawest. And it's nice to be part of it – I look back on those days and realise how much of an effort it took from everyone involved, what we all put into that jersey, and I think it saved the Lions at a point when it was in real danger of becoming an irrelevance after 2005. And even though again we lost with the last kick of the game, to look back and know you've been part of such a momentous game, it's pretty special.

'But there's also a lot of regret. We should have won that game, should have been up more points at half-time than we were. But there are always those situations, aren't there? You know, woulda coulda shoulda. When you lose two centres, two props, you're always going to be up against it when you're unloading your bench and players are coming on that haven't trained in those positions or haven't ever played in those positions in their lives. So you have to make the most of your circumstances and they managed to do it a bit better that day. I think you can always look back with some form of regret when things haven't gone right and wish you could have changed things, but that's life. I think we do that in rugby, in our family lives, in our working lives, whatever we do, it's just part and parcel of looking back and realising that you left something behind. But it's all part of the experiential piece of making sure that when you do get the opportunity the next time round that you put that right, and they had that chance the following week;

I didn't play in the third Test because I was out with concussion, but the other guys had another shot to show what the Lions jersey meant to each of them.'

'I think that was a key focus for the final week,' says Geech. 'We had come so close in those first two Tests and it would have been criminal if we'd gone home 3–0 down. I said in my speech to the players before the third Test that they had a chance to leave the jersey in a good place for the players who would put it on four years later. They had a chance to show the power of the jersey and what it meant to each of them to wear it. We did very little training that week, we were a lot of bodies down, but the quality of the squad shone through and even though we made a load of changes, those players showed what it was to be a Lion. They went to Ellis Park, the spiritual home of rugby in South Africa, and they smashed the Springboks in the third Test. We lost the first game in the series by five points, we lost the second by three and won the third by nineteen. We were superb. And that was down to Paul's leadership and the quality of the players that we had.'

It had been agonisingly close and agonisingly compelling, and both sides had produced some of the finest rugby I've ever watched. The Lions may have lost the series 2–1 but they had also saved the concept from extinction. Geech and Gerald Davies and Warren Gatland and Paul O'Connell and Brian O'Driscoll and all the other leaders and players and coaches had played their part in rescuing the Lions after the debacle of 2005 and set the Lions back on track.

But the pressure was on in a different sense now. Australia awaited in 2013 and while the Lion was revived it was not yet safe. They needed a series win to stay truly relevant in the modern age.

SEVEN

RETURN TO THE TOP

2013

SAM WARBURTON'S DAD was a fireman. One day, when Sam was fourteen, his old man came back from the station brandishing a sheet of paper which he'd been given by one of his workmates.

'Sam,' he said, 'my mate's son needs this questionnaire filled out for his homework. Can you do it? Just write down whatever you want, and I'll give it back to him.'

Young Sam went to the kitchen table and unfolded the sheet. It was a simple questionnaire about sports that kids played. There were five boxes to fill out.

Name:
Age:
Sport:
Position:
Ambition:

He began to write.

> *Name:* Sam Warburton
> *Age:* 14
> *Sport:* Rugby union
> *Position:* Open-side flanker

He paused for a moment over the last question. Then he bent his head and wrote:

> *Ambition:* To be a British and Irish Lions rugby legend.

Satisfied, he handed the sheet back to his dad.

'I'd actually completely forgotten about that story until my dad reminded me of it recently,' he tells me. 'And I'm not saying I achieved it – the legendary status – but I always wanted to go on a Lions tour, and not only that, I wanted to be one of the best players on that tour. I wanted to lead the Lions. I wanted to win multiple tours. I didn't want to be just one of the crowd. I wanted to stand out.'

'And that was always your ambition?'

He nods. 'I remember back in 2005 my dad bought me a Lions shirt with a number seven on the back. And I put it away in my wardrobe and I wouldn't wear it. After a while he asked why, of all the replica jerseys I had, I wouldn't wear that one. And I said that the next time I wore a Lions number seven jersey, I wanted it to be a real one.'

I sit back in my chair and I can't help but smile. There's no arrogance or bravado in these stories; that's not Sam Warburton's way. Indeed, he is visibly cringing as he relays them. Instead, they reveal a childhood dream that he followed with passion and a furious dedication and one that, ultimately, he achieved. And is there anything more beautiful than that?

But chasing such an ambition can also carry a heavy burden. Because if you are on the road to achieving your childhood dream, what will the consequences be if you falter and fail? What if you don't live up to your own expectations?

'I think that's probably why I felt so much pressure,' he says. 'Because I just lumped it all on myself to try and achieve those things. And at times it could be excruciating. At times I wondered if it would be too much.'

'But,' I say, 'who ever said that achieving your dreams would be easy?'

*

In late 2012, the Four Home Unions Committee announced, via Andy Irvine, the Scotland and Lions great who had been named as the next tour manager, that they had appointed Warren Gatland to the head coach position for the 2013 Lions tour to Australia.

While some in the media began to speculate whether the Lions were headed for a similar disappointment to that suffered in 2001, when another Kiwi had been placed in charge, the difference this time was how embedded Gatland was into British and Irish rugby compared to Graham Henry, as well as his experience as assistant coach with the 2009 Lions under Ian McGeechan.

Gatland had begun his coaching career shortly after retiring from a hugely successful playing career for Waikato, who he represented 140 times, yet his rugby life had also been tinged with great frustration as he had spent the best part of a decade in and around the All Blacks, making seventeen appearances, yet never winning a full cap. He sat on the bench twenty-nine times for New Zealand behind Sean Fitzpatrick, yet the iconic captain never once made way for him. It was a different era with regards to substitutions, and Fitzpatrick would never show a chink in his mighty armour by going down injured or dropping out of the fight. But being so close to achieving his dream had been a hard pill for Gatland to swallow.

'Those experiences with the All Blacks,' he tells me from his home in New Zealand, 'I think, ultimately, they made me a better coach. It was pretty hard at the time, and frustrating – I was sitting on the bench and I backed myself to perform if I ever got the chance. But in those days, you only came off the bench for an injury and that bugger Fitzy was never injured. That All Blacks side was also going through this incredible run of fifty or so matches undefeated, so how was I ever going to get ahead of him? There were only two scenarios: either the team lost and played poorly, and you didn't really want that to happen; or Fitzy got injured. And he never did. So it was pretty tough from that point of view. But as I say, it made me a better coach. It definitely gave me an understanding about my role in the All Black squad.

'I expect my players to be really disappointed about missing out on selection because I expect them to believe in themselves and want to be selected, but it's how they respond to that disappointment afterwards that shows me their character. A player can never say to me, if he isn't selected, "You don't know what it's like to be sitting on the bench or not to be selected." Yeah? I know exactly what it's like, mate. I was this close to playing for the best team in the world, but it never happened. And from that point of view, I expect the players to be disappointed but then say, "Right, what's my role and responsibility now? My role is to get out there and support the starting XV to give them the best preparation that they can have to win that next match." You've got to put that disappointment behind you, because the team is bigger than the individual.'

When he hung up his boots, Gats headed to Ireland. He coached Galwegians in Galway before being offered a job with

Connacht. From there he was catapulted into the Ireland job – aged just thirty-four. The way that gig ended is still a painful matter for him, a sense that he was deliberately undermined by his assistant, Eddie O'Sullivan, who was then promoted to the top job in his stead.

From Ireland he headed to Wasps, where he forged a dynasty with the likes of Lawrence Dallaglio, Simon Shaw and Rafael Ibanez, guiding the club from the relegation zone in 2002 to the Premiership title the following season – and repeating the feat for the next two seasons, while also adding a Heineken Cup to the trophy cabinet in 2004.

After a disastrous 2007 World Cup campaign, the Welsh Rugby Union went out hunting for a new coach to replace Gareth Davies, chequebook in hand, and brought Gats and his Wasps defence coach Shaun Edwards to the Millennium Stadium. In their first season in charge they won a Grand Slam and, three years later, were one Leigh Halfpenny penalty kick away from playing in the 2011 World Cup final. Another Welsh Grand Slam was landed in 2012 before Gats was asked to step back into the Lions camp for the 2013 tour to Australia.

Right from the off, he proved that he was never going to be ruled by sentiment. Shaun Edwards had done a hugely impressive job with the defence at Wasps, Wales and on the 2009 Lions tour, but Gatland didn't ask him to reprise the role in 2013, even though it risked causing a rift in their relationship with Wales.

Instead he was keen to work with coaches from other countries, and recruited Andy Farrell from England to run his defence. Graham Rowntree, Rob Howley and Neil Jenkins returned to the fold as forwards, backs and kicking coach respectively, having performed those jobs in 2009, and the bulk of the medical and strength and conditioning team from that tour were also brought back together.

'From a selfish point of view, in both 2013 and 2017 I wanted to work with one or two other coaches that I hadn't worked with before,' says Gats. 'I had a huge amount of respect for Faz [Andy Farrell], the work he'd done with England as well as that rugby league background of his. He'd captained Great Britain when he was nineteen, he understood the team ethos, the team environment, what a winning culture looks like; he does it in a different way to some other coaches I've worked with and he's very smart from that perspective. So as I say, it was just a chance to work with someone different, and the Lions gives you that opportunity. It was actually hugely important to my longevity with Wales because it freshened things up for me.'

Both Paul O'Connell and Brian O'Driscoll would be touring again but, as with Edwards, Gatland wasn't going to be swayed by sentiment to give either the Lions captaincy for a second time. Instead he went for the young man who had led his Wales team since June 2011: Sam Warburton.

'We had a group of some young, talented players coming through with Wales in 2010 and 2011 and Sam was among them,' says Gats. 'He was incredibly talented, very professional, really dedicated and he reminded me of Richie McCaw in a lot of ways. And because he broke through at a very young age, I saw that he was potentially someone who could be in that role for a long time – two or three World Cup cycles. It was a close call with him and Alun Wyn Jones for the captaincy of both Wales and the Lions, and they had very different styles of leadership.

'The outside impression of Alun Wyn is probably, you know, that he's not always the easiest character to deal with – he's very much his own man, thinks outside the box, he can be challenging at times. He's probably mellowed a little in the last few years, as he's got a bit older and had children and stuff. But he's an incredible warrior and because he's so competitive he'd be the guy starting fights at training and that kind of thing. As he's got older, he's developed into the role as a much better leader and a better captain, but Sam had those qualities already – and I knew that Alun Wyn and the other players who'd been around a bit longer would be really supportive of Sam from a leadership perspective.'

'I'd played really well that season,' says Warburton as we reminisce about those heady days, 'but two months before the squad was announced I got injured and it was touch and go about whether I'd be fit enough to go.

'I hadn't spoken to Gats for probably six, seven months, because he'd been off Wales duty so he could concentrate on the Lions. About a month before the squad was announced, his name flashed up on my phone and, because I was injured, I knew it was going to be an all or nothing call. He was either going to ask me to be captain or was calling to respectfully tell me, "Right, we think with your injury status at the moment, we're not going to pick you to tour – you need to go on tour with Wales, and if you get fit we can maybe call you up." I knew they had rung Jonny Wilkinson to ask him if he was available, so I thought it might be the same sort of thing.

'So I answered and we had a chat for about five minutes, him asking about the Cardiff Blues, my injury and things like that, and then he asks me the question: "Will you captain the Lions this summer?"

'And I just burst out laughing. It was such a surreal moment to hear that question being asked. I used to wear all the Lions kit as a kid and, as you're growing up, the Lions are the gods of British and Irish rugby. So suddenly to be asked to be captain . . . I needed a couple of seconds to process the question and laugh, and then there's no other answer apart from "Yes" because it's just the greatest privilege. Even though I knew it was going to come with a lot of pressure and expectation, it was a ridiculous privilege to have.

'But I was also terrified to do it, because I was only twenty-four at that time. And to be honest, I didn't want the captaincy, I felt I was too young. I knew Brian O'Driscoll, Paul O'Connell, Gethin Jenkins and Alun Wyn Jones and those boys would be going on their third or fourth tour with eighty caps' more experience than me. I didn't think I was the best guy, but obviously I did it. I said yes – because what else are you going to say?'

It was a punchy call from Gats, particularly with Warburton still racing to regain fitness, but he knew that the young captain was a charismatic figure who would flourish in the Lions environment and, crucially, he would have a huge support network of experienced players around him.

'It was a very similar scenario to the one I'd been in four years earlier,' says Paul O'Connell. 'And just as Drico had been hugely supportive of me as captain having done it before, I wanted to be as supportive as I could with Sam. And to be honest, I was just delighted to make the tour at all. I'd had a back operation on New Year's Eve, and I was under pressure to get back in time for the tour. Luckily for me, Munster had qualified to the quarter-final of Europe, I played a game against Harlequins and Gats and Graham Rowntree were there and I played well and we won and that kind of got me on the plane. It was bonus territory for me to be there and, same as Drico, I'd been captain of my province for a long time and I enjoyed being captain, but I really enjoyed not being captain, as well. And for Sam's sake, it wasn't ever in my nature to sit back and be quiet if I wasn't captain; I still probably behaved as a captain, just as Drico did – but we didn't do the coin toss, we didn't do the media. We helped Sam lead in training and on the field and with words in the changing room. I would still speak to the players the same as if I was a captain, and tried to help Sam with that and enjoyed that part of it. So I really enjoyed the 2013 tour and one of the reasons I think I really enjoyed it is because I wasn't captain – just as Drico had found in 2009.'

'So how did you approach the Lions captaincy?' I ask Sam. 'No one gives you a book when you're made Lions captain and goes, "Here's the leadership bible, read it and embrace it all; this is your manual for the next few weeks." It doesn't happen like that. Was there anything that you wanted to do or felt that you should do? Did you just say, "Well, I'm Lions captain, this is my way of leading," or did you get a bunch of the more experienced guys around to help you?'

'Listen,' he replies, 'I'll tell you what I did, actually. I sat down with a mental skills coach before the tour and said, "Right, I need to write down every possible negative scenario that might happen, and I'm going to think in my head now, a month in advance of the tour, how I'm going to handle it." So it might be things like players complaining about the food in the hotel, or somebody comes up to me saying they're exhausted from playing midweek and weekends. It might be something that's happened in the press where there's some negative stories going around, or someone's pissed off about not getting to play enough – all those kinds of things, and then we would come up with answers of how I would deal with them. So, for example, it might be making sure that I had a good rapport with the press officer so I knew if there was a bad story about to come out about someone, we could then come up with a plan about how we would manage it, to take the pressure off that player and make sure it wasn't a distraction for the rest of the squad.

'So there were all these things that I tried to pre-empt. The good thing was, it was like an exam: I then went into the tour feeling really well prepared. And what was even better was that I didn't

LEGACY OF THE LIONS

have to refer to it once, because the tour was run so well; there were as many members of the management and security as there were players. If anyone was getting slightly out of hand on a night out, they'd get a tap on the shoulder from one of the security guys, who would whisk them back to the hotel. So in the end, I had nothing else to focus on apart from my own individual performance on the pitch and preparing the team. Everything else was looked after, so it was actually a lot easier than my time with Wales. But I took those steps to prepare and I would recommend any future captains doing the exact same thing.'

He pauses for a moment and gazes out the window. 'You know what,' he continues, thoughtfully. 'I think the most crucial thing I learned as a young captain was not to fall into the trap of believing that being a leader suddenly means that you know everything – because you don't. And being able to delegate and lean on other people is a sign of strength, not weakness. I think some people perceive it as weakness and they feel they have to do everything themselves, call all the shots themselves; actually, it's much better to incorporate a larger group of people to help you and have a leadership group.'

'That's very wise,' I say, thinking of both Fin's words and my own thoughts about not trying to be all things to all men when you're a captain. 'So how did you incorporate that with this brand-new squad of players, many of whom you didn't know?'

'One of the first things we did was that we sat down and we created a whole load of committees to help share the workload, but to also make sure that loads of players felt involved in what we were doing. Players get so much done for them these days, but I think the Lions had learned from previous tours that it was important not to get too big-headed about being on the tour. So we had a laundry committee who would liaise with the people who did the laundry in every hotel we got to, so everyone knew where to drop off their kit, where their bags were, what they had to do to get their kit washed. We'd have a food committee, who'd liaise with the chef and the nutritionist about the menus and things like that, so the boys got what they wanted. We had a rooming committee, entertainment committee, fines committee, music committee, all sorts of things. We got guys from each country to tell us what worked best in their teams and we adopted them, and I tried to get a good cross-section of players from each country on these committees so that it integrated the group, and it gave people responsibility and a little bit of leadership as well. It was great and it helped us all mix straight away.'

'It sounds like classic touring,' I say. 'I like it a lot – taking responsibility for yourselves and not just leaving it up to the management to sort it all out for you. And how about the team-building exercises, did you do them before you left?'

'We did,' he says, 'but all these formal team-building exercises they do within a corporate environment, they're fine . . . but nothing has ever got a team together like a good piss-up. It sounds so trivial, but you go out for a few drinks and the night always starts off slow at first. But it picks up and picks up, and obviously you can't get completely out of control, but it really breaks the ice between the players. Boys are singing, they're dancing with their tops off, everyone's just pissing themselves laughing. Then you come down for breakfast the next morning and all you can hear is the clanging of cutlery and laughing and talking, because everyone's reminiscing about the night before, all the barriers have come down, you've got to know guys probably ten times faster than if you just carried on doing your normal thing, and suddenly you're looking after each other on the next night out and it just brings the team together massively. Those nights are gold dust for getting the team together, absolute gold dust. It sounds so old-fashioned, but it's what the boys want – and it just works. You can have a guy in their early twenties who is now teammates with a guy twelve years older than him who has been on three tours, but after a couple of beers you're all exactly the same. There are no egos and reputations are out the window; you're just blokes, enjoying each other's company. And it sounds so obvious, and there's nothing scientific about it, but it works every time without fail.'

Gats nods when I raise this with him. 'I think my attitude has always been that the most important thing I could focus on with the Lions wasn't what was happening on the field, but what was happening off the field,' he says. 'If we could bring all those people together and create some harmony off the field, then we would achieve harmony on the field.

'You've got a group of players who all know each other by reputation, but they've been bashing the crap out of each other in the Six Nations and other competitions for four years or more and you've got to bring them together and put those rivalries to one side. Having nights out together is paramount to achieving that. We tried to get that balance right between working hard and enjoying ourselves and having a bit of fun. It's the end of a long season, so I tried to keep training sessions relatively short with quite a high intensity, trying to give the guys a little bit of a break. You learn all that from looking at what has and hasn't worked in the past. Some hugely talented squads have come up short because they over-trained and didn't have the work/fun balance right.

'Again, going back to my experience sitting on the bench behind Sean Fitzpatrick,' says Gats. 'One of the things I've always said to the players is that everyone will get a start in one of the first three games, if you're fit. So, in some positions you've got three No.9s, three No.10s, three hookers, so if I'm going on a Lions tour and the coach says to me that I'm going to start in one of the first three games, then I kind of feel like, "Well, it's up to me now, I've got a chance to prove myself and if the team plays well and I play well, I've got a chance of being involved in the Test side." And that isn't necessarily ideal for a coach in terms of preparation for the Tests, as you have fewer opportunities to put combinations together, but from a team harmony point of view, I think that's been one of the crucial things we've done.'

'These are exactly the lessons that came out from 2001 and 2005,' I say, 'which you've then mixed with the lessons from 1997 and 2009 about having fun and keeping the whole squad involved.'

'It's not a guaranteed recipe for success,' says Gats, 'but it gives you the best chance. You have to make sure the players care for each other and that they'll give every last ounce of themselves for the jersey. If they like each other, feel they've been given a chance to prove themselves and no one has been handed anything, you've got a chance. Of course, it gets harder and harder with every tour because there are fewer and fewer matches to give everyone a decent run-out while also bedding in combinations, but it's what you've got to do. I spoke to a lot of people about the Lions, and they all said that you needed to have harmony between the Saturday side and the midweek sides and to avoid cliques. You're not going to get it all right all the time, but that's the ambition.'

'Paul O'Connell said that he was astonished by how much effort Geech put into selecting the right mix in the squad – of great players but also great tourists, great team players,' I say.

'Yeah, he's right – it's one of the most important things I learned from Geech in 2009. In past tours, things have gone wrong when the wrong kind of character has been selected. In 2009, 2013 and 2017 we went through a lot of the individuals as a group of coaches, and there were probably two or three players that we didn't take on the tour because the general consensus was, if they were in the Test side, they would be great; if they were not in the Test side, not in the twenty-three, they could have a negative influence on the group, and so we didn't end up taking them. We didn't get them all right; there were one or two who were dickheads and I don't personally have a lot of time for, but you try and go through that process to get as good a mix as you can.'

*

The 2013 Lions' preparation was hamstrung by the continued refusal by the domestic leagues to provide any extra time for the Lions by changing their fixture schedules. It meant that the full squad of players didn't meet up until six days before the first game, against the Barbarians in Hong Kong. This game, played in sweltering conditions with over eighty per cent humidity in the air, was hugely sapping for both teams, but the Lions won at a canter, 59–8. While unusual in its setting, the game had served several purposes – it satisfied the corporate needs of the main sponsor, HSBC, it gave the Lions a much-needed run-out and it provided them with another opportunity to socialise before they hit Australia to begin the tour in earnest.

The Lions flew into Perth for their game against Western Force, the weakest of the Australian Super Rugby franchises, and swept them aside 69–17. Two good wins clocked, albeit it against moderate opponents, but already the Australian media were getting edgy.

'I remember a lot of the stories coming out that were pretty dismissive about our rugby ability,' says Drico. 'They called us slabs of meat and stuff like that. They were obsessed with this idea of "Warrenball" and that all we could do was run straight and hit contact. But the skill level in our squad on that tour was incredible. It was funny being back in Australia twelve years after being there before with the Lions. We'd over-trained on that tour and run out of steam by the end; by 2013, the game had moved forward a long way and training was short and intense and that helped keep us fresh. And the skillsets that everyone had made training so enjoyable – and really pushed each player to produce his best. That's the magic of the Lions, it pushes you into a new level because there aren't just one or two stand-out players in the team, as you might get with your club or international team; *everyone* is at that level with the Lions and it just pushes you on.'

'The preparation must have been hard, though,' I say, 'if you only have a few days together before playing your first game?'

'The one thing I would say about the Lions is, the premise it's built on doesn't exist anymore,' says Drico. 'It's built on the amateur game, going away for long periods of time, an opportunity to build up a head of steam, and then ultimately play one of the best teams in the world in a three- or four-Test series. You look back to the earliest tours and they were away for six months or more.

'But subsequently, even going back over my four tours, they got increasingly shorter and increasingly more challenging because of the level of organisation of the opposition that you're playing against, and to try and knit a team together in what is really just a four-week window before you play that first Test match seems crazy in the modern game. But because of the history and the prestige that comes with the Lions, there's buy-in from players, and provided you leave your nationality at the door – which is a hugely important component of becoming a Lion – you soon realise that with the quality of the team and the fact that it's been done in the past, you have as good a shot as any to win a series.'

'How do you manage yourself in these scenarios after a long season?' I ask. 'Because you want to go full-bore for the Lions, but you've obviously got to manage your body and your form over that seven-week period.'

'It's more challenging than any other environment,' says Drico. 'I think you have to be willing to give a little bit more of yourself on a Lions tour than you might give from a national point of view. Some people won't like hearing that, but it's the nature of the tour, which still has elements of an amateur ethos, even though it's professional, where players are going to have to back up a Wednesday and a Saturday game at least once on tour, maybe twice. That's just necessitated by the squad size because otherwise you're going to have to have forty-five/fifty players on tours and you're going to lose out on the bond between those players – as we did in 2005.

'So, as a result, you have to give a little bit more of yourself. You've got to get yourself out of bed after playing a really tough game and hold bags and help prepare the next team for the next game. You need to be a bit more selfless on Lions tours. You have to get your aching body recovered after a match so you can sit on the bench three days later. But, you know, the carrot is substantial: the opportunity to play in a Lions team, have the jersey, have those teammates, have the experience, and potentially win a series and be remembered forever is pretty special. It's not a whole lot to give up for a seven-week period.'

From Perth, the Lions crossed the country to Brisbane to face the Reds at the Suncorp Stadium, where they would return to face Australia in the first Test. Although Wallaby coach Robbie Deans had insisted on withdrawing his international players from all of the warm-up games – thus diluting the quality of many of the matches – this third game was full of blood and thunder and the Lions were pleased to have been tested on their way to a 22–12 win. The midweek side then played another virtual walkover against Combined Country in Newcastle, putting sixty-four points on their opponents while managing to keep a clean sheet.

Match five pitched the Lions against the Waratahs at the Sydney Football Stadium and the tourists upped their game to another level a week out from the first Test, thumping their opponents 47–17. In the process, however, they lost the giant Welsh centre Jamie Roberts to a worrying hamstring injury. Roberts was permitted to stay on tour and James Robson was tasked with working his magic to get the player of the 2009 tour – who had been in great form again in 2013 – back on the field in time to play a role in the series.

The midweek team had one final challenge before the first Test: the Brumbies at Canberra Stadium. With injuries mounting and a desire to protect the front-runners for the Tests, Gatland brought in some fresh legs for this game, flying former world player of the year Shane Williams in from Japan, where he was playing club rugby, and handing starts to England's Christian Wade, Brad Barritt and Billy Twelvetrees, who had all just arrived on tour, while also picking Scottish full back Stuart Hogg at stand-off. The selections raised some serious eyebrows as the backline had only managed one training session together before facing Australia's best Super Rugby team, which was being coached by 2007 World Cup winner Jake White.

The result was a disjointed and disappointing performance from the Lions, while the Brumbies were swashbuckling and spirited, with a number of future Wallabies – including Jesse Mogg, Henry Speight, Tevita Kuridrani, Matt Toomua, Scott Sio and Scott Fardy – stamping their mark on the game, which they won 14–12.

'Listen,' says O'Connell, 'that Brumbies game was a tough one. Not much would have been made about it if we'd won, but because the midweek guys lost, suddenly there was a lot more said about flying in Shane Williams and playing those combinations that had hardly trained together. But it was the risk/reward the management gambled on by taking a smaller squad. It was the same in 2017 with the Geography Six – which I'm sure you'll talk about when you come to that tour. Gats wanted a smaller initial squad so that we could bond and really get to know each other, but he knew he would probably have to bring other people out later on. A really important part of the decision-making process when it comes to picking the initial squad for the tours since 2005 has been around wanting to keep the group pretty tight – but, in the end, I think every tour has ended up having almost as many players as Clive selected. So again, Clive's thinking in 2005 made sense on paper, it was just too big and unwieldy from the start. But you ultimately still need those players – and this has been Gats' way of doing it.'

'As much as you'd love to win every game on tour,' says Alun Wyn Jones, 'it's not actually about that. If you win the Test series then no one remembers a loss in a provincial game – or, at least, it becomes immaterial to the overall success of the tour. And it doesn't matter if you lose or draw one of the Tests, it's about winning the series. One thing I will always remember from 2009 was Paul O'Connell saying that if we ever wanted to be looked at in the same way as Willie John McBride, Martin Johnson and any of those other rugby royalty types, then we had to win a Lions Test series in the southern hemisphere. That's how Lions tours and players are ultimately judged and remembered.'

'The Lions need to win one in every three tours to maintain a relevance,' says Drico. 'That's the harsh reality of it. Winning reinforces the concept of why it's so brilliant, why it's so special to fans and why, to players in particular, it is the ultimate – that's why you test yourself to play against the best players.'

'And the pressure at this stage?' I ask.

Drico laughs. 'Well it was my fourth tour and my last chance to win a series, so the personal pressure was huge. But it was also pretty heavy for the Lions in general because the challenge wouldn't be getting any easier with New Zealand waiting for them four years later and then South Africa waiting for them in 2021 – which, as we now know, would see the Lions coming up against the world champions on both occasions.'

The colour, the pageantry, the spectacular drama and the tries scored at the Suncorp Stadium in Brisbane were all a match for that incredible opening Test between the Lions and the Wallabies in 2001. It was hugely unfortunate for the hosts that they lost their play-making centre and primary goal kicker, Christian Leali'ifano, to concussion in the opening passage of play and would be savaged by injuries throughout the game, losing full back Berrick Barnes, wing Digby Ioane, centre Adam Ashley-Cooper and eventually having to deploy open-side flanker Michael Hooper in the midfield. But despite these considerable setbacks, the Wallabies were right in the contest until the final seconds after the new cross-code sensation Israel Folau, making his rugby union Test debut, scored two scintillating tries, and it was only thanks to Kurtley Beale slipping on the slick turf as he lined up a potentially match-winning penalty that the Lions secured their victory, 23–21. Despite Beale's late miss, the Lions had been worthy winners. George North – still only twenty-one years old – scored one of the great individual Lions tries from within his own half, which was followed by a beautifully taken score by his compatriot, Alex Cuthbert, early in the second half. Ultimately the sides had been separated by the excellence of Leigh Halfpenny's boot.

'The Wallabies missed several kicks at goal in the first Test,' says O'Connell, 'so in many ways they were unlucky not to win. You then throw the injuries they had on top of that and we knew it could easily have gone against us – so there was no resting on any laurels before the second Test.'

'They weren't the only ones to suffer injuries though, were they?' I note.

O'Connell nods grimly. 'I broke my hand,' he says. 'It was a hairline fracture and I thought I'd just got bad bruising. Doc Robson came on with five minutes to go, put the sponge on my arm, told me I was fine – and I *was* fine – but it was a little bit hard to grip afterwards. I was taken for an X-ray and I genuinely thought it was just a box-ticking exercise, because my hand was functioning fine and it wasn't that sore. And I came out of it and the doc just said, "You've got a fracture; if you get another bang on that, it'll break and you'll be in big trouble, so you can't play next week; you're out for the tour."

'It was very hard to take, but as I said before, I was in bonus territory just being there. I felt I was lucky to get picked in the squad, I'd managed to play well in a few of the games, played really well against the Waratahs, and we'd won the first Test. The difficult thing was that I hadn't managed to be part of a winning Lions tour yet, and now I was out of it.'

'Drico says that the worst thing he did in 2005 was stay on tour,' I say. 'He thinks he should have gone home. But you decided to stay on in 2013 – why was that?'

'2005 was a tough tour,' replies O'Connell. 'The last week or so was very, very tough going, so I can understand why he wanted to go. He was also captain, so it was a different scenario. Andy Irvine asked me to stay in 2013; I was helping out with the lineout and I suppose the fact that I had been captain previously and had experience meant I would be useful to have around, and because I wasn't captain on this tour it wasn't such a big thing me staying. Also, unlike Brian in 2005 – and in 2009 when he went home after being knocked out in the second Test – I was still able to train. I trained quite a lot on the side of the pitch, because I'd only just come back from injury and I didn't want to lose my fitness. So I was happy to stay on, I wanted to be part of it, I knew I was never going to go on a Lions tour again. We were 1–0 up in the series, we'd a good chance of winning from here; I probably wanted to be around when we won.'

'I'd been in that situation before – 1–0 up in a Lions Test series against the Wallabies,' says Drico. 'I said to the boys: "We need to finish it next week because it's a hell of a lot easier to win a series in two games than it is in three. The pressure goes through the roof if it goes into a deciding third game."'

'So how did it feel,' I ask, 'when you go to Melbourne and have almost a mirror-image game? Really close, tit for tat for most of the match, then they make a breakthrough and score a good try and you guys have a chance to win it in the dying seconds, only for Leigh Halfpenny to miss and you lose by a point?'

Drico shakes his head and begins to laugh. 'It was horrendous! You're sitting there going, "Oh, man, what's happening here? Am I jinxed or something? Is history repeating itself?" Jesus, all the pressure was now on this final game, just as it was back in 2001.'

One-all in the series, the travelling circus rolled back to Sydney for the decider. It had been sixteen years since the Lions had last triumphed in a Test series. With momentum now with the Wallabies, how could the Lions wrestle it back and prevent another disappointment?

'Emotionally, the Wallabies had put a hell of a lot into that second Test win,' says Gats. 'You could see them at full time – James Horwill, the captain, was in tears and they were screaming the place down. They'd given their all to stay in the series. So we looked at that and said, "Can they back that up? They've just emptied the tank, do they have enough about them to go again?"

'We went and had a very light training week up in Noosa. We got a fair bit of flack for it because it was a holiday resort and we gave the boys several days off, but we needed to do it to refresh them and get them refocussed on the final Test. Again, we'd learned from the past, particularly in Australia in 2001, not to flog the players because otherwise they'd be running on fumes coming into that last game.'

'Noosa was good for the lads, but it wasn't a brilliant week for me,' says Drico.

'We had some tough choices to make about the Test team,' says Gats. 'Jamie Roberts was back fit and we felt our best centre pairing was Jamie and Jon Davies, who'd played in the first two Tests alongside Brian. So then we looked at the bench and had to weigh up who was going to have a bigger impact in the last quarter of the game – was it going to be Brian O'Driscoll or Manu Tuilagi? We opted for Manu.'

'You took some amount of shit for that decision,' I say.

'The abuse was pretty vitriolic,' says Gats. 'And it lasted a long time. It's funny, though, there's only ever been one person blamed for leaving Brian O'Driscoll out and that's me. But I can tell you that the five coaches were a hundred per cent unanimous that it was the right decision. Once we'd made the selection for the starting team we looked at the bench and we could have made the soft decision to put Brian on the bench, and everyone would have gone, "Oh, it's a difficult call but at least he's on the bench, and he'll get to come on," and that would have alleviated a lot of the criticism that was levelled at me. But I had to put that to one side, because my job, my whole focus, was to pick the best team that we thought could win a Test series. And when we pictured ourselves in a situation where we had ten or fifteen minutes to go, and had to imagine who could have the massive impact that was required to beat Australia if we needed a try, it was Manu that we settled on.'

'Still, it was a huge call,' I say.

'It was – but that's my job. As a Lions head coach, your main role is selection. And there are sometimes really, really tough calls that need to be made, and you've got to put the emotion to one side and you've just got to look at it and say, "What's my job; what have I been tasked to do?" And it's to pick the twenty-three players in any given match that I think can win that match. That's your leadership moment.'

'Of course, I was aware that there was a chance that I might not be selected for the final game, because I hadn't played particularly well in the second Test,' says Drico. 'And there's always that chance on a Lions tour that the coaches might need to freshen something up in a third Test. But I was put out to talk to the media on the Sunday and that's usually a good sign that you'll play the following week.

'And then, just before the team meeting on the Wednesday, I got called into the room by Gats and Howlers [Rob Howley]; I could see the scowls on their faces, and I thought, "This isn't good news." I sat down and was quickly told: "We don't have a place for you and you won't be in the twenty-three," and that was pretty much it. You've nothing to say; you're not going to try and convince them. It's like talking to a referee who's just given a penalty against you. You're not going to get them to change their mind there and then, so you just have to suck it up. I was never really a bench player, you know. Manu played a bit of wing and centre, so I could understand that he covered more than one position; I wasn't a bench player – I'd only ever been on the bench once in my Test career.'

'Rhys Long, who was the analyst at the time, was with Brian in the lift,' says Gats, 'and Brian basically said, "I've talked the talk, now I've got to walk the walk." Over the years Brian will have had that conversation with Irish players who had missed out, saying, "Guys, your job now is to support. You haven't made the twenty-three, so now you've got to get over that and your role over the next three or four or five days is to do everything you can to help this team prepare for the weekend." And he was brilliant. Not everyone is capable of walking the walk, but he did. He was obviously hugely disappointed but he went and did what he could and supported the team for that third Test match.'

'Over the course of my career,' says Drico, 'I always talked about the strength of the non-playing side, the bag-holders. They're the ones that ultimately prep the team for battle at the weekend and the onus is on them to do as good a job as they can. So I kind of thought to myself: "I've got to live that now. I can't be a turncoat just because it doesn't suit me anymore." So I remember trying to train as well as I could, I still spoke in the huddle afterwards, and we had a community visit to give that afternoon, when news had gotten out, and I was like, "You can't be going around feeling sorry for yourself; these kids don't care about that." So I tried to put on a brave face and be excited and energised with teaching them – but inside, you're crying about not playing in your final Lions game.

'But ultimately, you know, the decision goes with the coach and you have to respect that. You don't lose hope until the first whistle is blown, in that someone might get injured and you want to keep yourself fresh, when maybe it would have been easy to have gone and drowned my sorrows, but doing that on a Wednesday or a Thursday before a Test match is not a reality if you still might be called in late.'

O'Driscoll and O'Connell weren't the only senior players to be racked with disappointment about missing the final game, however. The tour captain was also out.

'I was jackling for the ball late on in the second Test,' remembers Warburton, 'and I got cleared out and as I fell backwards I remember thinking, "Oh shit, this isn't good," and my hamstring went. I was hoping that James Robson might be able to work some magic and get me back – he'd got Jamie Roberts back from his hamstring injury and somehow got Tommy Bowe back despite him breaking his hand – but deep down I knew it wasn't going to happen in a week and that my tour was over.

'I was gutted. All you want to do is be in the fight to the very end. On the sidelines, you have no control whatsoever and it's agonising to watch. The pressure on a Lions tour is immense. As a captain, as you'll know, Gav, if you don't perform at a level of seven or eight out of ten in every game, the hammer comes down, because you've got so many world-class players who could step in and take your place. So the pressure to perform individually is massive but it suddenly shifted focus in that last week because the enormity of what it would mean to succeed or not succeed was so big for all of us as a group and for the Lions in general. It had been sixteen years since we'd last won a series. If we didn't win in '13, people were looking at the New Zealand tour four years later and not giving us a chance. So then you'd end up at the 2021 tour for your next real chance to win a series, which would be a twenty-four-year gap since the previous victory in 1997. So suddenly the pressure is just massive, massive, massive on us doing the job in 2013. And I couldn't do anything but watch on from the sidelines, which made it about a billion times worse.'

So this was it, time to make history or become another footnote.

Andy Farrell perhaps summed up the challenge – and the privilege – of being a Lion with his pre-match speech which has since gone down in Lions folklore. Like Jim Telfer's 'Everest' speech in 1997, Farrell's is now known simply as the 'Hurt Arena'.

'Last weekend was a good effort,' says Farrell in the meeting room. 'A good effort as far as D [defence] is concerned. A lot of pressure was coming on us, especially on our own line and they kept pounding away and pounding away and it was a gallant effort boys. All right . . .' He pauses for a moment and his expression hardens. 'That's what I would say to you if I was your club coach or if I was your international coach. But I'm not. We're your Lions coaches and a gallant effort, good defence or good spirit ain't good enough at this level.

'On D, we cannot afford our emotional energy to dip whatsoever. You know why? Because there is no tomorrow. There is no tomorrow. We are taking them boys to the hurt arena this weekend. Because our mentality is going to be a different mentality than what the British Lions teams have had over the last sixteen years, right? A different mentality. Because over the last sixteen years it's been about failure.

'You shock yourself by taking yourself to another level. Because that's what being a Lion is about. It ain't about anything other than that . . . ain't about taking part, ain't about being here – it's about winning. They won't have that. They won't have that. Make it your point of difference.'

'Ah, it was great, wasn't it?' says Gats, smiling fondly at the memory. 'He plans those speeches and he prepares really well for those sorts of things, and he's smart. He's very good like that.'

'The speeches,' says O'Connell, 'they're part and parcel of the whole magic of the Lions. I fell in love with rugby – not just the Lions, but rugby itself – because of the 1997 *Living with Lions* documentary. Hearing Ian McGeechan speak in that environment in 2009 was incredible for me and we had him speak to us before the first Test in 2013. If I were the Lions committee, I'd get him involved in some way in every single tour until he can't go anymore, because he just gets it. And Faz's speech was tremendous. He gets it too. He's been there and done it in rugby league with Great Britain, he knows what it takes to win at the highest level. And when you have a great team, sometimes you just need a little emotional kicker to push you off the edge to do something special, to produce a special performance. And that's what the Hurt Arena did for the team in 2013.'

'There's only a few people I've heard who can speak like that,' says Graham Rowntree. 'I'd say Andy Farrell, the way he speaks, is very similar to Jim Telfer. We were up against some stuff. We'd lost Sam and we'd lost Paulie. James Horwill had got off a disciplinary hearing for stamping and was available to play. So everything was pushing away from us. We'd had a few days off, so we hadn't done a lot of training. We'd come back to Sydney. And we were up against it for many reasons and Andy spoke to the guys the night before the game and I'd say that speech was up there with Telfer's.

'You knew what was coming. Games like that, your mind knows what's coming – the intensity. You've got the fear. Your stomach's churning, you can hardly eat anything the day of the game, you know what's coming. I don't miss that feeling as a player. It's just absolute anxiety and your great leaders are the guys who can encapsulate that, pull people's minds together and pinpoint what you're thinking and help you navigate a way through that anxiety. Jim did that in 1997 and Faz did that in 2013.'

'The whole coaching team were good,' says O'Connell. 'And they prepared the players brilliantly that week even though they didn't have a lot of time on the training paddock. I remember Graham Rowntree and I went through the videos from the previous two Tests and we picked out eleven things we were going to show the players that we felt we needed to work on, and Graham was to present them in a team meeting. So he goes up to the front of the room – but he only showed three clips. And after the meeting – and I mean, the meeting was like ninety seconds long – after the meeting, I said, "What have you done? You've left out loads of the detail." And he said, "Gats came up to me beforehand and asked me what I was showing, and I said, 'Well, look, I'm showing these eleven clips here,' and Gats just said, 'You're only allowed to show three of them, pick whatever three you want,' and he just walked off!"

'It was actually brilliant, because it made Graham Rowntree think, "What is absolutely vital here? We've got a group of players here from Wales, Ireland, England, Scotland; they're knackered; the pressure is massive and I don't want to overload them with detail, so what's really important here?" and the way Gats did that was just brilliant, like. He didn't even care what three clips Graham showed.

'There have been a few things like that down through the years with Gats, where I would have been big on detail and big on the lineout complexity, and he would say, "Listen, if you have guys that are thinking too much about the game, thinking too much about the detail, they won't be able to deliver physically." And he said, "If there's one thing these Welsh boys can do, they can deliver physically." And I remember that being a big moment, and even now, as a coach, to this day, I think of that all the time: "What's important? Am I actually doing this meeting for me or for the players?" So that one always sticks out to me.'

Led by Alun Wyn Jones, the Lions stepped out under the lights on to the ANZ Stadium, and they roared. With just one minute on the clock, loose head Alex Corbisiero rolled over the line to score. By midway through the first half, they held a 19–3 lead. Australia responded with a James O'Connor try in injury time before the break and then narrowed the gap further with two penalties early in the second half – but then the Lions took the Wallabies to the hurt arena. Leigh Halfpenny kicked his fifth penalty of the night and then broke the Australian defensive line to set up Johnny Sexton for a try under the posts; George North scored a third try soon afterwards and then Jamie Roberts put the icing on the cake, slicing an angle off a lineout that sent him straight through the Wallaby defence to score. As Romain Poite, the referee who would play a major role on the next Lions tour, blew his final whistle, the Lions had forty-one points on the board and an historic series win in the bag.

'Was there a moment after that third Test when you wanted to stick two fingers up at everyone who had criticised you?' I ask Gats.

He smiles ruefully. 'In fairness, some journalists came back and went, "Fair play, we got it wrong, you cooked it right." I understood that the story had given them an opportunity to build some drama and hype ahead of the Test, which sells papers and get clicks – but I took a lot of shit for it. Well, depending on where you came from. I went back to New Zealand and everyone there was just like, "Well, that's a coach's decision; that's what you get paid to make the calls about." No one there saw an issue with it – while I was basically excommunicated from Ireland. I had to go back there on the *Late, Late Show* a year or so later and get down on my hands and knees and beg for forgiveness. Brian and I also had to talk it through. He presented the jerseys before the first Test in 2017 and he made a joke about it, which was good – and we're good.'

'Not playing that final Test was a difficult one to take,' says Drico, 'but ultimately the team result is what matters, and the fact that they won the series and I was two-thirds part of that series win was far more important than any individual accolade of playing in a team that goes on tour and loses. So to finally be a Lions series winner was very important for me. I'd finally done it – and we'd finally done it. It was a good way to leave that jersey behind – we'd put it in a good place for the guys who would wear it in New Zealand four years later, and that's all that you can ever really hope to do.'

EIGHT

INTO THE PRESSURE DOME

2017

THE TWELVE-YEAR wheel turned and, in 2017, the Lions headed back to New Zealand. The ghosts of 2005 haunted every step of the build-up to this tour – and haunted many more once the team arrived in New Zealand. But if the 2005 Lions thought they had been up against it, their experiences were nothing compared to challenges that confronted the class of 2017. While Clive Woodward had demanded the earth in 2005 – and got everything he asked for from the Lions committee – Warren Gatland, on his second tour as head coach, seemed only to be offered the bare minimum with which to prepare his team. The squad met up in full just two days before their departure from Heathrow and they played their first game three days after touching down in Auckland. Their jet lag had jet lag.

And the challenges didn't stop there. For the first time in sixteen years, the host union released Test players to the provinces for the warm-up matches. The Lions would then face one of the most formidable teams the game has ever known in the Test series.

New Zealand had won back-to-back World Cups in 2011 and 2015, and although they had lost the services of Richie McCaw, Dan Carter, Keven Mealamu and Tony Woodcock to retirement, and Conrad Smith, Ma'a Nonu, Victor Vito and Ben Franks to pastures new, they had replaced the seemingly irreplaceable with more jaw-dropping talent. Anton Lienert-Brown, Waisake Naholo, Rieko Ioane, Codie Taylor and Ardie Savea all came into the team, while Beauden Barrett, the heir to Carter in the black No.10 shirt, won World Player of the Year in 2016 and would go on to win it again in 2017.

After demolishing Australia 34–17 in the 2015 World Cup final, many believed there would be a decline in New Zealand's fortunes as they transitioned to a new playing roster. But, terrifyingly, they actually seemed to get better. They whitewashed Wales in a three-Test home series before marching unbeaten through the 2016 Rugby Championship, scoring forty-two points in Sydney, thirty-six in Buenos Aires, fifty-seven in Durban and notching up 164 points in the return fixtures at home. They looked unstoppable. Only a match against Ireland in Chicago was to spoil their perfect record that year. All Black head coach Steve Hansen would later bemoan his players' loss of focus as they enjoyed the carnival atmosphere in the city as Chicago came to a standstill to celebrate the Cubs winning the World Series. The Irish players had also enjoyed the pageantry, but they had remained laser-like in their preparation for the game at Soldier Field, which would produce one of their most famous results ever and perhaps the greatest Irish performance of all time. Having come agonisingly close to defeating the All Blacks in Dublin in 2013, this time Joe Schmidt's charges did the job, dismantling the world champions in every facet of the game to record a storied 40–29 victory.

That night Chicago turned green and the Irish players celebrated like there was no tomorrow. The All Blacks, meanwhile, regathered, refocussed and turned their attention to the rematch in Dublin two weeks later. This time there were no parades to distract them, no traps for Ireland to spring. The All Blacks dished out a staggering physical backlash, thundering into every contact with a frightening mania. They were lucky to avoid at least one red card, but there was no luck involved in the rest of their dominance as they repaid the loss at Soldier Field with a 21–9 victory.

As the key players from each side left the field at the Aviva Stadium, they knew that the next time they would meet would be in the red-hot furnace of a Lions Test series.

These Ireland/New Zealand games gave Warren Gatland much food for thought. Although the All Blacks had exacted revenge in the second Test, he had seen how unsettled they had been by a hard-pressing and physical defence at Soldier Field. He had seen how they had struggled when the breakdown was fiercely contested. If he could find a combination of players to repeat those tactics – and have the physical and mental resilience to stand up to the backlash – then the 2017 Lions party might defy the expectations of every level-headed punter in the world who could only foresee an All Blacks series win. If he could do that, then the 2017 party might join John Dawes' team of 1971 as the only other Lions side in history to win a series on New Zealand soil.

Selection, as Gats now knew well, would be crucial. As would his leader. He had just the man in mind. Someone who felt that he had unfinished business in a Lions shirt.

'The third Test in 2013 gnawed at me for a long time,' says Sam Warburton. 'Standing there on the sidelines watching was horrible. I just felt helpless.

'I remember being in my blazer while all the boys were popping champagne in the changing rooms. I mean, I enjoyed it, and I was in all the photos and stuff, but unless you've gone through the physical pain of eighty minutes, and all the psychological prep from the Monday to Saturday, the nervousness that you get as a player, all those emotions in the week, it doesn't feel the same. It was great to lift the trophy with Alun Wyn at the end of the game and all that, but really my only thought was: "I have to go to New Zealand in 2017. I won't be happy unless I go to New Zealand and play in three Tests and finish there as a winner." So for me it felt like unfinished business – even though we'd won in Australia, I had to go and finish the next series. As captain, I needed to be there on the pitch in the last game.'

'So when did Gats tell you that he wanted you to lead the team again for the next tour?' I ask.

'As I told you before,' he says, 'I didn't really want the captaincy in 2013. I was nervous, I didn't feel ready. But in 2017, I really wanted it and, without wanting to sound arrogant, I genuinely felt I was the best guy for the job – I was very experienced at that point, I'd done two World Cups, a Lions tour, eight Six Nations campaigns. And the speculation around it was huge. You know what it's like, as soon as one Lions tour is over, people start talking about potential Lions from the next autumn campaign onwards and it builds and builds over the next three and a half years. Once the World Cup is out the way, it's pretty much all anyone talks about whenever there's a game. So about two months before the squad announcement, everywhere I went everyone was asking me – I reckon six to ten times a day, whether it was on a dog walk, in the supermarket, family friends, it happened constantly – "Are you the Lions captain again?" And I'd say, "I don't know." And people were like, "You must know. You are captain, aren't you?" And I was like, "I don't, I promise you, I don't fucking know." It was really winding me up. I honestly wanted to go and live under a rock.

'I went with my wife to the supermarket to get a couple of bits and pieces one afternoon and when we arrived I asked her if she wouldn't mind doing the shopping because I just couldn't handle the cashier or anyone else asking me about the captaincy again. So she went in and by pure coincidence I looked at my phone. "Calling: Gats". It was a similar situation to 2013; I'd had one of my best Six Nations campaigns but I'd got injured shortly afterwards. So again, I thought: "It's all or nothing; he's going to tell me I'm going to be captain or he's going to tell me I need to get fit before I can go on tour again." So I answered and he didn't waste any time, he just said: "Hi Sam, I'm just calling to see if you want to be Lions captain to New Zealand." It sounds crude, but the first thing I said, because I felt so desperate to do it, was: "Fucking right I do." And he started laughing, and he said, "We'll beat 'em," and I was like, "Yeah, a hundred per cent." And that was literally the conversation. He said, "Right, I'll be in touch," and that was it. We didn't mess around. I think that's why we got on so well: we didn't live in each other's pockets, we both knew we had our own roles to play, and he knew deep down, and vice versa, that we were both extreme competitors who believed we were the best at what we did and would compete for everything. We had one goal in mind: to go down to New Zealand and beat them. We wanted to make history. That was it. Pure and simple.'

The tour schedule was the shortest in Lions history, reduced to just ten matches. Preparation time, as already referenced, was also cut to the bare minimum, and with the New Zealand Rugby Union opting for matches against Super Rugby teams instead of provinces, the tour looked set to be one of the most challenging ever for the Lions – if not the most challenging.

Forty-eight hours after an arduous journey from London – which took in a stopover in Dubai and a six-hour layover in Sydney before the hop across the Tasman to Auckland – the

Lions convoyed up to Whangerei for a welcoming ceremony. Twenty-four hours later, they were in action in their first game against the Provincial Barbarians at Okara Park in Whangarei.

Every player who took the field in a red jersey that night talks about running on empty, their legs heavy, their minds scrambled, overcoming the effects of jet lag almost harder than defeating the men opposite them. The Provincial Barbarians, for their part, took the game to the Lions from the first minute, with Bryn Gatland, son of the Lions head coach, pulling the strings in the No.10 shirt and future All Black wing Sevu Reece causing all sorts of problems out wide. The Lions, still very much feeling their way in terms of combinations, were far from impressive – but what else could be expected from them? In the end, thanks to the kicking of Johnny Sexton, Owen Farrell and Greig Laidlaw and a neatly taken try from Anthony Watson, they pushed through to win 13–7.

Large swathes of the media, seemingly oblivious to the Lions' hamstrung preparations, were quickly sharpening their knives.

'I have to admit that the stuff in the press really took me by surprise on that tour,' says Gats. 'I think I headed out there with some romantic notions in my mind about the reception I'd receive. It thought it would be: "Here's a New Zealander, an ex-All Black, coming back to coach the Lions, who only come here once every twelve years; we know what the fans are like, it's going to brilliant, this special team coming to play the world champions." And Jesus, right from day one, I had some critical stuff in the media trying to upset me – and it worked. It threw me. I was taken aback by the stuff that was written and said.

'I had a press conference the day before the Provincial Barbarians game and they asked if I'd spoken to Bryn. I said we'd spoken and that he probably expected to make a few tackles. The next day, the headline in the *New Zealand Herald* was: "Gatland

v Gatland: Warren aiming at Bryn in Lions opener" and the
story was all about us targeting him with our runners as some
kind of weak link. It was so out of order. I was disgusted with it,
to be honest. But it made me realise that this was maybe going to
be the tip of the iceberg and that the media were going to go out
and try and unsettle me throughout the rest of the tour.'

'So how did you handle that?' I ask.

'I kept it very separate from the players – and that was easy
enough because they didn't see as much of me as some of the
other coaches – but the other staff and coaches knew it was
going on and they were all very supportive. I didn't make one
comment about it during the tour. I never, ever let anyone see
that it affected or upset me. And probably what it ended up
doing was motivating me and making me more determined. It
was very disappointing, but it wasn't a reflection of the tour in
terms of the atmosphere at the games or the hospitality which we
experienced, both of which were incredible. We just had a small
element of the media trying to be personal and critical of me,
trying to upset me, and that was a challenge from a leadership
perspective to overcome that, but I think we managed it.'

I call Greig Laidlaw to talk about the tour. He is in a flat in
Ichikawa, just to the east of Tokyo, where he is playing for the
Shining Arcs in Japan's Top League. 'We all saw the newspaper
stories,' he says, thinking back to some of the greatest weeks of
his career. 'But Gats was very good and he didn't let them affect
anything we were doing in the squad.

'He was interesting to work with on that tour – he was clearly
a real competitor, and a winner but, interestingly, he wasn't as
hands-on when it came to coaching as I thought he'd be. He
seemed to just sit above it all and oversee everything and then
step in during the last couple of days in the lead-up to matches
when he would speak really well and give the team a lot of

confidence in what we were doing. I think that was very much his leadership style: to stand up in front of the team and give them that confidence going into games. The detailed coaching then came from the likes of Steve Borthwick, Andy Farrell and Rob Howley. It was a good blend of people in the management, all with different skills and different personalities that blended and worked well together.'

'It was clearly a challenging tour, though,' I say. 'After that Provincial Barbarians game, you got into a fixture list that pitched you against each of the Super Rugby teams, the Maori and then three Tests against the All Blacks.'

'It has to be the toughest match schedule ever,' says Warburton. 'We played the Auckland Blues in the second game, barely a week after arriving in the country, and they had several All Blacks playing for them – Sonny Bill Williams in the centre, Rieko Ioane on the wing, Ofa Tu'ungafasi and Charlie Faumuina in the front row, Steven Luatua in the back row. We put out a strong team, but those guys were the difference and broke us at crucial moments – Sonny Bill getting a try after chasing down a kick at goal, then he and Luatua combined with some incredible hands to put Ihaia West through for the match-winner. We lost 22–16 and it was a massive disappointment, but you don't have time to really dwell on it. The coaches analyse where things went well and what needed work, but you're almost instantly preparing for the next game three days later and trying to get combinations bedded in and the set piece working and so on. We had the Crusaders next – one of the best teams on the planet, so you just have to suck up the loss and move on.'

I call Kieran Read, the All Black captain from the series, who is also out in Japan – playing for the Toyota Verblitz – to discuss his memories from the tour.

'I didn't play in that Crusaders game, but I was involved in the camp in the build-up,' he says. 'I was pretty jealous not to get to play, to be honest. It's a once-in-a-lifetime opportunity to play in a Crusaders jersey against the Lions, and for the guys that will never play in a Test match, this is an international game, so it's huge for them. It was rightly built up as one of our biggest games of the year, and we wanted to play well. We'd seen the Blues go well against the Lions, so the team was pretty pumped to go out and see what we could do as well. It was actually a really good game, but the Lions' defence really suffocated us.

'Richie Mo'unga would later establish himself as the All Black No.10, but he wasn't there yet in 2017. I think he probably took a lot of lessons from that game, especially around game management, territorial kicking, marshalling kick-chases and so on. He pushed on after that game and has been one the best players in New Zealand in the years since. So yeah, for a lot of our guys, it was one of the highlights of their career in the Crusader jersey; it was huge.'

'That was a huge result for us,' says Warburton. 'We beat them 12–3, which wasn't a big score, but the performance was very good against a top-class side. It was a greasy surface and it came down to our kicking – Faz [Owen Farrell] was outstanding – and our defence, which was solid. I think it was the least number of points they'd ever scored at home. They had a very, very strong team out. Kieran Read was coming back from injury but the rest of their All Blacks played – Sam Whitelock, Joe Moody, Codie Taylor, Owen Franks, Israel Dagg, Matt Todd, loads of them.'

While the Saturday side had two wins from two, the midweek team struggled a little more. Having lost to the Blues, they then lost by a point to the Highlanders in Dunedin. A strong Saturday side then dismantled the Maori 32–10 and it seemed clear that the two sides were diverging in terms of those putting their hands up for Test selection and those who would be relegated to permanent dirt-tacker status. Crucially, however, unlike on previous tours, this demarcation between the teams did not divide the squad.

'I think there were a couple of things that contributed to that sense of harmony,' says Laidlaw. 'The first was with Warren Gatland and the way he coaches. To be fair to him, I think he genuinely sees every player as an equal and he's never been afraid to make big calls, regardless of who he is dealing with. If he feels X is playing better than Y, he's going to pick X. So even though the midweek side were struggling with results to begin with, there was a real sense that it wouldn't necessarily discount you from staking a claim for the Test side if you performed well within that – plus there was a recognition that the Super Rugby sides were all really well-prepared for us, while we were still trying to get used to playing together, so no one ever took major flak for us losing games.

'Then the other thing was key guys within the squad working to keep things enjoyable, making sure everyone was working together and having fun. Rory Best was massive with that. He became a real leader both on and off the field and led a lot of the social stuff. James Haskell had come in as a replacement for Billy Vunipola before we left and I think a lot of boys from outside England were a bit wary of him – there's this persona we saw of him on social media and the way he carried himself on the field that would maybe rub you up the wrong way if you didn't know him, but he was brilliant fun. A lot of energy, always performing. I'm not sure how much time I could spend with him in one go, but he was very important for the tour morale. Joe Marler was the same – carried himself very well, worked hard, didn't gripe about being a midweek player. Sean O'Brien, much the same mould, albeit a Test starter. Good fun and understood the importance of the whole squad having a good time and not feeling isolated at any stage.'

Having spent large sections of this book analysing how a divided squad had derailed past Lions tours, it was a huge relief to hear this. Yet the management of the tour wasn't without controversy, as the episode around the so-called Geography Six was to prove.

Ahead of the Maori game, Gats called up six players who would remain in camp for just ten days. This was all pre-planned, just as it had been ahead of the Brumbies game in 2013. Gats knew that more bodies would be required at that stage of the tour to relieve some of the workload on the rest of the squad and to ensure the Test twenty-three didn't pick up any midweek injuries, but had learned from 2005 that it was a bad idea to have too big a squad from the outset. Nevertheless, the strategy did not go down well with much of the squad, especially as there was a perception that the players called up had been selected based on where they were in the world rather than where they were in the Lions pecking order. Kristian Dacey, Tomas Francis, Cory Hill and Gareth Davies were called up from the Wales squad touring New Zealand at the same time, while Finn Russell and Allan Dell were flown over from Australia after Scotland's summer tour victory over the Wallabies in Sydney. It was felt that England's players touring Argentina and Ireland's touring Japan were too far away to fly over for such a short period of time. While the Geography Six were made to feel welcome by the squad when they arrived, when it came to playing, there was a different attitude.

Dell came off the bench against the Chiefs on the Tuesday before the first Test – a comfortable 34–6 victory for the Lions – when Marler was sent to the sin bin, but when the dirt-trackers played the Hurricanes a week later, there was a decision made among the starting XV that they would only come off if they were injured or sin-binned – otherwise, if a call came from the sidelines for a change, they would refuse to make way. Consequently, the Lions went from leading 31–17 against the Hurricanes to drawing the game at full time when they ran out of steam in the final fifteen minutes. Of the Geography Six, Finn Russell was the only one to play, when he came on to cover Dan Biggar while the fly-half went for a head injury assessment.

'The whole Geography Six thing wasn't good,' says Laidlaw. 'And I think it was almost worse for the players that came in, to be honest, because you had the situation of coaches trying to sub players during the games and then the players refusing to go off because they felt so strongly about it. In fairness, a couple of the Geography Six players were probably the next in line to be called up anyway – but in my opinion if you're called up to the Lions it should be because you're the best of the best, not just because you're nearby. Part of the whole challenge of going on the tour is the backing up of one game after another. It's old-school. Yeah, you've got player welfare and stuff to think about, but playing for the Lions is a one-off. So as I say, I almost felt more sorry for the players coming in. I went round and made sure they were happy with everything that was going on on the field, especially with Finn and Allan Dell, because as Scotland teammates I wanted them to feel welcome, and part of the tour. It was a tough job for the boys, but I think all of them handled themselves really well, which was a credit to them.'

'It was tough for a couple of them,' says Warburton, 'because they were probably the next guys off the rank having just missed out on the original squad, but they were there with other guys who definitely weren't and they were all lumped in together and that was the problem. I met with Gats after the tour and I told him the Geography Six thing couldn't happen again. I said that if it had been me and I'd been the next in line to be called up, I would have flown halfway across the world to just sit on the bench for a midweek game for the Lions. I would have missed a Test for Wales if it meant I got just one minute in a Lions jersey – and I'm sure the guys playing for England in Argentina and Ireland in Japan would have felt the same.'

'I can understand that guys in the original tour party might have felt like having the Geography Six there devalued the jersey a little,' I say, 'but that wasn't those six guys' fault.'

'No, you're right,' says Laidlaw. 'And it was a tough one because we were well ahead against the Hurricanes but boys were out on their feet by the end and the Hurricanes came back to draw the match. If we'd used our bench we'd probably have won the game, and in the end, that's what we were there for: to win games of rugby. So, as I say, the whole experience must have been tough for those guys coming in – they knew how the guys around them were feeling, they didn't get used in the games and then they had to leave the tour.'

'I have to hold my hands up and say, "Look, I don't always get things right,"' says Gats. 'The Geography Six thing wasn't received well and it was tough on everyone involved. It's another lesson, I suppose. It's a balancing act because you can't have a huge squad at the beginning – 2005 taught us that – but you also need bodies so the Test players can be fresh – and 2001 and 2009 taught us that.'

'People were critical,' I say, 'but your job was to win two out of three Test matches. That's what you were paid to do, and I guess the end always justifies the means, so if you felt you needed to do that to help out the Test players, then so be it. The Tests were the main part of the tour and you were now there; you'd reached the series. How were you feeling going into the first Test? How was the pressure?'

'It was pretty intense,' he says. 'Maybe more so than any other Lions series I'd been involved with because I was bringing the Lions back to play in front of my own people. You know, I was blown away by the New Zealand perspective on it. I had a conversation with Steve Hansen and some people from the New Zealand Rugby Union, and they were saying that the two most important things on the rugby calendar are the World Cup and the Lions. They saw those as the most significant and important aspects of the rugby calendar; not the Six Nations, not the Rugby Championship; the World Cup and the Lions were number one and number two. I was taken aback that that was the reaction from the southern hemisphere.'

'Mate, it's a massive thing,' says Kieran Read. 'The Lions are so special, and I truly appreciated the tradition and how tough a team they are to play against. And with the fans travelling around the country, and how our fans were responding to them, the vibe was very similar to the 2011 World Cup. It was an amazing time. Going into the series, I was hearing a lot from our media about how we were going to give them a hiding – but I couldn't quite figure out how they'd come up with that idea. The international game had got really close at the very top end and anyone could beat anyone. Yes, the Lions were a brand-new team but they were also the best of the best from four of the world's top sides.'

'Do you think that media response had a lot to do with 2005?' I ask. 'Or the fact the Lions had lost some of the provincial games before the series?'

'From a media perspective, maybe,' Read concedes, 'but we as a team never dismissed them. I watched how they were playing in the build-up and they weren't playing a style of game to win provincial midweek games; they were building a game to win Test matches – and those are two very different things. I could see that and I recognised what a massive challenge they presented us, because their game plan was very well suited to a Test match, which is just so tough and there's not the space that you get normally in any other kind of game. They had a suffocating defence, they contested the breakdown, they box-kicked and chased really well. That kind of thing is Test match rugby.'

'So how did you respond to that within the All Black camp?'

'It was months in the planning,' he replies. 'Throughout the Super Rugby season we were having meetings every month as a leadership group to talk about how we were going to approach the series. So all the planning was in place, and then we had a warm-up game against Samoa to get ourselves ready for the first Test. It was good to get into camp, because you do all the planning and everything, but it's about getting there and getting into it. There was so much excitement because the stakes were so high and everything was a lot more ramped up with the fans than a usual Test match.'

In many ways, the narrative leading into the game was a tale of two captains struggling with injury. Sam Warburton was still trying to regain full fitness and Kieran Read was coming back from thumb surgery. In the end, Warburton made the decision that he didn't feel he was fit enough to start the first Test, so took up a place on the bench and the captaincy was passed to Peter O'Mahony; Read, meanwhile, felt ready to go – albeit he had to play with a brace on his hand.

'The anxiety was quite intense before the series,' says Read. 'I only played three or four games in the entire year before I broke my thumb, and then went into the first Test against the Lions with six or seven weeks of no rugby under my belt – so I wasn't exactly battle-hardened! But I think you get to a stage in your career where you don't need the warm-up games anymore; you can kind of switch yourself into Test gear pretty quickly, and I was at that point where I knew I was going to be able to handle it physically, because I could handle it mentally. I don't think you should really change how you lead if you're injured or you're not – you always start by focussing on your own game and then you have a voice around the team. I guess I was lucky that I had a lot of leaders around me so that I could really just concentrate on having a good game first up to start the series well.'

'I felt the same in terms of the leadership,' says Warburton. 'I knew that I could still lead the squad as the tour captain, but there were loads of other great leaders around me who could take up the mantle while I worked my way back to full fitness. I just wasn't ready to start that Test match. I always needed two or three good hit-outs before I was match-fit and I didn't have them under my belt by then. I knew that if I played I wouldn't be doing myself or the jersey justice, so I sat on the bench. I remember sitting down after the anthems and looking around at the others on the bench and it was one of those magic Lions moments when I looked at Kyle Sinckler, Ken Owens, Maro Itoje, Johnny Sexton and Leigh Halfpenny sitting next to me. I remember thinking, "This is the bench! Shit! This is a joke how fucking good this team is."'

The first Test was played at Eden Park, the great bastion of New Zealand rugby. Despite the huge pressure of the occasion and the slippery surface, both teams played with impressive attacking intent, with numerous surges to the line only stopped by desperate last-ditch defence. Eventually, a quick tap penalty on the Lions' five-metre line and two long passes across the field freed All Black hooker Codie Taylor to slide in at the corner to break the deadlock – which the Lions responded to with one of the greatest tries in their history. Just before half-time, Anthony Watson gathered a kick in his twenty-two and passed to Liam Williams who sidestepped a chasing Kieran Read to skip into space. Ben Te'o ran a neat blocking line on Sonny Bill Williams to open a gap for Liam Williams to scythe through the chasing defensive line and the ball then switched between the supporting Jon Davies and Elliot Daly before Davies took a second touch of the ball and fed Sean O'Brien to score. The sea of red in the stands roared so loudly that the foundations of Eden Park itself must have been shaking.

Coming out for the second half and leading 13–8 thanks to Beauden Barrett's boot, the All Blacks upped the pace of the game. Read then produced a moment of sublime skill that put paid to any suggestion that he might be rusty after so long out of the game. In the fifty-fourth minute, the All Blacks had a scrum in the Lions' twenty-two. The home pack powered forward and earned a penalty advantage as the Lions front row crumbled and wheeled. Just as it seemed that referee Jaco Peyper was about to blow his whistle, the ball bobbled loose at the base, Read pounced for it and, with the ball just an inch from the turf, the No.8 executed an exquisite scoop pass to his scrum-half Aaron Smith. The Lions defence was caught on its heels and quick hands across the All Blacks' back line freed Rieko Ioane to score in the corner. Barrett added the touchline conversion and then slotted another penalty five minutes later.

At 23–8 down with ten minutes to go, the road back for the Lions was a long one – and it became an impossible task when TJ Perenara sent up a box kick from his twenty-two which was badly guddled by Liam Williams. Ioane was the first to the bouncing ball and burst down the left touchline, showing electric pace to leave Watson and Elliot Daly in his wake as he collected his second try of the night. Although the Lions would pull back a late consolation try from replacement scrum-half Rhys Webb, all it did was avoid total humiliation on the scoreboard. The game ended 30–15 to the All Blacks.

If Gatland had felt the New Zealand media had been critical before, it was nothing compared to the heat he suffered after the first Test. The *New Zealand Herald* featured a cartoon caricature of the Lions head coach dressed as a red-nosed clown beneath a headline that read: 'If the nose fits, Warren'. It was perhaps the tamest of the attacks on his coaching ability.

'To be honest, the way the press behaved almost ruined the tour for me,' says Gats, clearly still upset by the episode. 'I had a lot of support from Kiwis as well as Lions fans, but it was tough seeing that kind of thing every day.'

'Did it galvanise you at all?' I ask. 'As a squad and as a management team?'

'Yeah, I think it did a bit,' he says. 'But we were pretty galvanised anyway. We had one shot to stay alive in the series, so that focusses the mind pretty well!'

'What was the pressure like that week?' I ask.

'Massive,' says Warburton. 'Absolutely massive. It was sink or swim time. We made some personnel changes – Johnny Sexton started at stand-off and Owen Farrell moved to centre; Maro Itoje came in for George Kruis; and I started. I felt that I'd made a difference when I'd come on the previous week and I felt good enough physically to start. But God, the pressure. I couldn't sleep the night before the second Test. I remember it got to around two or three in the morning and I phoned my mum. I said, "Mum, I don't think I can do this. I don't think I can handle the pressure." If someone had told me I could have jumped on a flight home I think I might have done it. But she said, "Calm down, you can do this. You have two games to go – just do them, get them done, and if you want to finish you can finish then."

'The fight or flight instinct kicks in around these big games, and you've just got to slap yourself around the face and choose to fight. People come out with phrases like, "He's a big-game player," but what does that mean? For me, it's a mentality thing. It's facing up to that fight or flight instinct and overcoming the fear. You're under a massive, massive amount of pressure, but that's why the Lions selectors pick teams based on the highest-profile games in the Six Nations and domestic and European finals – you need to see how players handle themselves under the extreme pressure. A part of you might want to hide away and hope everybody's going to carry you, but you've got to front up and step up. That, to me, is the mentality of a big-game player. And luckily in that Lions team, we had a lot of big-game players.

'But the pressure was savage. I think it was because I was so desperate to win. All my thoughts were: "I want to beat New Zealand in New Zealand, I don't give a fuck about anything else, that's the only thing I want to achieve right now – I want us to be arguably the greatest Lions team in history." I was so desperate to achieve that. I think that's why I felt the pressure, where some guys would probably have been happy to go on tour, play midweek and enjoy the experience more. But that wasn't why I was there.'

The rain poured over Wellington, casting long lances against the floodlights at the Westpac Stadium. The red wall of Lions supporters were unperturbed, though, shouting and singing and cheering their warriors with a deafening roar as they took the field. I remember sitting in the stands and despite the rain and the wind and the nerves, the warmth from the crowd and the energy that was being generated by them created the kind of staggering atmosphere that I have only ever experienced at a Lions Test match.

'The fans are incredible,' says Warburton. 'Bloody hell, I was in the emotional washing machine as we ran out in Wellington, I was all over the shop. But at the same time, that's what drives you on to want to win. You don't want let all these people down who've travelled halfway across the world and are all united under the Lions banner. People say, "How do you unite as a team?" I'm like, "Exactly the same way you do as a fan. We all just jump on the Lions bandwagon and we love it, so it's a very easy thing to do." But the impact of those fans on the players is extraordinary. You're away from home, you haven't got any of your home comforts, you're in an alien country, you're surrounded by a lot of people you don't really know, you miss your family and friends, and then you get this huge lift from the crowd and all those worries just melt away. You feel empowered. Powerful. You ride that wave of energy they give you. It's extraordinary.'

The conditions played a big part in stifling the attack on both sides – but so too did the shuddering collisions, ferocious contests at the breakdown and the swarming line-speed from both defences. The turning point in the game undoubtedly occurred in the twenty-fifth minute. Anthony Watson ran on to an offload from Taulupe Faletau and was half caught by his opposite number, Waisake Naholo. Sonny Bill Williams joined the tackle, but led with his right shoulder and clattered Watson in the head. The Lions fans erupted in fury while the players in red around Watson raised their arms in an appeal to the referee, Jérôme Garcès.

'Owen and Johnny were screaming at me to speak to the ref,' says Warburton. 'But I was like, "Boys, leave him alone." Over the years with Wales, I'd taken time to speak to the likes of Nigel Owens, Wayne Barnes, Craig Joubert, Romain Poite, all the top referees, and I said to them, "Surely if I'm talking to you all the time, it's just going to wind you up?" I looked at it in the same way as any other line of work: if somebody beneath you is constantly telling you you're doing something wrong and questioning you, you're just going to get wound up and their words are eventually going to become white noise. So constantly carping on at the ref isn't going to have any value to your side whatsoever. To a man, they all agreed with my point of view.

'So every time I played, I'd tell the referee at the coin toss: "Mate, you'll hear from me two or three times a half, max. I won't bother you more than that." So I'd only go up to them if I had to, and if I hadn't spoken to the ref for twenty minutes, I'd catch him after a penalty kick or something and say, "Anything we could do better? You happy?" And if he said, "No, no, I'm happy," I'd go, "Great, no problem," and I'd leave it there; I wouldn't try and make conversation just for the sake of it.'

'I always had great feedback from referees about Sam,' says Gats. 'They were always incredibly complimentary about him, about how approachable he was, how he wasn't aggressive, how he picked the right moments to speak to them, that he was brilliant to deal with, very polite, asked all the right questions. His management of the referees was always outstanding. A couple of the top referees in the world had also said to me pretty early on in his career that he was as good as Richie McCaw and David Pocock over the ball at the breakdown, and those accolades don't come around that often. So as a leader, Sam was tremendous. He had respect from the referees in terms of the way he played, how strong he was on the ball, putting his head in places where most people wouldn't, and then with the way that he conducted himself when he spoke to them. He's one of the all-time greats, no doubt.'

'I looked at the Sonny Bill incident,' says Warburton, 'and I knew I didn't need to speak to the ref. He had the crowd screaming at him, his assistants in his ear, he didn't need my voice adding to it all and annoying him. The rules were very clear: if a shoulder hit a head with force, it was going to be a red card. The replay was on a screen the size of my house in the stadium, the crowd were going nuts, I could see the referee looking up at it. I just said to the lads, "Don't go up to him. Leave him alone, let him make the decision himself. We don't need to waste a chip here."'

It didn't take long for Garcès to reach his decision and he brandished his red card at Williams, making him only the second All Black in history to be sent from the field.

Despite having a one-man advantage, the Lions didn't immediately make it tell and the teams were locked at 9–9 going into the break.

'It was frustrating that we were still level on the scoreboard,' says Warburton. 'But we knew they would tire in the second half and we could make that tell.'

And what was it like in the opposition changing room?

'One of the great challenges in sport is to back up a decent performance and do it again,' says Read. 'We'd had a good week preparing for that second Test, but that all gets blown out of the water when you lose a player after twenty-five minutes. It was raining and we were down a man, so we tightened things up in attack and kicked more, but looking back on it, maybe that was the wrong way to go. That's not the natural way that All Blacks teams play. We should have done the opposite and played more footy. It was a tight, tight game and I think they got some lucky breaks – particularly at the end – but they were a good enough team to get themselves out in front and take the series to Auckland.'

Beauden Barrett kept his side in the fight until the bitter end, landing four second-half penalties, but these were countered by two brilliantly taken tries by Faletau and Conor Murray, the latter of which was converted by Farrell. And it was the Lions No.12 who kicked the late match-winning penalty after Kyle Sinckler jumped to take a pass from Murray and was tackled in the air. As Read alluded to, the Lions were fortunate to have been given that shot at goal, but so often in the past such luck had deserted previous tourists and they were undoubtedly worthy winners at full time.

Auckland awaited for the decider. One-all in the series, could the Lions join the immortal team of 1971?

They spent much of the following week in Queenstown, pulling back on the training schedule, just as they had done at Noosa four years earlier. One meeting they did have that week, however, was to discuss the backlash that would be coming their way from the All Blacks. On this occasion, Gats asked a leader who had the most recent experience of this scenario to make a presentation to the squad. Rory Best had captained Ireland to victory over New Zealand at Soldier Field, and he had then captained them in the return fixture in Dublin.

'After the win in Chicago, we thought we could play the same way in Dublin and beat them,' says Best, 'but they shocked us with their physicality in the first twenty minutes of that second game. Gats asked me to speak to the lads about those experiences ahead of the third Test and I said to them, "You think you know what kind of animal is coming at us on Saturday, but prepare yourself for a shock. We were shocked in Dublin; don't let them do that to you at Eden Park. Gear yourself up for a physical onslaught."'

It reminded me of the stories the '97 Lions had told me about playing the Springboks. They knew that the Boks would come at them at a hundred miles an hour in the opening quarter of the second Test, and it was key that they weathered the storm until it blew itself out.

'I think that's exactly it,' says Warburton when I relay this story to him. 'It's impossible to play at that intensity for eighty minutes, so you've just got to hang in there and hang in there until that frenzied start subsides.'

'Having gone through all those emotions ahead of the second Test, how did you manage things ahead of the return to Eden Park?' I ask.

'Michael Johnson said a really good quote,' says Warburton. '"Pressure is the shadow of great opportunity." If you're in a hugely pressurised situation, it's because there's something amazing to be won or to be achieved, and that's what you've got to focus on. Don't worry about what you could lose: focus on the carrot of what you could gain. And that's just the mentality you've got to have when you're being thrown into high-pressure situations. From a leadership perspective, I wanted to focus my mind on that goal of winning the series and potentially achieving greatness and relay that same feeling to the rest of the team. The pressure was intense, but it was one more game and then the pressure would be released one way or another.

'I think you've got to go through a bit of adversity in life; if you come through it, it helps you grow as an individual, and that's what the Lions did for me. I look back with fond memories of my tours and there are times on the campaign when you have a lot of laughs, but when it comes to business time and winning games, shit me, it's hard. The pressure's so intense, particularly with the press and all the thousands of fans around, and then there's the weight of history on your shoulders.

'Having come through all of that I feel that it's made me into a much more rounded person who can take on a lot of challenges that get thrown at me in my life post-rugby, because nothing compares to the pressure I felt on a Lions tour.'

'Take me into the changing room,' I say. 'Just before kick-off. What was going through your mind?'

Warburton smiles and I can see his eyes unfocus for a moment as he transports himself back through time. 'I remember looking around,' he says slowly, 'and thinking: "There are hundreds of thousands of rugby players in the four countries represented by the Lions, and you've got the best twenty-three right here – the best athletes, the most competitive animals, the strongest wills, the most talented players out of all those four countries." And I was like: "We can't lose. I just cannot see how we're going to lose." To be in that dressing room was such an immense privilege, because you realise: "This is one of the best teams, if not the best team, in world rugby." The two sides going into that match were the two best twenty-threes in world rugby at that moment in time. What an occasion. What a challenge. I couldn't wait to get out there.'

In the neighbouring changing room, the feeling was mutual. 'It was tough losing the second Test,' says Read. 'I think coming out of it, I was like, "Okay, we haven't played our best, we were a man down for an hour and we lost to a late penalty. We can do this. Let's get going again for the next week." So that was our mindset. And playing at Eden Park is a special thing for us. We hadn't lost there since 1994. We were confident we were going to go out and do the job. We'd had some injuries in the second Test and brought in Jordie Barrett at full back and Ngani Laumape in the centre for their first caps, but I had every confidence in them and in our system and I was certain that we were going to win.'

'How did you manage those young players throughout the week?' I ask. 'It's a hell of a big ask for them to make their Test debuts in a match like that.'

'I think you try and shelter the young guys as much as you can,' he says. 'I think the biggest thing is to try and keep your focus inside your camp and try not to read too much of the news, which is very hard with the young guys these days with social media. Then I tried to really just give them as much confidence as I could – that was my way as a leader. I'd say to these young guys that they were there for a reason: "You're playing for the All Blacks because you're talented and because you're a great footy player. You've been chosen because you're ready." So I really tried to build them up.

'It's tough, though: you're playing in a Test match that's equal to a World Cup final in terms of the pressure and expectation and the huge numbers watching. I also had the added incentive of it being my hundredth cap, but I didn't really want to think about that; I just wanted to do what I could for the team.'

'And what was it like out there, playing that game?'

'I think once we got into it, both sides were trying to manage the pressure as much as they were managing the game,' says Read. 'In many ways it was like the 2011 World Cup final which was really cagey and saw guys making errors that they wouldn't normally make because of the pressure. I remember Julian Savea was put away down the touchline and he was in open space but he dropped the ball. Any other day, he'd have caught it and scored without a second thought, but that's what pressure does to you.'

The pressure was exacting, but the attack from both sides was electric, as it had been throughout the series. It took fourteen minutes for the first try to be scored – and it was the debutants combining for the All Blacks that made it happen. Beauden Barrett sent a cross-field kick to his brother, Jordie, who rose above Daly to tap the ball down to Laumape to score.

The All Blacks were 7–0 up but two penalties from Farrell reduced the deficit to one point before Jordie Barrett again showed extreme calm under pressure to sprint on to a wide ball from Anton Lienert-Brown deep in Lions territory. Unlike Savea, the debutant held the pass and slid over to score the All Blacks' second try of the night. His brother was unable to convert and the teams went in 12–6 at half-time.

Just fifty seconds into the second half, the Lions were awarded a penalty inside their own half, which Daly stepped up to convert. It was a monstrous kick on a cold winter night at sea level, but Daly hit it as if he were on the high veldt in South Africa. From sixty metres out, he cleared the bar with ease and the Lions edged closer. Then, in the fifty-ninth minute, Farrell drew them level. Game on.

'When I look back on that series,' says Read, 'and think about what we could have done better from the leadership perspective, I think that we maybe focussed a little too much on the Lions, looking at their box-kicking strategy and their defence, which maybe inhibited some of the younger guys. We should have looked at ourselves more and said, "Okay, let's back ourselves and back what we can do."'

The All Blacks might not have been attacking with quite the same deadly efficiency as they usually did, but they were far from underperforming. With the Lions utilising a venomous rush defence and kicking with pinpoint accuracy, the All Blacks had to dig into another part of the armoury to find a way to get an edge in the game. In the sixty-sixth minute they returned to the basics and brought their scrum power to bear, just as they had in the second Test. The Lions had a put-in just inside their twenty-two and the front rows, both recently refreshed with substitutes, collided. Conor Murray fed the ball, the front rows oscillated then Kyle Sinckler hinged at the hips and collapsed. This time Read didn't try to force any miracle plays from the base, but pointed to the posts. Barrett obliged with his kick and the All Blacks were up 15–12.

Many other teams might have crumbled at this stage, but not this Lions side. They kept up the pressure and with seventy-six minutes on the clock, it was the All Blacks' turn to crack as they tried to illegally slow the ball down at a ruck. Poite was alert to the skulduggery and blew his whistle in the Lions' favour. Owen Farrell, as he had been all tour, was absolutely nerveless as he kicked the penalty to tie the scores again.

And then, of course, came the controversy around the offside penalty awarded against Ken Owens being downgraded to a scrum to the All Blacks. At the end of such a compulsively engaging series, a draw may have satisfied few but it was the least that each side deserved.

'I guess on paper, from an All Blacks point of view,' says Read, 'you would look at a drawn series and see it as a failure. But you know, there was nothing but positivity from a lot of people around New Zealand, which I think shows that people accepted the result because they understood how good a series it was.'

'I think that in years to come,' I say, 'you'll look back on that Lions tour and you'll think, "You know what, that was a pretty special moment in my life," and okay, you didn't win, but you didn't lose either, and for anyone who watched it, it was the most compelling series. It was magical, and for me it summed up the Lions: playing against the best team in the world, no quarter asked nor given. And then there was just total respect for each other afterwards. It was a monumental, epic battle and it was fantastic. You can argue that rugby was the winner; I certainly think it was.'

'You know, there's a memory that I'm very fond of recalling from those last few minutes of the third Test,' says Warburton. 'Kieran and I were standing together while we waited for Romain Poite to make his decision. I wasn't in the mood to speak to anyone, because I was just waiting to find out what Romain was going to do. I remember listening to him and the fourth official talking it all over, and I could hear the hysteria of the crowd and I just knew, with two minutes to go in the third Test, what an enormous moment this was in the history of the Lions and in my own career. I was standing next to Kieran, who I've got to know pretty well over the years, but you don't talk to each other during a game, not in a friendly way, anyway, but he just nudged me with his elbow and went, "How awesome's this? This is the pinnacle, isn't it? Take it in." And I looked at him, and I laughed, and said, "I know, this is crazy," but I thought, "What an amazing, grounded bloke, just to be able to take a step back in this environment, even though we're both desperate to win, and take stock of the moment." He was like, "Mate, look what we're doing – look at this, this is special." Just to have that moment on the pitch with him and realise that we were at the pinnacle of world rugby . . . it was incredible.

'I think that kind of sums up the magic of rugby for me,' he continues. 'On the pitch, rugby players will hit you as hard as anything, but when you're off it, there's just utmost respect for each other. Because there's nothing personal on the pitch: it's just a game. It doesn't matter what number's on your back, you play fierce and then you have a beer with your opposite number afterwards. It's the way it's always been and the way it should always be.

'When the trophy was about to be presented, Jerome Kaino came up to us and said, "Boys, do you think we should all mix in?" and I was like, "Yeah, that's a great idea." Jerome Kaino, another top bloke. And so we all mixed in together for the trophy lift, and I am really proud of that moment, that we were in that photo together, we all mixed in with our arms around each other. In the years since the series, I've thought about that moment a lot. I still don't know another sport where that would have happened, where you would have competed that fiercely and then all mixed in and had a laugh, right at the end. I think that's just what rugby is all about. That one picture alone of New Zealand and the Lions mixing in, after one of the most competitive Test series that there's been in the modern age, that we all mixed in like best pals afterwards, I think that sums up our game better than anything else I've seen.'

'You look at that Lions team and what we achieved in those few weeks together,' says Gats, who wore a clown nose to the press conference after the third Test as a final riposte to those that had been so critical of him during the course of the tour. 'And I remember thinking, "Christ, if we could keep this team together for another six or seven weeks, they would be just awesome. Unstoppable." It makes you wish you could go back in time to the old touring itineraries where the Lions were away for twenty matches or more. If we'd had that amount of time together, we'd have been the best team in the world. But that's part of the challenge – you have to bring the guys together, create a really simple structure for them to play within and cut as many corners as you can because you don't have the time to do anything else.'

'You know what,' I say, 'I think it's remarkable that since 1983 – with the very obvious exception of 2005 – the Lions have won at least one Test match per series. As I said to Graham Henry when we spoke, the margin between being successful and not successful at that level is miniscule. I would never say that the teams of 1993, 2001 and 2009 failed because they were within a whisker of winning – so failure is the wrong word to use, they were just not successful. And even then, only just. It was the same in 2017 and if you look at the schedule you had, the quality of the opposition, the time you had to build that team, it was the most remarkable achievement that you won the second Test and drew the third to tie the series. It's right up there with the achievements of the tours that won their Test series.'

'I think that's right,' says Gats. 'And it's what makes it all worthwhile. The work is unbelievably hard on a Lions tour. You finish a game, do the press, check on the players and while the guys who just played get into recovery mode and have a few beers, you're immediately on to preparing for the next game three days later while also dealing with the travel and everything else. It's the hardest task in the game because there's nothing else like it – nothing comes close. It's just relentless. But that's all part of the magic, isn't it?'

'I still feel in awe of the fact that I represented the Lions,' says Warburton. 'Not even being captain, just having played for them. And even though the Lions was just four months of my career in total, when I look back, I think eighty per cent of my rugby memories come from Lions tours because that's what's almost defined me as a person. It was the most pressurised, under-the-microscope environment in the highest-profile games I ever played. And it was my childhood dream to wear that red jersey in a match.'

I think back to that fourteen-year-old boy in Cardiff, with a 2005 Lions shirt lying untouched in his wardrobe, who filled out a form for his dad's mate.

Ambition: To be a British and Irish Lions rugby legend.

I think it's fair to say that Sam Warburton is among the greats in the Lions pantheon. That third Test would turn out to be his final game of rugby. The following year he would admit defeat to injuries and so he bowed out at the top, surrounded by the best of the best from Britain, Ireland and New Zealand. Along the way he learned many lessons – about rugby, leadership and life – just as all the Lions and their opponents who spoke to me during the course of writing this book have done. Only a fraction of those lessons have been passed on in these pages, but I hope that they have been as enlightening, interesting and enriching to you as they have been to me.

And the conclusion? As a concept, the Lions shouldn't function in the modern game, but they remain the twin pinnacle to lifting the Webb Ellis Cup. Lions tours present the most testing, challenging and exacting examination of a rugby player, coach, manager, administrator and back-room staff member; they are brutally hard but can also be life-changing and life-affirming. They distil every challenge in the sport into a condensed period of a few relentless weeks on the road and, as this book has shown, provide myriad lessons in leadership which can be transferred to life beyond the game as well as to different sporting environments and businesses everywhere.

In short, the Lions are magical. Long may they roar.

Gavin Hastings
Lion #606

ACKNOWLEDGEMENTS

THE BRITISH & IRISH Lions change every four years, but their legend lives on and, indeed, grows with every passing tour.

I have always been fascinated by the changing dynamic and how some tours are able to build a winning team more easily than others. In order to find out why, who better to ask than those who have been at the coal face of each successive Lions tour since 1989? I would like to thank Lions captains Fin Calder, Martin Johnson, Brian O'Driscoll, Paul O'Connell and Sam Warburton for sharing the learnings from each of their tours. I also wish to thank Sir Ian McGeechan and Warren Gatland for their wonderful insights, as well as Sir Graham Henry for being so honest with his thoughts relating to 2001 and 2005.

Huge thanks also to a host of other great Lions, including Jerry Guscott, Lawrence Dallaglio, Keith Wood, Greig Laidlaw and Richard Hill, as well as Dr James Robson. Giving an alternative insight into leading their teams into battle against the Lions were John Eales, John Smit and Kieran Read and I would like to place on record my huge thanks to these giants of the game for their generous time.

It is remarkable that, with the exception of 2005 when the All Blacks were as fine a side as any in the modern era, the Lions have managed to win at least one Test match on every tour against one of the southern hemisphere superpowers since 1989. Any supporter who has witnessed that experience first-hand will tell you just what it means to have been there and, on behalf of all Lions players, we wholeheartedly salute your unwavering support.

A special thanks to my brother Scott, who I shared all my international career with and enjoyed the privilege of touring alongside with the Lions in '89 and '93.

To Pete Burns, my Publisher (and ghost writer), a special thanks for all your support, knowledge, advice and guidance in order to get this book to press on time. I hope it has been worth it.

And, finally, to Carson Russell who gave me the energy to get this project off the ground and, had it not been for the Covid pandemic, would have been even more involved, a thousand thanks for igniting the spark.